Counselling for sexual abuse

A therapist's guide

to working with

adults, children, and families

KATHY MACDONALD

IAN LAMBIE

LES SIMMONDS

OXFORD UN. ERSITY PRESS

Oxford   Auckland   New York

OXFORD UNIVERSITY PRESS NEW ZEALAND

Oxford New York
Athens Auckland Bangkok Bombay
Calcutta Cape Town Dar es Salaam Delhi
Florence Hong Kong Istanbul Karachi
Kuala Lumpur Madras Madrid Melbourne
Mexico City Nairobi Paris Singapore
Taipei Tokyo Toronto

and associated companies in
Berlin Ibadan

OXFORD is a trade mark of Oxford University Press

Edited by Maria Jungowska—Scope
Cover design by Paradigm
Typeset by Desktop Concepts P/L, Melbourne
Printed through Bookpac Production Services, Singapore
Published by Oxford University Press,
540 Great South Road, Greenlane, Auckland, New Zealand

FOREWORD

Knowledge about sexual abuse has been ignored historically and in some cases actively suppressed. The last 20 to 30 years, however, have seen a sharp change in the recognition that it does occur and in the discovery and description of the effects of sexual abuse on its victims. Nevertheless, the forces of disbelief and denial that kept sexual abuse a well-kept secret for so long have continued to exert their pressure, and have shaped the response to emerging knowledge. Social-service resources have been disproportionately committed to assessment, diagnosis, and legal responses to abuse. The cost has been to the pace of development of effective therapy. This book, while not ignoring issues of assessment and legal interventions, is a response to the need for practical therapeutic responses — the task of helping people to heal.

The challenges to knowledge of sexual abuse in the 1970s were to the claims of the high prevalence of sexual-abuse occurrence. Systematic research has continued to show that prevalence is indeed high. In the 1980s the major challenge was to the credibility of children as reporters of sexual abuse. Subsequent research has shown that some false allegations do occur, but they represent only a small proportion of the total of abuse allegations.

In the 1990s the challenge has been to the reliability of adults' memory of childhood abuse, in particular where the memory has been recovered from total amnesia for the events. Recent research shows that the majority of sexual-abuse survivors have always retained some memory at least of abuse events. Those who do recover memories often have the events corroborated subsequently.

As with children, false allegations by adults do occur, and some may be based on false recovered memories. Yet in terms of the total number of genuine cases of sexual abuse, such allegations comprise a small proportion.

Much energy has been dedicated to addressing the issues of the prevalence of sexual abuse and the credibility of those who disclose it. Gradually, however, knowledge about the effects of sexual abuse has emerged and has been accepted. Along with other forms of childhood abuse, sexual abuse is now recognized as a major contributor — in children and in adults — to problems of mental disorder, drug and alcohol addiction, criminal offending, and relationship difficulties. Therapeutic services for those affected by abuse are now considered to be justified and essential.

Counselling for Sexual Abuse is a response to the need for appropriate counselling. While other books exist that describe therapy for abuse, this text provides a particularly practical and instructive resource. It is rich in ideas and free of dogma or jargon. Furthermore, it recognizes that abuse affects not only the individual who was abused. It recognizes that family members may also be victims and may need assistance. Families can also provide inestimable support and help for the abused person, directly contributing to their healing.

The Leslie Centre has a strong tradition in family therapy. Traditionally, therapy or counselling has been dominated by individual-oriented models. This book provides a valuable balance and extension to previous work. The methods of therapy described here derive not only from family therapy, however; techniques from other therapeutic models are included. This is sensible. In decades of research on the effectiveness of therapy, no single model of therapy has been proved to be more effective than another. What matters most are factors common in all good therapy — the ability of the counsellor to be empathetic or understanding, and their skill in building rapport and a good therapeutic relationship.

Effective therapy outcomes depend on the quality of the relationship between therapist and client and the presence of mutually agreed upon goals to which therapy is directed. These process issues are dealt with in this book. The numerous suggestions about what to do in therapy in terms of tools and techniques will assist counsellors to be confident and creative. The description of how to deal with process issues will help remind them it is not just what they do but how they do it that ultimately determines success for their clients.

Strong features of the approach to abuse counselling in this book include the emphasis on education, empowerment, and the avoidance of pathologizing people. Not everyone who has been abused will be severely affected and need to suffer long term. Overall this is an optimistic book. It does not in any way trivialize the effects of sexual abuse but the message is that people can and do heal themselves. The extent of help that they need in counselling will vary, but should be a choice left in their hands.

Fred W. Seymour, Ph.D.
Senior Lecturer in Clinical Psychology
University of Auckland

Contents

7 **GENERAL ISSUES FOR COUNSELLORS
AND COUNSELLING** 281

ACKNOWLEDGEMENTS

Many people contributed to making this book possible.

All the staff at the Leslie Centre, Presbyterian Support Services, Auckland, gave it the priority required to allow us to take time away from other work.

Special mention is due to the Director of the Leslie Centre, Gay Bayfield, for her belief in the value of this book, and for her unfailing support through receding deadlines.

Molly Matheson and Lorraine Owens provided us with valuable feedback and encouragement as they tirelessly typed and retyped draft copies of the manuscript. Christine Leach and Sue Ingram provided essential administrative support and assisted Molly Matheson in the tedious task of compiling the Index.

Lindsay Barron was a member of our original team. She helped to prepare and present the workshops on which this book is based. Her influence can be found in every chapter.

Eileen Swan was responsible for the development of a team for working with sexual-abuse survivors at the Leslie Centre. She instigated our work in this area, with her encouragement, her expertise, and her foresight in appreciating the need for quality services.

Since then many people have contributed to the development of our ideas, although it is not possible to acknowledge all of them. Many are listed amongst the references at the end of the book.

We give special thanks to Ruth Jackson and Heather McDowell for the inspiration and support they have provided. We have consulted them for help with our clients and for help with this book. From their reading of draft chapters they have provided valuable feedback. Gail Ratcliffe read the chapter on offenders and made useful comments.

We consulted with Laurie Hinchcliff and Antony Williams for help in clarifying our theoretical framework. We acknowledge their expertise and their input.

Some people have contributed through training and workshops they have provided. Particular mention should be made of Bridget Busck, whose workshop on Milton Erickson helped us to incorporate strategies derived from his work.

Don Reekie helped in the development of psychodrama skills, and in relating theory to practice. Astrid Heger and Lucy Berliner contributed to our general knowledge of sexual abuse through their workshops conducted in Auckland.

The Auckland Savings Bank provided funding to assist with the final preparation of the book, and we gratefully acknowledge their contribution.

Most of all we would like to acknowledge our clients, from whom we have learned so much of what we know. We are frequently humbled by their courage, wisdom, and perseverance.

Kathy Macdonald, BA; B.Soc.Stud. (Sydney)
Ian Lambie, R.Cp.N; MA (Hons); P.G.Dip.Clin.Psych.
Les Simmonds, Dip. Natural Therapeutics; B.Soc.Sci.

INTRODUCTION

When we began counselling people who had been abused, we discovered that very little practical information was available for therapists. Much has been written about counselling generally, and an increasing amount of research material relates specifically to sexual abuse. But remarkably little has been written to provide sexual-abuse counsellors with the resources they need for their work. How do we know what our clients need? What therapeutic options are available? How do we put the various methods into practice? What background information do we need about sexual abuse? These are some of the questions we address.

This is a book written by counsellors, for counsellors. It is intended to be a practical guide to sexual-abuse counselling. We have gathered together a wide variety of therapeutic tools, and combined them within a consistent theoretical framework. Numerous references are provided for those who wish to know more about theory and research, but the focus remains on practical issues of what to do, how, why, and when.

The book arose from a series of workshops that we presented in 1992, as staff from the Leslie Centre in Auckland, New Zealand. The workshops provided intensive training over four days for counsellors working with adults and children who had been sexually abused. The goal of the workshops was to provide counsellors with information about sexual abuse and practical ideas which they could incorporate into their work.

The workshops clearly met a need within the community, and the overwhelmingly positive response to them has encouraged us to make the information more available. In doing so we express our commitment to those who have been abused and those who wish to help them. We are also committed to sharing knowledge in a way that empowers people to solve their own problems.

The Leslie Centre is part of Presbyterian Support Services, and has developed a reputation for high-quality therapy both in New Zealand and overseas. As an agency, we work predominantly with families where children are involved, and cover a wide range of problems. Over recent years help for survivors of sexual abuse has become an increasing part of our workload, and one in which we have had to develop some expertise. The 1992 workshops were a way of sharing this expertise with other counsellors, and thereby extending the services available for those who have been abused.

As this book has been written for counsellors, it assumes some basic knowledge and experience of counselling techniques. Those who will find it most useful will be experienced counsellors who wish to know more about the specific skills required for work with sexual abuse.

For people who have been abused and for their families, the book may be helpful in providing an understanding of sexual-abuse therapy. It is not, however, intended to be a self-help manual. It is essential that the ideas described here are combined with experience and skills in counselling, as well as appropriate supervision, before being put into practice.

We have collected basic background information about sexual abuse in Chapter 1, and include a theoretical rationale for our work in Chapter 2. Chapters 3 and 4 explain the stages of healing and therapy respectively. The following seven chapters provide a very comprehensive description of the skills and methods required for work with adults, children, and their families. In order to make the book more accessible we include examples throughout and try to avoid jargon as much as possible.

We conclude with a section on offenders, and two chapters on issues for therapists and for sexual-abuse counselling generally.

In the development of our framework for therapy we rely heavily on systems theory combined with a feminist perspective. The tools we use have been drawn from many different areas. Details of our basic theoretical assumptions are provided in Chapter 2. One of the most important is reflected in our emphasis on therapy being as brief as possible, whilst ensuring that the necessary help is provided. Effective therapy is not necessarily long-term.

Another basic assumption is inherent in the way we consider the whole-family system and, at least in the case of children, emphasize the need to involve families in therapy.

We also emphasize the need to empower those who have been sexually abused, rather than to pathologize them. Inherent in this is a belief in the power of healing and the potential for people who have been abused to leave their abuse experience in the past.

The model we present is a combination of individual and family therapy. We also acknowledge the value of group work for sexual-abuse survivors, either for support or as a part of therapy. Along with other successful techniques not included in this book, we leave it for those with more relevant experience to describe group work elsewhere.

The team which first put together the ideas for this book comprised two men and two women with extensive experience in family therapy, and with formal qualifications from the fields of psychology, social work, and teaching. Culturally we are New Zealand, British, and Australian citizens of Celtic and Anglo-Saxon origins, who have worked predominantly with clients of a similar cultural background.

We believe that therapy must be culturally appropriate and do not consider ourselves experts on therapy for people from cultures other than our own. Feedback from colleagues and participants in our workshops, however, indicates that many of the ideas in this book may be adapted across cultures. We suggest that counsellors select from the book what is useful for them and their clients.

Nor do we consider ourselves experts on issues relating to gay or lesbian clients, whom we would generally refer to counsellors with specialist knowledge of their concerns. In this book we have confined ourselves to dealing in detail with issues with which we have had extensive clinical experience and made brief reference to other issues with which we have only limited experience.

The gender balance of our team is not accidental, but based on a deliberate policy of women working with female survivors of abuse, and men working with male survivors. We believe that this is important in most individual therapy, but particularly relevant with sexual abuse. The client's comfort in talking about sexual matters is more likely to be achieved with a therapist of the same gender. Furthermore, there is a danger of replicating the power issues underlying sexual abuse if a client is seen by a therapist of the opposite sex. Gender issues in sexual-abuse counselling are addressed in detail in Chapter 2.

Teamwork is an important part of our style of working. We appreciate that not all counsellors have the luxury of working as a team, but it has undoubted benefits for therapist and client. In Chapter 13 we discuss teamwork in detail.

In many ways there are few original ideas in this book, and we have acknowledged our sources wherever possible. What is new is the way that we have put the ideas together in an integrated model of therapy which deals with the people who have been abused, their families, and the offenders. We set out the steps involved in both healing and therapy, and provide practical ideas which can be used at each stage. We have placed a new emphasis on work with the family, which we see as an essential part of therapy with children, and often helpful in work with adults. Chapter 6, which relates to work with the family, is therefore pivotal to understanding our model and way of working.

A brief explanation of some of the terminology used is important. The names 'therapist' and 'counsellor' are used interchangeably throughout. While people may choose either title, both are relevant for work with sexual abuse. We avoid describing our clients as 'victims' because this word has implications of pathology. It is a vital assumption of our work that our clients have many strengths, and that many aspects of their experience are quite separate from sexual abuse. We therefore prefer to use such terms as 'people who have been abused', 'survivors', or 'clients'.

The word 'survivor' has implications of strength which the word 'victim' lacks, while the word 'client' helps to define our professional, co-operative relationship with those seeking our help. As we work from a solution-based health model rather than a pathology-based model, we would never use the word 'patient', with its implications of pathology and hierarchy.

The one context in which we find the word 'victim' useful is in work with sexual offenders. It is important that abusers understand that the effect of their behaviour is to victimize others. When they appreciate the full impact of the word 'victim' in relation to their own abusive behaviour, they have begun to develop a useful perspective for creating change.

Frequently we use the word 'offender' to designate the abuser. It is a word we also use in our work, because it very clearly lays responsibility for abuse with the perpetrator. It underlines our unambiguous belief that abuse is morally and legally wrong.

In the examples quoted, the offender is most frequently male. This reflects the reality that the majority of abusers are men. Our examples of those abused, however, include both males and females. It is important to provide therapy which meets the needs of both.

The chapter on offenders (Chapter 12) is not intended to be a detailed guide to work with abusers, but provides general information about who the offenders are and some of the factors which lead to abuse. A brief description of methods of assessment and treatment is included. This information is useful for those trying to gain a better understanding of sexual abuse, be they therapist, survivor, or family. Those wishing to learn more about work with offenders are referred to books which specialize in this area.

The last section includes a number of issues which commonly arise in sexual-abuse counselling, such as therapist survival, protocols for dealing with disclosures, networking with other counsellors, and discussion about the importance of evaluating our work.

We have not attempted to describe the assessment or 'diagnostic' techniques used, particularly with young children, to determine whether sexual abuse has occurred. This could be the subject of a whole book in itself. We focus our attention rather on therapy for children and adults who are known to have been abused when they come for counselling. This book is about clients who have memories of sexual abuse and who need assistance to deal with its effects.

Exactly how sexual abuse is defined varies considerably in the literature. For us the essential factor is that one person misuses a position of power to involve another person in some form of sexual behaviour. The power difference is often, but not always, reflected in a difference in age. It may involve coercion, bribes, or threats. The second person may even appear to co-operate, but would not have willingly participated had their relationship been more equal. Abuse can occur between children, between adults, or, more frequently between adult and child. We believe that any satisfactory definition of sexual abuse must include a wide range of sexual behaviours by the perpetrator, and a wide range of subjective experiences of the person abused.

It is important that we address here the needs of therapists who have themselves been sexually abused. Given the prevalence of sexual abuse it is inevitable that many counsellors reading this book will have personal experience of abuse. Some will have been drawn to their work by a desire to use their own experience to help others.

To those readers who have been abused we have an important message: It is possible that reading about the experiences of others in this book may trigger strong emotions about your own abuse. If this happens we urge you to consider what you need to complete your own healing. Otherwise these emotions are also likely to be triggered in a counselling session by a client who is relying on your assistance. Only when we have taken adequate care of ourselves are we in the strongest position to care for our clients.

For all our readers, our hope is that this book will provide you with a sound knowledge base, practical ideas, and the inspiration to develop your own creativity. In this way we combine our efforts with yours, to take a more powerful stand against sexual abuse and its effects on the lives of our clients.

PART 1

AN OVERVIEW

SEXUAL ABUSE:
Facts and Fallacies

Therapists working with clients who have been sexually abused need to keep themselves well informed about the issues involved. When our work is based on a solid knowledge of relevant facts we are much clearer about what help our clients need and how to plan therapy to provide it most effectively.

We are also in a much better position to provide our clients with the information they need for their healing. This might include information about resources, and about options available. It might also include reassurance about fears which are crippling our clients' lives, or affirmation of the steps they have taken towards healing. They need to know, for example, that they are not alone, that abuse happens to other people, and that healing is possible. A solid base of knowledge will empower us to speak with the confidence our clients need.

Perhaps more than with therapy for many other problems, therapy for sexual abuse almost always includes a significant educational component. In cases where a client has not been severely traumatized by abuse, providing information may constitute the major part of therapy. By sharing our knowledge we can help many clients and their families to understand their experience. We do not dispute the reality of their experience, but provide a different perspective which helps them to see their responses as normal rather than pathological. This process of normalizing can be very therapeutic, and is described in more detail in Chapter 5.

With information we can guide parents as to how best to help a child who has been abused. Particularly with younger children the role of parents and caregivers is paramount in the therapy process, and the primary role of the therapist may be to inform and support the parents.

Providing information does not mean that our therapy sessions turn into lectures. Rather, we take opportunities as they arise to share our knowledge, one or two facts at a time. This is known as 'seeding' information and is described in detail in Chapter 5.

In this chapter we have gathered together the information which we find most useful. This comes from a variety of sources which we have acknowledged whenever possible. Original sources are not always known when the information presented has moved into the domain of assumptions commonly held by sexual-abuse therapists.

With some issues therapists would be advised to seek regular updates on the information provided, as new research and information continually reinforce and extend our knowledge base.

PREVALENCE

A significant body of research has been undertaken over recent years, studying the prevalence of sexual abuse. Conclusions differ according to the definition of abuse, the methods used, and the sample studied. It appears, however, from an examination of comparable studies, that incidence does not vary significantly between countries within the Western world. In a review of the literature Anna Salter (1988) concluded that the more comprehensive and rigorous the research, the higher the incidence of abuse reported.

Recent detailed research into sexual abuse in New Zealand confirmed results from the more thorough studies in Australia, Britain, Canada, and the United States. A survey of women's health in Otago, New Zealand (Anderson *et al.* 1993) found that nearly 20 per cent of the 1660 urban women respondents reported sexual abuse involving at least genital contact before they turned 16. Another 6 per cent reported inappropriate touching or kissing, and a further 7 per cent reported sexual abuse which did not involve physical contact — such as exposure or being asked to do something sexual. This amounts to one in three girls under 16 experiencing some form of sexual abuse.

In addition, approximately a quarter of the women surveyed reported experiences of sexual abuse as adults (over 16), often by abusers they knew well, such as husbands or boyfriends.

In general, studies of male sexual abuse have reported lower rates than those found for females. A Canadian study by Badgley (1984), for example, in a typical result found that 5.9 per cent of boys had been molested under the age of 15, and 9.4 per cent under the age of 18. In Watkins and Bentovim's (1992) review of studies of male sexual abuse, they note the wide range in reported rates (3–31 per cent), and suggest that a current 'best guess' indicates that 2–5 per cent of the male population experience sexual abuse involving physical contact.

A growing body of research, however, supports the idea that reported rates of abuse of boys may be significantly underestimated (e.g. Finkelhor 1984, 1990; Watkins & Bentovim 1992). There is evidence that boys are less likely to disclose than girls (Watkins & Bentovim 1992), and some researchers (e.g. Baker & Duncan 1985) believe that the actual rate of abuse of boys may be comparable to that of girls.

Even if we accept figures currently available, research indicates that boys represent between one fifth and one third of all victims of sexual abuse (Watkins & Bentovim 1992). This is a significant problem which has been given inadequate recognition in the literature, in research, and in therapy. It reflects a serious need for more male therapists to work with the boys concerned.

OFFENDERS

Early research has indicated that the vast majority (96–98 per cent) of offenders are male (e.g. Farrelly & Sebastian 1984; Russell 1983). More recent evidence suggests that abuse by women is likely to be under-reported (Watkins & Bentovim 1992), but there is considerable controversy about its true extent. An interesting North American study by Faller (1987) found that 13.8 per cent of abusers in a clinical sample of 289 sexual offenders were women, but in the majority of these cases abuse had been initiated by men, and the women were drawn into it by coercion or persuasion.

The majority of offenders are known to their victim. A 1980 New Zealand study (reported by Saphira 1985) found that 89 per cent of sexually abused children had been molested by someone they knew. Nearly half of the offenders were relatives, and nearly a quarter were fathers or stepfathers.

According to Anderson et al. (1993), stepfathers are much more likely to abuse children in their care than are biological fathers. One in every ten stepfathers were reported to have sexually molested children in their care, as opposed to one in every hundred biological fathers. This finding is supported by Finkelhor et al. (1990) and Russell (1983).

A New Zealand survey of women's health (Anderson et al. 1993) also supported findings commonly quoted in research from other countries (e.g. Deisher et al. 1982) indicating that 25 per cent of offenders are teenagers, and nearly half are under the age of 25. Miriam Saphira (1985) reported that

82.5 per cent of offenders are under the age of 50, thus negating the common stereotype of the 'dirty old man'.

POSSIBLE EFFECTS OF SEXUAL ABUSE

The possible effects of sexual abuse have been widely reported internationally in reviews of the research literature (e.g. Beitchman *et al.* 1992; Browne & Finkelhor 1986; Saphira 1985). We present here a brief summary derived from the literature and from our own experience. It is important to note that these behaviours are not by themselves *evidence* of abuse. They are simply listed here as possible *consequences* of abuse.

Regression

Regression involves reverting to habits usually associated with a younger age group — such as using a 'security blanket', thumb-sucking, or 'baby talk'. It also includes loss of bladder or bowel control in children who have previously been clean and dry. Bedwetting at night after achieving dry beds for a significant period would be an example, as would wetting or soiling during the day. Sometimes more extreme behaviours are involved, such as smearing faeces or choosing inappropriate places for urination.

Sleep disturbances

Persistent nightmares or 'night terrors' (when a highly distressed or frightened person appears to be awake but often has no memory of the event later) fall within this category. Refusal to sleep alone and sleep-walking may also occur as a result of abuse.

Eating disorders

A wide range of eating disorders has been associated with abuse, from overeating to bulimia and anorexia. Feeding difficulties in infants and preschoolers may follow abuse.

Acute traumatic response

With children, trauma may be indicated by extreme fearfulness, clinging, frequent unprovoked crying, or constant irritability. Other symptoms which may also be present in adults include 'flashbacks', problems with memory or concentration, feelings of estrangement from others, and avoidance of social activities.

Behaviour problems

Extremes of behaviour in children, ranging from increased defiance and aggression to withdrawal or overly compliant behaviour, can occur as a result of sexual abuse. Behaviour problems may manifest in delinquency, and in running away from home in older children and adolescents. Inappropriate sexualized behaviour is a common problem in abused children of all ages, while difficulties with sexual relationships may be a concern for adolescents and adults who have been abused.

Social problems

Abuse survivors may have difficulty relating to peers as well as problems with self-care. A range of behaviours, such as poor hygiene, poor nutrition, and excessive washing, may lead to ostracism and social isolation.

School problems

Possible effects of sexual abuse on a child's performance at school include lowered concentration span, poor performance, attention-seeking, disruptive behaviour, fighting, and truancy. A child who tries to escape from abuse at home may habitually arrive early at school and/or leave late.

Long-term effects of abuse

Many long-term effects of abuse are reported in the literature (e.g. Beitchman *et al.* 1992; Browne & Finkelhor 1986; Finkelhor 1990). These include poor self-esteem, depression, guilt, anxiety, phobias, and self-destructive behaviour. Difficulties in sexual relationships, alcohol and drug abuse, difficulties with trust and intimacy, a sense of powerlessness, and vulnerability to revictimization have also been widely reported.

The long-term effects of abuse include the consequences of those responses exhibited more immediately. For example, the child who is unable to concentrate at school can grow up to become an adult who has been deprived of an education. The child who is aggressive in response to abuse can grow up to be an adult who is violent and lacking in social skills.

It may be that the long-term effects of abuse vary between men and women. There is some evidence from a number of studies reviewed by

Finkelhor (1990) that women are more likely to internalize the effects of the abuse and consequently to suffer more from depression and anxiety states, while men are more likely to externalize the effects, as demonstrated in higher rates of aggressive behaviour in sexually abused males. Differences in the socialization of men and women could account for different gender patterns in the effects of abuse. More research is needed, however, as not all studies have supported these conclusions regarding gender differences in response to abuse (Finkelhor 1990; Watkins & Bentovim 1992).

Medical indicators

There are a number of medical indicators of abuse, but it is important to remember that these will not be evident in the majority of cases. Astrid Heger* reported during a 1991 Auckland workshop that 75 per cent of those who are sexually abused present no medical evidence. Medical indicators include infection, bruises, inflammation, blood stains, sexually transmitted diseases, and pregnancy. Symptoms sometimes associated with stress can also occur, such as enuresis, encopresis, eczema, and asthma.

WHAT IS NORMAL CHILDHOOD SEXUAL BEHAVIOUR?

The behaviours listed above are possible effects of abuse rather than conclusive indicators. While any one of them may be an indicator of abuse, they can also be indicators of other difficulties. Therapists need to be alert to the signs of abuse in children but also be wary of jumping to conclusions.

A knowledge of the range of normal childhood sexual behaviours is invaluable as a reference point when suspicion of possible abuse is aroused, because inappropriate sexual behaviour is one of the most reliable indicators of abuse (Friedrich 1990). We need to take into account, however, the individual differences exhibited by children when we are considering whether a particular behaviour is 'normal'. These differences reflect their differing levels of maturity and exposure to adult sexuality. We should also be wary of using sexual behaviour as the sole criterion for determining whether a child has a problem (Johnson 1991).

It is normal for children of all ages to masturbate, and for some this can become a comfort or a habit. Parents may choose to ignore it, or to insist

* Professor Astrid Heger, Clinical Professor of Paediatrics, Director of Child Sexual Abuse Clinic, University of Southern California.

that it not be done in public. Obsessive masturbation, use of objects to rub the genitals, or penetration using either a finger or an object would be outside normal limits and would require further investigation.

Children are naturally curious about the differences between the sexes from about age two, and may want to see one another's genitals or show interest in how others urinate. They may ask questions about body parts or play games which allow them to study one another's genitals (e.g. hospital games). As they become older (about six) they may take part in mild sex play, but they are unlikely to display a detailed knowledge of sex unless they have observed (live, on film, or in magazine) or experienced it. Similarly, play which involves genital penetration, sexually acting out with animals and toys, or a preoccupation with sexual matters, goes beyond the limits of normality and indicates the possibility of sexual abuse. This kind of sexualized play may also be experienced as abusive by other children involved.

Interest in toilets and the different positions used by boys and girls to urinate is common in young children, as are frequent references to toileting and a lot of giggling about the subject. It is also normal for children to demand privacy for themselves at the toilet despite wanting to observe others. Some children are quite modest about undressing in front of people while others are unperturbed about it — both are quite normal.

FALSE ACCUSATIONS

The most reliable indicator of sexual abuse is a disclosure from the person who was abused. This may come as a direct statement or may be relatively indirect — as in, 'I don't like Uncle Bert', 'Mr Jones does funny things', or 'Daddy hurt my bottom'. Obviously indirect statements such as these are not by themselves evidence of abuse, but they do warrant further questioning.

Children rarely make false accusations of abuse. After a review of the literature Anna Salter (1988) concluded that false reports by children are rare and may occur in perhaps no more than 2 per cent of cases. She also reported that false reports by adults and children may total up to 8 per cent, leaving 92 per cent of allegations reasonably reliable. Lucy Berliner* in an Auckland workshop (14.2.92), stated that those few who do make false accusations usually have a prior history of abuse.

* Lucy Berliner, Research Director, Harborview Sexual Assault Centre, Harborview Medical Centre, University of Washington, Seattle; Clinical Assistant Professor, School of Social Work, University of Washington, Seattle.

Children and mothers are frequently accused of lying about sexual abuse, but the evidence suggests that this is a rare phenomenon (Salter 1988). While it is important that we determine when a child is lying and that we are careful not to support false allegations, the reality is that proving genuine disclosures and protecting children from repeated abuse is a much more extensive problem than protecting innocent adults from false accusations.

Women are not infrequently accused of lying when they make an accusation of abuse against an ex-partner at the time of a custody or access dispute. As Salter (1988) reports, however, there are a number of reasons why genuine allegations are likely to emerge at this time. A separated man under stress may be more likely to abuse, and may have greater opportunity. A child may be more likely to disclose abuse when the offender is no longer in the home. It would be a serious mistake to dismiss allegations made at this time as motivated by vindictiveness or ulterior motives without full and careful investigation.

Finally, with greater public awareness of sexual abuse, it is possible that there may be an increase in false or mistaken allegations. This needs to be monitored with further research.

NON-DISCLOSURE OF ABUSE

Not reporting abuse is a far more common problem than false allegations. The Otago Women's Health Survey (Anderson et al. 1993) found that only 40 per cent of women who had experienced sexual abuse as children had told anyone at the time. Other studies report similar or even lower disclosure rates. Watkins and Bentovim (1992) reviewed the literature and found that under-reporting of sexual abuse is a consistent and universal problem.

Only 6 per cent of the women in the Otago Study had reported to the police. Finkelhor (1984) found that frequency of reporting to an outside agency varied enormously depending on the relationship between the parents and the offender. Of those parents whose children were abused by a stranger, 73 per cent reported the abuse. When the offender was an acquaintance, only 23 per cent did so. When the offender was a relative, however, none reported the abuse. Clearly, police records cannot provide anything like an accurate guide to the prevalence of sexual abuse.

Of the women surveyed in the Otago Study, 20 per cent had disclosed abuse later in life, and a significant 28 per cent had not told anyone before responding to the survey.

With increasing resources and awareness of sexual abuse, there has been a significant increase in reporting rates. The number of cases reported, however, still comes nowhere near the actual rate of abuse as found in incidence studies.

WHY CHILDREN HAVE DIFFICULTY REPORTING SEXUAL ABUSE

There are a number of powerful reasons why sexual abuse may not be disclosed. An awareness of these reasons helps therapists to help abused clients and their families. The person who was abused may blame themselves for not stopping the abuse by telling someone about it. Parents may blame themselves for not recognizing indirect references to abuse, or may worry about why their children did not confide in them. Parents sometimes feel angry, hurt, or guilty when they discover that children have not disclosed abuse as it occurred.

When we understand the reasons why children find it so difficult to disclose, we can share this knowledge. This helps to remove the feelings of blame or guilt which children and their families may be experiencing.

Listed here are a number of reasons why children find it difficult to disclose:

- They may not know the words to describe what has happened;
- They may believe that they have done something wrong and be ashamed or afraid to tell;
- They may feel too embarrassed to talk about it;
- They may feel that they will not be believed;
- They may have been coerced with bribes or threats;
- They may have been told to keep a secret;
- They may be afraid of the reaction they will get;
- They may have had a bad experience of trying to tell and been ignored, disbelieved, or punished;
- They may want to protect their family from upset, anger, or breakup;
- They may want to protect the offender;
- Boys abused by men may fear being seen as homosexual;
- Boys abused by women may fear that their abuse experience will not be taken seriously.
- They may be afraid of the offender.

HOW TO RESPOND TO A DISCLOSURE

Therapists known to work with clients who have been sexually abused are often contacted by upset family members in crisis when a disclosure of abuse has just been made. Sometimes the initial disclosure, by either a child or an adult, is made to a therapist rather than to a family member.

At other times we see the family after they have begun to deal with a disclosure, and we need to be able to affirm them for any positive steps taken to help the person who was abused. Reassurance about how they have coped is therapeutic for the family and empowers them to provide further help as needed.

For all these reasons we need to be clear about how to respond in the most helpful way to anyone disclosing sexual abuse. Several factors are crucial:

- Stay calm;
- Believe what they say. Remember false accusations are extremely rare;
- Let them know that you are pleased they told you. If appropriate, affirm them for their courage in disclosing.
- Validate their feelings — whether distress, anger, confusion, etc.;
- Tell them that it was not their fault;
- Ensure that they are safe;
- Ensure that they get appropriate help, e.g. counselling, medical attention;
- Get adult support for yourself if needed.

REPORTING ABUSE

While reporting sexual abuse to the police or to child welfare services is not mandatory in all areas, it is advisable in most cases. Offenders are likely to continue abusing until apprehended by the police and/or forced to enter treatment (Salter 1988). Few admit freely to their offences when confronted, or enter treatment voluntarily. When family, friends, or associates believe that they can deal with abuse without involving the police they run a serious risk that the person who was abused may not be getting the help they need, or that an offender continues to pose a threat to others by not getting appropriate treatment.

RESPONSIBILITY FOR SEXUAL ABUSE LIES WITH THE OFFENDER

It is a basic premise of our work that a child is never to blame for being sexually abused. Responsibility for abuse lies totally with the abuser, who may be adolescent or older.

Prior to adolescence we would call abusive behaviour 'sexually acting out' or 'inappropriate sexual behaviour', although the other child may experience it as abuse. We take a strong stand that abuse by all age groups is unacceptable and must be stopped.

For preadolescent abusers, however, we would also be asking questions about where they learned their sexualized behaviour and investigating whether they themselves had been abused. There is a wide range of 'normal' sexual behaviour in children, determined by factors such as developmental levels, parental attitudes, and exposure to adult sexuality, explicit television, or videos. Increased sexual behaviour may also indicate that a child has been abused (Friedrich *et al.* 1988; Gale *et al.* 1988; Johnson 1991). This may provide an understanding of their behaviour, but should never be presented as an excuse. For adolescents and adults a history of abuse is not considered to be an excuse for becoming an abuser.

There are a number of reasons why children are never to blame for being abused. They may be physically too weak to resist. They may be too afraid or too confused by what is happening to them. They may be trained to be obedient to their elders and not know that they have a right to say 'No'. They may have been sexualized by previous abuse and have made themselves vulnerable to revictimization, perhaps even by initiating sexual behaviour. Whatever the reasons, children are not to be blamed. It must be remembered that they are always relatively powerless and dependent on adults to ensure that they are safe and that appropriate boundaries are maintained.

Historically both children and their mothers have been blamed in the literature for sexual abuse (Salter 1988). Women even blame themselves at times, wondering if they could have prevented abuse if they had been more vigilant or more sexually available to their partners. The truth is that an abuser may be in a sexual relationship with an adult at the same time as they are abusing children, or they may simply prefer sex with children. Lack of a satisfying sexual relationship with an adult is never an excuse for abusing children.

Women may sometimes have to take responsibility for not protecting a child from abuse, if, for example, they knew the abuse was occurring or generally failed to provide adequate care, but it is still the abuser who is responsible for the abuse itself.

ABUSE DOES NOT NECESSARILY LEAD TO ABUSING

One of the common fears of those who have been sexually abused — and their families — is that they will become abusers themselves. We need to be really clear that a history of sexual abuse is not an excuse for becoming an abuser, and that abusers are responsible for their actions in spite of their history. The important fact here is that the majority of children abused do not grow up to be abusers. Nor do all abusers have a history of being abused themselves.

Sexual abuse is a choice made by offenders, not forced upon them by circumstances. While some reports indicate that rates of offending may be higher amongst people who have been abused (e.g. Watkins & Bentovim 1992), it is also evident that abusive behaviour is not a necessary result of having been abused.

A number of studies (e.g. Johnson 1989; McCarty 1986) have found that the majority — if not all — of the female perpetrators they investigated had a history of being abused. Others, such as Faller (1987), have not found a history of abuse in female offenders to be significantly different from that found in similar studies of non-abusing women. At present there is insufficient evidence to draw any definite conclusions about this, apart from the fact that few women with a history of abuse sexually abuse others.

Lucy Berliner (see p. 8) stated in her 1992 Auckland workshop that some young women who had been abused may experiment with abuse as a means of trying to understand their experience and what it feels like to be an abuser. Unlike men, however, whose abusive behaviour is usually reinforced with immediate sexual gratification, it seems that women are not likely to persist with repeated offending. This is supported by Faller's (1987) finding that the average age of female abusers was almost ten years younger than that of male abusers.

Widely divergent rates of prior abuse have been reported in studies of male perpetrators (Watkins & Bentovim 1992). Becker (1988), for example, found that 19 per cent of perpetrators in her study had been abused themselves, while Seghorn *et al.* (1987), found a rate of 57 per cent in their sample of 54 child molesters.

It is clear that more than one factor (i.e. history of abuse) is operating when a victim becomes a victimizer (Finkelhor 1986).

ABUSE DOES NOT CREATE GAYS OR LESBIANS

Another very common fear, is that a history of sexual abuse will make the abuse survivor become gay or lesbian (Watkins & Bentovim 1992). This is most prevalent in adolescent boys who may be heterosexual but who have experienced arousal in response to abuse by another male. It is also a fear commonly held by the families of boys who have been abused. It is a fear so common that it is often wise for the therapist to offer information on this subject even if it is not raised by the client. In doing this we do not imply any judgement of those who are gay or lesbian, simply the lack of connection with sexual abuse.

We can state with confidence that sexual orientation is not determined by abuse. The majority of gays and lesbians have not had inappropriate experiences in childhood, and are not interested in children sexually (Finkelhor 1984). An abusive act perpetrated on someone of the same gender does not indicate that the perpetrator is homosexually oriented (Watkins & Bentovim 1992). The majority of sexual offenders are in fact heterosexual males (Saphira 1987). For some clients, getting this information will be a major step in their healing process.

At times we will be working with people who are gay or lesbian. They need a counsellor who is able to validate and support them in their sexual orientation. Heterosexual counsellors are well advised to offer these clients a choice of seeing a gay or lesbian therapist who is likely to be more aware of the issues involved.

LIFE AFTER ABUSE

One important fact that is often overlooked as we become more aware of the effects of sexual abuse, is that some people who have been abused experience no serious trauma or symptoms. In his review of the literature, Finkelhor (1990) concluded that almost every study of the impact of sexual abuse found a substantial group of survivors who were relatively symptom-free. It seems from Finkelhor's survey that between one-quarter and one-third of sexually abused children have adequate psychological and social resources to cope without experiencing serious trauma or long-lasting effects.

From Finkelhor (1990) and Beitchman *et al.*(1992), we learn that there are two major factors contributing to the impact of sexual abuse. One is the nature of the abuse itself, and the other is the response to it once disclosed.

The effects of abuse are less likely to be serious if the abuse does not involve force or violence, if there is no penetration, if it is of relatively short duration, and if the abuser is not a father or father-figure (e.g. stepfather).

In addition, parental and social attitudes toward the child and towards the child's role in the event are important determinants of the long-term effects of abuse. Prognosis is likely to be best for those who are believed, who are not blamed, who have family support, secure relationships, a stable home environment, co-operation between home and school, and who get appropriate counselling as needed (Friedrich 1990).

Friedrich (1990) reports on several US studies which identify revictimization by the socio-legal system. This can occur, for example, through poor handling of cases, lack of treatment in order to avoid 'contamination' of a legal prosecution, or removal of a child from the home without family counselling aimed at their return. Giaretto (1982) claims that such revictimization can be even more negative than the abuse itself for some children.

The behavioural response of the child is another factor that contributes to the impact of the abuse. Behavioural changes as a result of abuse (e.g. aggression) create their own difficulties (e.g. social isolation). These can continue after the abuse has ceased (Friedrich 1990) and may need specific attention within child and family counselling.

Information and assistance given to families is therefore crucial for the recovery of a child. Sometimes this will include reassurance that their child has not been traumatized and can continue to lead a normal life. Other times the reassurance will be that both children and adults can heal from sexual abuse if given the help they need. This does not mean that it will be forgotten. Rather, it becomes a part of the survivor's history, always with them, but not preventing them from living a happy and fulfilled life.

2

BASIC THEORETICAL
ASSUMPTIONS

It is important that we are clear about the assumptions and values underlying our methods of therapy. In making our assumptions and values explicit
we hold them up for examination and discussion, and also explain why
we choose to work in a particular way.

We make a basic distinction between the model which guides the way
we think about abuse and therapy, and the many models of therapy from
which we have drawn the techniques that we use.

We think about sexual abuse therapy within a coherent theoretical
model based on a combination of systems theory and feminism. However,
the tools that we use to achieve our therapeutic goals come from many
sources. As we describe these tools throughout the book, we acknowledge
where possible the models from which they have been drawn. We do not
provide an exhaustive description or critique of these models, but references are given for those who are interested in reading more about them.

We believe that both the systemic and feminist perspectives are necessary
for an understanding of abuse, and, like Goldner (1992), believe that the
apparent contradictions between these two perspectives can be contained.
There is no single politically or clinically 'correct' position which can explain
the very different ways that individuals experience sexual abuse and its
effects, or that meets the very different therapeutic needs of each client.

In this chapter we describe briefly the influence of both the systems and
feminist perspectives on our work, the issues that arise from combining
the two, and our ideas about how change is facilitated in therapy.

THE INDIVIDUAL AS A SYSTEM

From systems theory we understand that individuals, families, and social groups are each made up of various parts. The parts interact with one another, so that change in one part will affect other parts. When we think of the individual as a system, for example, we understand why helping a client to change some aspect of their behaviour might influence the way in which they think about themselves. Changing a *belief* can influence *emotions*, while techniques which help to deal with such feelings as anger, anxiety, and grief can ultimately affect *beliefs*, *physical symptoms*, and *behaviour*.

Therapists working with people who have been sexually abused have adopted techniques for dealing specifically with the various effects of abuse. Some methods focus, for example, on relief for such physical symptoms as psychosomatic pains. Some offer behavioural techniques to target such responses as aggression, overeating or alcohol abuse. Many different ways are used to challenge unhelpful beliefs or to develop new perspectives. Any method that focuses on a specific problem can indirectly alleviate difficulties in other areas.

THE FAMILY AS A SYSTEM

Thinking about the family as a system helps us to understand the pivotal role the family plays in the healing of one of its members following sexual abuse. Abuse affects the whole family, and the family's response in turn has a major effect on the person who was abused. This response will be determined by the various perceptions each family member has about the offender, the survivor, and about sexual abuse generally.

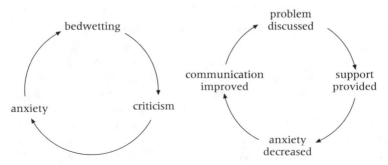

The trauma of abuse is either compounded or minimized by the reactions of others.

One of the basic premises of family systems theory is that the effect of any action by one person can be magnified or decreased by the way others respond to it. For example, anxiety triggered in a child by abuse is likely to be increased if caregivers respond with criticism or blame to symptoms such as bedwetting or night-waking. On the other hand, effects of child abuse may be alleviated by a caregiver who believes a disclosure and takes immediate action to provide safety and support. In each case a circular pattern develops in which the trauma of abuse is either compounded or minimized by the reactions of others.

This pattern is widely known in the family therapy literature as 'circular causality'. It is, however, more usefully applied as a description of what is happening than as an explanation of the causes of behaviour.

CIRCULAR CAUSALITY

The notion of circular causality has been misused in the past to imply that abuse is a two-way process in which the survivor shares responsibility. This in no way recognizes the unequal power relationship between survivor and offender.

One of the basic tenets of our model of therapy is that the perpetrator is totally responsible for sexual abuse. The notion of circularity effectively eliminates blame and thus makes it a useful concept for dealing with the effects of abuse, but not for explaining the abuse itself. For a fuller understanding of abuse we reject the neutrality implied in the concept of circular causality, and turn to feminism which allows us to make judgements on moral issues. This is explained in more detail later in the chapter.

CIRCLES THAT HELP
AND CIRCLES THAT HINDER

One useful application of circular causality is in understanding what has become known colloquially as 'vicious' and 'virtuous' circles. These are cycles in which we notice information which strengthens existing beliefs and behaviours, while ignoring evidence which might support other ways of thinking or behaving. For example, a person who has been abused may believe that they are responsible for what happened and consequently develop a poor opinion of themselves based on shame and guilt. They are then more likely to interpret their behaviour in terms of weakness or failure. As their strengths and successes are ignored, the poor opinion of themselves is reinforced over time in a 'vicious cycle'.

Conversely, by helping clients to notice their strengths and successes, we can start a helpful or 'virtuous' cycle, in which small changes can lead to major positive shifts in perception and behaviour. This is one of the main tasks of therapy.

WORKING WITH THE FAMILY

The major implication of systems thinking to therapy for sexual abuse is the importance of involving the family. In work with children the response of the family is vital to healing, so concurrent work with a child's family is an integral part of our model of therapy. Where necessary we work with family members to develop ideas and responses which are most effective for their own healing, and for the healing of the child. As in individual work with the survivor, this involves conveying information in such a way that it enhances the development of those perceptions, feelings, and behaviours that facilitate beneficial change.

In our work with adult clients, we are influenced by systems theory in our awareness of the influence of family, partners, and friends, although the client will not always choose to involve others directly in the therapy process. By exploring with the client the family's responses to the abuse and how this has affected them, we imply that other perceptions and responses are possible. Similarly, we can invite our clients to consider other ways of responding to their family's influence if this has not been helpful.

Beliefs about sexual abuse (e.g. beliefs about who is responsible and how people are affected) are crucial to the healing process, because they play a major role in determining how each person's behaviour, feelings, and physical reaction are influenced by their abuse. We have drawn from the different models of therapy various ways of addressing unhelpful beliefs and may use any or all of these methods with a particular client. Not surprisingly many of the tools we use are derived from the various schools of family therapy, because these are all based on a systems approach.

THE INFLUENCE OF THE STRUCTURAL SCHOOL OF FAMILY THERAPY

From the systems perspective we gain an understanding of sub-systems within the family. Any combination of family members may be regarded as a sub-system. The siblings, for example, form a sub-system, as do the parents, grandparents, parent and child. An awareness of family sub-systems is useful in our assessment of the client's situation and their particular needs. We need to know, for example, where the client gets their support, who is closest to whom, and where the power lies. With adult clients we ask how/if the abuse affects their adult relationships and the parenting of their children.

The idea of sub-systems has been developed most within the Structural School of family therapy, pioneered by Salvador Minuchin (1974). Minuchin believed that appropriate boundaries between generations are necessary for the healthy functioning of the family. According to this notion there is a hierarchy of power within the family, with the parental sub-system having authority over the children. Sexual abuse by a parent-figure is obviously a misuse of that power, but there are many examples of appropriate use of parental power. When we encourage parents to take control of their children's unacceptable behaviour, for example, we imply that it is their right and responsibility to use their power in this way.

Structural family therapy provides a clear guide to dealing with families where incest has occurred, because it advocates appropriate boundaries between the various sub-systems and provides an unambiguous perspective on responsibility for abuse lying with the adult perpetrator. It is particularly helpful in families where the abuser remains within the home (as is not uncommon in brother–sister incest) or when the abuser returns to the home — for example, when a husband and wife are reconciled after a period of treatment and/or imprisonment. Therapy with such families will focus at some stage on defining the behaviours which constitute appropriate boundaries and the ways in which these can be maintained.

In cases where the family is generally unsupportive, the boundaries may be drawn between the client and the family, or at least between the client and particular family members. Such boundaries provide protection by defining the limits of the relationship and by helping the client to develop a stronger sense of self, while finding other sources of support outside the family.

THE WIDER SOCIAL SYSTEM

From a systems perspective we see the client not only as part of a family, but as part of a wider social system which impinges on their world-view in a multitude of ways. Effective therapy takes into account such influences as culture, religion, education, and gender. From these our client will have developed perspectives which influence both their response to abuse and their needs in therapy.

Feminism provides us with an understanding of the ways in which the wider social system influences the beliefs of both client and therapist. This is because it adds to systems thinking an analysis of historical, political, and social processes that affect our beliefs and our position in society. These in turn impinge on therapy in a number of ways.

Beliefs which do not award women an equal place in society, for example, can reinforce the sense of powerlessness and incompetency experienced by our female clients as a result of abuse. Socialization processes which teach women to nurture others before themselves, or which teach men that tears are a sign of weakness, may prevent people from expressing their needs and getting help. Sexual stereotypes which dictate how men and women should look and act can stop them from asserting themselves and feeling good about the way they really are.

For some people, politicization can be part of therapy. Understanding the influence of social and cultural norms through discussion and reading helps to remove self-blame, and can empower clients to make changes in their own lives and perhaps also to help others. Women may find a new perspective on their lives in the feminist literature, or may decide to join together in groups to promote awareness of issues relating to abuse. Men may also get involved in various groups, or, for example, in work with offenders.

Awareness of the wider social system also helps to determine the therapist's world-view, and determines which type of therapist is likely to be most effective with a particular client. For this reason it is almost always helpful for therapist and client to be matched for culture and gender. The therapist then can fully appreciate the major influences in the client's life.

Matching culture and gender also helps the client to relate to the therapist, because we cannot help but reflect the beliefs and habits acquired within our own culture. When these are not the same as those of our client, they may impede development of the therapeutic relationship. (See also 'Gender-appropriate Counselling', p. 23.)

In many ways society helps to perpetuate beliefs and practices which contribute to sexual abuse, and which are unhelpful for the healing of survivors. In therapy we need to challenge such beliefs. We may also choose to take political action outside the therapy room to create change, just as our clients may find political action to be a positive and therapeutic option.

THE THERAPIST AS PART OF THE SYSTEM

Finally, systems theory provides us with a useful framework for examining the role of the therapist in sexual-abuse counselling. The therapist becomes part of a system which includes client and family, and works with them in

a co-operative way to produce change and healing. In our model of working the therapist also has a very clear belief and value system about abuse, including basic assumptions about survivors not being to blame and healing being possible. We do not hesitate to share these beliefs, and where necessary to take on an advocacy role for a survivor whose family may have accepted in part or whole the meaning ascribed to the abuse by the perpetrator (e.g. 'She led me on', 'He wanted it', 'It didn't do any harm').
It is sometimes very difficult to keep a balance between the need to work co-operatively with client and family, and the need to be clear about our own beliefs and values, but this is essential if we are to be helpful to our clients.

FEMINISM AND SOCIAL ANALYSIS

From feminism we have gained an understanding of the way in which power is distributed unequally according to gender. This occurs both within the family and within society generally. These differences in the distribution of power combine with gender differences in socialization to make women and children more vulnerable to abuse, and men more likely to be the abusers. Statistics strongly support this inference (see Chapter 1).

The feminist analysis of society informs our work, and provides an understanding of sexual abuse within its social context. It encourages us to raise moral issues and to make judgements which condemn abuse. It ensures that we act as advocates for those who have been abused, and as advocates for social change. Feminist ideas also provide a different perspective to help our clients understand their experience. Appreciating the social context of abuse helps them to abandon any ideas of self-blame and feelings of shame. It may also empower them by encouraging a proactive stance against abuse of themselves and others. They might choose to participate in self-help groups or in activities designed to create social change. These include courses in self-assertion, self-defence, support groups, or lobby groups.

FEMINISM AND SOCIAL PRESCRIPTIONS

Feminist analysis identifies societal prescriptions for females which not only make them more vulnerable to abuse but also compound its effects. These prescriptions include ideas that women should be nurturing and put the needs of others before their own, that they should make themselves sexually attractive to men (according to specified stereotypes), and that being strong and assertive is unfeminine and therefore desirable only in men.

Similarly, certain behaviours are commonly prescribed for men. They are expected to be 'strong' and in control, and their socialization does not encourage them to be so sensitive to the feelings of others, or so free to express their own feelings. Furthermore, in most cultures sexual 'conquests' of women are sanctioned and even acclaimed by men. These factors not only contribute to male sexual abuse of women and children, but also contribute to specific difficulties experienced by males who have been sexually abused themselves.

FEMINIST FAMILY THERAPY

Feminist family therapists such as Deborah Leupnitz (1988) have pointed to the importance of understanding the origins of problem behaviour rather than just treating symptoms. This idea is essential in sexual-abuse therapy, where tracing a survivor's responses back to the abusive act and validating their feelings about the abuse are basic to the healing process. Treating symptoms, and offering new perspectives are useful but are not sufficient. No amount of redefining will take away the fact that abuse has occurred, and therapy which proceeds without understanding or validating the client's experience of abuse is likely to fail.

Feminists have also brought to family therapy an appreciation of the importance of emotions. This helps us to avoid the tendency of some models of therapy to focus only on beliefs or behaviours. In sexual-abuse therapy we believe that it is essential to deal with the emotional response to abuse, as well as the physical, behavioural, and cognitive effects.

GENDER-APPROPRIATE COUNSELLING

The feminist viewpoint guides our belief in the importance of gender-appropriate counselling. Not only do we believe that female therapists have a better understanding of their female clients' experience of life, but they are also able to provide positive models for women without replicating the male/female power imbalance inherent in society and in most abuse of women. No matter how good a male therapist might be, there is a serious danger that his relationship with a female client may reflect the power imbalance determined by gender within our society. This works to compound the effects of abuse rather than to alleviate it, because imbalance of power is a major issue for those who have been abused.

Similarly, male clients are best seen by male therapists, who can relate to their experience, communicate in familiar ways, and provide models of sensitivity and nurturing. With a male therapist men can learn to take better care of themselves and one another, rather than perpetuating dependency on women to meet their needs.

NEUTRALITY AND MORALITY

It should be clear from preceding comments that we do not adopt a neutral stance towards either sexual abuse or change. Our basic assumptions include beliefs that sexual abuse is wrong, that it is the responsibility of the abuser, and that therapy is about helping our clients to make changes. Furthermore we have clear ideas about the sorts of changes we want clients to make, and we direct our therapy towards specific goals. These include helping clients to build self-esteem, to reject shame and guilt, and to deal with any effects of abuse which are impairing their enjoyment of life. Our values inform our work and impel us to challenge rather than reinforce dominant patriarchal norms.

We need to be careful, however, that taking a strong stand against abuse does not alienate those clients who still have feelings of loyalty or even love for the abuser. As Goldner (1992) points out, the danger of blaming the victim with a systemic perspective can be replaced by shaming the victim with a feminist perspective. Clients can feel ashamed and guilty if they do not agree with inflexible ideas about what is 'politically correct'. It is always important for therapists to demonstrate understanding and respect for the client's world-view before trying to facilitate change.

POWER ISSUES IN THERAPY

In recent years the therapeutic literature has reflected concern and controversy about the role of the therapist and the distribution of power between therapist and client. While we acknowledge that these are important issues, we do not agree with those who deny the legitimacy of expertise, or the inevitability of power inherent in the role of 'therapist'. We agree with therapists as diverse as Goldner (1992) and Minuchin (1991) that all therapists are in an elevated position of power relative to their clients. It would be dishonest to pretend that the skills we attain in our training and the fact that people seek our assistance do not confer us with some 'expert' status.

The issue is not whether therapists have power, but how we use it. Clients are entitled to make informed choices about the type of therapy we offer, and to question the assumptions and values on which we base our work. They are certainly entitled to go elsewhere if we do not provide the assistance they seek.

Nor do we assume absolute power. 'Therapy is indeed a limited arrangement; a relative degree of power is provisionally designated in a restricted context for a prescribed period of time' (Minuchin 1991, p. 50). While we have ideas about the goals of therapy, we discuss with the client the particular goals they have for themselves. We cannot make them change, but we can facilitate change.

The type of relationship we aspire to with our clients is one in which we agree on goals and empower them to make the changes they want. The power for change resides in the client. We respect the fact that the client will choose the time and the pace at which change occurs. We develop a co-operative relationship based on our expert knowledge of therapy, and the client's expert knowledge of themselves. We know about good therapy, but we do not necessarily know what is good for a particular client.

THE GOALS OF THERAPY

In our experience it is not difficult for therapist and client to agree on the goals of therapy. This is because we believe that everyone has a natural desire for growth and healing. It is one of our basic assumptions that clients have many inner resources which can assist them to overcome the effects of sexual abuse.

The goals that therapist and client are likely to agree on would generally include the following:
- To assign responsibility for sexual abuse to the perpetrator;
- To assign shame and guilt to the perpetrator;
- To put the client in touch with their strengths and in this way increase self-esteem;
- To deal with any negative effects of abuse on client and family (i.e. any unhelpful behaviours, emotions, beliefs, or physical symptoms);
- To ensure that the client has the support they need from others;
- To plan for future safety;
- To consider the social and cultural context of abuse;

FACILITATING CHANGE

As for many family therapists, our ideas about how change is created can be traced back to the work of the anthropologist Gregory Bateson (1972,

1979). For Bateson, any change in living systems (which includes humans) is brought about by information, i.e. by a difference that is noticed.

Although we are not always aware of or in control of it, through our senses and thought processes we are continually responding to the vast amount of potential information which surrounds us. Some is selected to be noticed and some is not. Those events, feelings, ideas, etc. that we do select as significant information become the experiences with which we construct our individual maps of reality.

In order to facilitate change, it is necessary to find ways of helping our clients to make shifts in the images, beliefs, values, behaviours, etc. that constitute their experience of reality. Clearly, providing information and advice is not sufficient or therapy would be much simpler and therapists immensely powerful. Some of our suggestions will be rejected as inconsistent with clients' views; others will be ignored because they seem irrelevant or unhelpful.

To create change therefore, we attempt to provide our clients with what Bateson calls 'news of difference' (1979). This enables our clients to consider different ideas, different images, different feelings, or different responses. To do this we provide information in a way that is noticed, and in a way that is not rejected or ignored.

This is a difficult task, and inevitably some of our efforts will not be successful. In order to create 'news of difference' for any one client, we may need to try many different ways, and to try some ways several times. Creating change through therapeutic conversation and questioning is reflected in many of the ideas presented in this book. But change in the meaning that individuals ascribe to certain events (i.e. attitudes and beliefs) can also occur through experience, behaviour, symbolism, and non-verbal communication (Coale 1992). We therefore rely on a variety of methods (see chapters 7 & 11), including behavioural interventions, action methods, and art, as well as methods that rely on dialogue. We believe that this variety of methods makes our therapy more accessible to a greater range of people, in particular those who are less verbally skilled (e.g. children).

THE DEVELOPMENT OF PROBLEMS

It is our belief that people do not choose to have problems, and that they do their best to overcome them. They certainly do not choose to be sexually abused, nor do they choose from the variety of ways and degrees that sexual abuse might affect them. Their response to abuse depends on what happened, on their own perceptions, previous experiences and inner resources, and on the responses of others involved.

Like Milton Erickson (Erickson & Rossi 1979) we believe that our clients have many abilities which can help them to overcome their problems. They may, however, be trapped in belief systems which do not allow them to explore and utilize their abilities to best advantage. Therapy is a way of helping clients to explore their potential and develop their abilities.

THE THERAPEUTIC RELATIONSHIP

Before therapy can proceed it is essential that a positive feeling of understanding and mutual regard exists between therapist and client. Creation of this is what we refer to as 'joining' or rapport. It requires that the client feels respected and understood by the therapist, and that they in turn understand and respect the therapist. Without this feeling the client will not be able to attend fully to the therapist, and will not be free to consider the different perspectives and beliefs which therapy offers, and which are essential for change to occur.

PART 2

PRINCIPLES OF HEALING AND THERAPY

THE
HEALING PROCESS

Therapy is about healing, so it is essential that therapists consider the healing process when they are assessing the needs of each client and planning the next stage in their therapy. This is important through all stages of therapy.

Each individual's experience of sexual abuse will be different, so therapy must be designed to take into account the effects of abuse for each individual, and their particular needs. We can, however, describe the stages which frequently contribute to the healing process, and have chosen to identify these stages as follows:

- Acknowledging that Sexual Abuse Occurred
- Making the Decision to Heal
- Talking to Others about the Abuse
- Placing Responsibility where it Belongs
- Dealing with the Loss and Sadness
- Expressing Anger
- Working through the Difficulties Caused by the Abuse
- Building a Future.

We emphasize that clients differ in the rate at which they go through this healing process, and in the significance that each stage has for them. Some experience elements of different stages at the same time, some need to spend only a brief time at a particular stage. But for most it is necessary to negotiate each stage, though not necessarily in the order described below.

It is not our intention to describe the healing process in exhaustive detail, and we refer those interested in reading more on the topic to *The Courage to Heal* (Bass & Davis 1988), which was written especially for women, and *Victims No Longer* (Lew 1988), which was written primarily for men.

ACKNOWLEDGING THAT SEXUAL ABUSE OCCURRED

Before healing can take place the survivor needs to acknowledge that abuse occurred, and to recognize at least some of the effects it has had in their life. While this may seem obvious, some people who have been abused never reach this stage. Some may have little or no memory of the abuse, perhaps because they were very young when it occurred, or because it happened a long time ago. For some the memories are too painful to confront, or have been blocked out in various ways (e.g. drugs, alcohol, leading a busy life). Some will acknowledge that something occurred, but will deny to themselves and others the extent of the trauma experienced.

It is important here that we distinguish between people who have no memory of abuse and are not significantly affected by it, and those who are affected by abuse but who have coped by blocking out some of the memories. The former group have no need for healing, and are not the people referred to in this chapter. Throughout this book we refer to those who know that they were abused and who are consequently seeking assistance to deal with this.

Denial of abuse is not a cause for blame or criticism. It can be positively reframed as a way of coping with painful memories, or as a helpful stage at times when it is necessary to get on with other areas of one's life.

Acknowledging abuse and its effects can make the daily lives of our clients difficult. Strong emotions may be experienced for the first time, or may be relived with memories of the abuse. Clients may experience feelings similar to those felt when the abuse occurred, including fear, anxiety, helplessness, nausea, or depression. It is important that the therapist normalizes and validates such feelings, and helps the client to understand them as memories and not re-abuse. It is also helpful if we normalize experiences which might otherwise lead clients to doubt their own sanity. These might include mood swings, a flood of emotions, or uncontrollable crying. Clients need reassurance that a wide range of emotions and reactions are normal at this stage, that some of their behaviour may be out of character, and that this stage will pass. In our work with children, parents often need the same reassurance.

For some clients this is a crisis stage, when a cautious assessment of risk from careless, impulsive, or self-destructive behaviour is indicated. The therapist needs to check what support is available for these clients, and to help them plan ways of taking care of themselves. If there is a risk of suicide, specific action must be taken by the therapist, as described in Chapter 11.

Other clients will experience relief when they acknowledge the abuse and its effects. It may be the first time that they can make sense of their emotions and behaviours, and so can begin to see themselves in a more positive light. Where previously they may have thought of themselves as 'mad' or 'bad', they can now begin to see themselves as normal people reacting in a normal way to an awful experience.

Part of acknowledging that the abuse occurred is for the survivor to learn to trust their own perceptions of what happened. For many this is not easy, as the abuser and others may have consciously distorted what was happening. The survivor may have been told that the abuse did not happen, or that they were partly, or even fully, responsible.

Explicitly or implicitly, the survivor may have got the message that they are worthless, or bad, or that their feelings do not count. Learning to trust their own intuition may take a long time, but is an enormously liberating process as the survivor learns to say, 'This happened to me, it is part of my life story, and this is the way I feel about it.'

It can be very difficult for people who have previously coped by denying abuse when they begin to face the memories of what happened. Therapists can sometimes help by explaining that a lot of energy goes into maintaining denial, and that this energy can now be redirected and used as a resource for healing. We believe that our clients' potential for creativity and development can be greatly increased when their energy is no longer tied up in denying memories of abuse and in minimizing the effects of the abuse on their lives.

Some clients have unclear memories of sexual abuse, and struggle to recall more details of their experience. Recall may be facilitated by therapy, by returning to the place where the abuse occurred, or by any number of triggers associated with the abuse. These might include seeing something on television, or hearing about the abuse of someone else. Some recall their own abuse when they discover that one of their children has been abused, or when their child reaches the age that they were when their abuse occurred.

Some will experience flashbacks which are powerful visual memories, and often very traumatic. When this occurs it can be useful to help the client to make a clear distinction between the memories and the abuse. This is the first step towards developing strategies to deal with the memories and to prevent retraumatization.

Memories of abuse occur at a number of levels. The client may recall only that the abuse occurred, or they may recall the details of what happened. They may recall the actions, or they may recall other aspects, such as emotions, sights, sounds, smells, or tactile details. Working through one set of memories might allow space for the recall of others.

It is not necessary for every client to recall the details of the abuse. Healing can occur without clear memories, and it is important not to push people to remember more than they can recall accurately, or more than they are ready to deal with. Particularly for people who have been traumatized, however, some memory of the abuse and acknowledgement of its effects can play an important part in healing.

MAKING THE DECISION TO HEAL

The decision to heal is a positive response to the memories of abuse. It involves choosing hope over resignation or despair, and making an active commitment to change.

For many adults in particular the decision may involve putting aside other demands and allowing time to experience emotions, to think about the issues, and to get the necessary help and support. For some it may be the first time that priority has been given to addressing their own needs.

In our work with children, the decision to seek help is usually made by an adult. A child may not consciously make a decision to heal, but it will be evident from their response to therapy whether they are ready to take this step.

The child who refuses to discuss their abuse or to co-operate with therapy may be signalling that they have not reached this stage in their healing. They may not wish to acknowledge that abuse happened, or they may be afraid to confront their memories for a variety of reasons. They may have no sense of hope that changes can be made. For these children considerable effort and support must be put into making connections, building trust, and helping them feel empowered to cope, before further progress can be made.

In many ways, making a decision to heal is taking a step into the unknown. Unexpected issues may arise, and emotional responses may not be predictable. Things sometimes get worse before they get better. A person's ability to function in their everyday life is often affected. They may find it difficult to cope at work, for example, or they may experience extra pressure on their relationships. They may find themselves in a constant emotional turmoil from which they have no confidence that they will emerge.

The therapist needs to affirm the decision to heal, and to ensure that the client has the support and guidance they need to face the unknown. While we acknowledge the difficulties, we must also convey our confidence that this stage too is only temporary, and that it is part of the healing process.

We convey our belief that the client did not deserve to be abused, and does not deserve the ongoing effects the abuse has on their lives. They do, however, deserve the time and effort that giving priority to healing requires.

We tell them that they have already survived the worst part of their experience, and that they have a lot of strengths and resources which will help them to cope with the issues and emotions which arise during healing. We reassure them that it is part of our job to help them to get in touch with those strengths and resources.

The decision to heal will be made by different people in very different circumstances. For some it is a choice made when the survivor is feeling particularly strong, positive, and energized to make changes in their lives. For others it will be a response to desperation or despair, to the breakdown in relationships, or to ongoing personal problems. They may decide that change is necessary because the alternative of not changing has become intolerable.

For some people the decision to heal is easy; for others it is one that is agonized over for many years. It may be a matter of making a time in their lives when it is possible to give healing the priority it deserves. The important factor is that some form of active commitment is made.

The client who wants to heal but does not become fully engaged in therapy may be communicating a lack of trust in the process, a lack of understanding of what is involved, or a lack of readiness to change. While we respect their desire for change, we may need to explore with them the restraints that prevent them from making this active commitment. These might include anxiety about the power of emotions which might be released, lack of confidence in therapy, fear of the consequences for close relationships, or a need to maintain some stability in order to meet commitments to work and family.

Anyone who has been badly affected by sexual abuse will want to make changes, but not everyone will feel ready to take action. The therapist supports those clients who feel ready to make changes, and respects those who feel that the right time for change has not yet arrived.

In order to make the active commitment required for healing, some abuse survivors need considerable support. Others will need more help once the decision is made, when they are putting it into practice. These are times when the therapist checks on the availability of support people, and on the other pressures in the client's life. It is helpful if our clients are well prepared with strategies for taking care of themselves, and if they have a place to go where they feel safe. They may need encouragement to ask for help when it is needed, and permission to say 'No' to demands which are likely to create additional stress in their lives.

Putting the client in touch with a support or therapy group where they talk to other people with similar experiences, can be particularly useful at this stage, because it helps to validate their feelings. It also helps them to perceive their reactions as normal when they see others responding in a similar way.

For many survivors the decision to heal is associated with a personal sense of spirituality. While this is experienced in very different ways by different people, its overall effect for the abuse survivor is to provide a sense of self-worth, and of connection with a positive power beyond themselves. Spirituality is an invaluable source of strength in the healing process. It is helpful therefore, for the therapist to explore ways of putting clients more in touch with their spirituality. A belief in a positive force, such as God, Nature, or Allah, helps the client to have faith in the power of a higher strength, and ultimately in healing itself.

TALKING TO OTHERS ABOUT THE ABUSE

Telling other people what happened can be extremely difficult. For many clients, abuse is associated with shame and self-blame so it is very threatening to talk about it. Others feel embarrassed and have difficulty finding the right words. Breaking the silence about abuse is a vital step towards reducing its power. It provides an opportunity for the abuse survivor to receive the help they need and to have their feelings validated. It helps them to challenge any feelings of guilt or shame, as they acknowledge out loud the fact that they were abused and that it was not their fault.

The therapist can help the client to talk about their abuse by sharing their understanding of the difficulties, by talking about how normal they are in the circumstances, by affirming efforts made, and by finding creative ways of facilitating the client's communication. For clients of all ages this could include writing, drawing, action methods, or demonstrating with dolls.

It is also important that we prepare our clients for the different reactions they may get when they begin to talk about their abuse outside the therapy room. Many people in our communities are ill-informed about sexual abuse, have difficulty understanding its effects, appreciating where responsibility lies, and even in accepting that it occurs at all. Some of the people our clients may wish to talk to will have their own reasons to deny or minimize the abuse. They may have been abused themselves and not wish to acknowledge this. They may have feelings of loyalty to the offender, or they may feel defensive because they believe that they are being held responsible in some way.

It is important that clients are selective about whom they talk to about their abuse. The therapist can help to clarify the reasons for choosing to speak to a particular person. We need to discuss with clients what they hope to achieve when we help them to prepare for making a disclosure or confrontation in the most positive way.

The reasons for a client wanting to talk to a particular person about their abuse help to determine just how useful this is likely to be. For example, a client who wishes only to express their anger to an abuser or to an unsupportive family member will be satisfied with a response different from that wanted by the client seeking an apology, understanding, support, or a closer relationship.

It is important that the survivor talks about their abuse with people who will validate their experience, who will support them, and with whom they want a closer relationship. They need to be selective in choosing people with whom they feel safe, in choosing the right time to talk to them, and in choosing how much they want to say. Talking about different aspects of the abuse over time, rather than trying to say everything at once can help to build up trust. This way the survivor feels safer and more comfortable, and the other person is less likely to be overwhelmed by the information and the emotions it engenders.

When relevant, the client can be coached to tell the other person what it is they want from them when they make a disclosure. This might be silent listening, a supportive hug, information, understanding, or even an admission of responsibility.

We help our clients assess how realistic their expectations are when they decide to make a disclosure. We can also help them to plan strategies for coping if these expectations are not met, or if they get any negative reaction.

If they do not get the response they want, the survivor might need to be prepared with something to say to themselves. They could say, for example, 'I know it happened and I know how it affected me.' They might need a support person to be with them or to contact immediately after a disclosure. They might need to be prepared to get out of the situation quickly if it is not meeting their needs. In many different ways abuse survivors need to take care of themselves when talking about their abuse, and to have the support of the therapist and others in doing this.

Despite all the preparation, talking about abuse is often a very difficult part of healing. It can also be a tremendous relief, and can be exceptionally therapeutic when followed by validation of feelings, affirmation, and support. It opens the way for a change in the way that clients perceive themselves and their future.

PLACING RESPONSIBILITY WHERE IT BELONGS

When survivors are able to place total responsibility for the abuse with the perpetrator, they have taken another vital step towards healing.

For many it is difficult to fully accept that they were not at least partly to blame for what happened to them. They may feel, perhaps, that they co-operated because they did not say 'No', or because they did not tell someone at the time. This would not be surprising, as such a view is a common misunderstanding and can be reinforced by other people within their social network. Information to help combat these beliefs is included in the section 'Responsibility for Abuse Lies with the Offender' in Chapter 1.

Some clients have ambivalent feelings towards the offender, which makes it difficult for them to accept the enormity of the abuse of trust that has occurred, and the responsibility of the offender for perpetrating this abuse.

Some have experienced positive feelings of intimacy or sexual arousal associated with the abuse and consequently feel confused, guilty, or responsible. Some of the people we have seen who have most difficulty putting responsibility where it belongs are locked into shame and guilt because they experienced some form of sexual arousal while being abused. The therapist may need to go over this issue many times before the client is able to accept that sexual arousal is a normal, physical response of their bodies, which in no way implies complicity or wrongdoing. Ideas for dealing with this issue are described more fully under 'Shame and Anxiety Relating to Sexual Arousal' in Chapter 10 (pp. 197–198), and are equally applicable to work with adults.

Shame and guilt can also be problems for those who believe that they should have been able to prevent on-going incidents of abuse. They may hold themselves responsible for not being able to stop the abuse once they could anticipate it.

Another common source of shame and guilt for the survivor is the breakup of a family. When family members become divided by an allegation of abuse, or when separation occurs, the survivor can feel responsible. They may also feel responsible for the emotional, social, and legal consequences faced by the perpetrator.

From a very early age, children in most cultures learn that there is something very wrong about sexual abuse. This is evident from the secrecy in which it occurs, as well as from their own responses of pain, fear, and confusion. For most it is only a small step from knowing abuse is wrong to feeling shame and guilt for being part of it. For some this feeling is exacerbated by adult perpetrators who tell them that they are bad or evil for being involved. The big step which needs to be taken for healing to occur is to separate the survivor from the shame and guilt, ascribing these elements totally to the abuser, where they belong.

Some groups are likely to have particular difficulties in placing responsibility where it belongs. Men are more likely to have been brought up to value strength and power, and may consequently find it more difficult to admit to having been vulnerable and relatively weak. Adolescents are also more likely to feel threatened by the idea that they were in a situation which they were unable to control.

A need to be seen as being in charge of one's life will seriously impede an ability to shift responsibility for abuse onto someone else. One way that the therapist can help is with questions that challenge such belief systems. Examples of questions which can be asked of all age groups are listed under 'Denial of Vulnerability' in Chapter 10 (pp. 195–197).

In placing responsibility where it belongs it is helpful for sexual-abuse survivors to understand how they were tricked, bribed, threatened, or coerced by the abuser. We call this the 'grooming' process, and help our clients to see it as a deliberately planned, often carefully orchestrated scheme which enabled the abuse to occur. For example, we might help them to see how an abuser made friends with them, gained the trust of their parents, took advantage of habits of obedience or needs for attention, and created opportunities to get them alone. Alternatively, an abuser may have used threats to keep them quiet, or played on fears or guilt to maintain their silence. Any questions which help to demonstrate how the abuser planned the abuse, tricked the child, and managed to keep them from telling anyone else, will help survivors to place responsibility where it belongs.

For many survivors it is devastating to realize that people whose job it was to protect and nurture them were unable to do so. This realization is likely to set off feelings of grief for the things they did not have, and anger with those responsible. It can also be a great relief, however, to accept that they themselves were not responsible for what happened, that they were relatively powerless to stop it, and that they have demonstrated many strengths in the way that they have survived.

DEALING WITH THE LOSS AND SADNESS

As the client begins to talk about their abuse and to put responsibility where it belongs, they may experience for the first time the power of many different emotions. At the cornerstone of these is the grief about what has happened to them, and what they have lost. They may grieve for the loss of childhood, the loss of innocence, or the loss of trust. They may feel incredibly sad about relationships that were not the way they wanted them to be, about happiness that was destroyed, or about their inability to grow up in the relatively carefree and secure way enjoyed by their peers. The effects of the abuse on their family, on their relationships, on their behaviour, and on their emotional well-being can constitute other forms of loss which they now begin to acknowledge.

It is important that our clients are able to get in touch with these feelings, and to share them with supportive people who they trust. They need to know that these sometimes overwhelming feelings are normal, and will not go on forever. They need a safe place where they are free to express their feelings, feel heard, and be understood. This may be particularly difficult for men, as their socialization often makes them feel more comfortable with anger than with the vulnerability implied by the expression of grief.

As with the other stages of healing, this step can be achieved in one conversation or can take weeks, months, or even years to work through. The therapist must find a balance between allowing the client the time they need, and helping them to move on to the next step.

Sometimes a client gets 'stuck' at this stage, and overwhelmed by feelings of depression or despair. They may get into a self-perpetuating cycle, where their relationships, work, etc. suffer even more, and the ongoing problems in their life feed into their depression. The therapist then needs to help them find ways of breaking this cycle. The depression might be externalized, for example, (see Chapter 5, pp. 57–58) and the client challenged to think about who 'wins' if they give up at this stage. They can be encouraged to take a stand against depression, and helped to get in touch with the times when they function competently and are not overwhelmed by their feelings. For some clients a limited course of antidepressant medication might be a useful way of breaking the cycle. Antidepressants may assist them to get on with their lives and to take practical steps to change their circumstances.

For other clients, the concerns that prevent their moving on to the next stage may need to be addressed. Questions may be asked, such as, 'What would you be doing if you were not feeling so unhappy and overwhelmed?',

'What would be scary/difficult about doing that?', 'Who might feel threatened if you were feeling stronger and more independent?'

We need to acknowledge that our clients have a considerable amount to grieve for, and to allow them the time and space to do this. But once they have effectively expressed these feelings we need to put them in touch with their strengths, and help them to move on to the next stage in their healing.

EXPRESSING ANGER

Once the survivor has placed responsibility for the abuse with the offender, they are free to experience the anger that goes with this awareness. Anger is a normal and healthy response to abuse, and the freedom to express it in an appropriate way is a very powerful part of healing. In 'Tools for Therapy with Children' (Chapter 7) and 'Tools for Therapy with Adults', (Chapter 11) we describe a number of forms that this expression of anger can take within therapy.

Some people see anger as a negative reaction, but expressed appropriately it is a source of energy for abuse survivors who are making changes in their lives. Directing anger at an abuser is also a positive step away from punishing oneself for abuse, and away from the feelings of self-blame, worthlessness, anxiety, depression, and despair which are inherent in this reaction. It enables clients to practise new roles and new responses more associated with self-assertion and strength.

Socialization processes which lead people to think of anger as a negative reaction can make its expression particularly difficult for women. Women are more likely to be socialized to internalize such emotions as anxiety and depression, than to externalize such feelings as anger towards someone else. The therapist needs to be aware of this and not try to force people to express their anger before they are ready, or in ways that are alien to them. For example, some women in therapy will prefer less physical methods of expressing their anger, such as writing or fantasy, rather than action methods, yelling, or addressing some symbolic representation of the abuser.

We draw a clear distinction between what we encourage our clients to do within therapy, and what is appropriate outside the therapy room. It might be therapeutic to cut up a drawing of the abuser, but it is not in anyone's interests for the client to literally attack anyone with a pair of scissors. By fully expressing their feelings in the therapy room, they are in fact less likely to want to act out their anger in inappropriate ways outside. We also draw a clear distinction between anger and retaliation. Anger is a normal response which can be expressed in many ways (e.g. assertive verbal statements, withdrawal, shouting, harmless physical activity, violence). When it takes the form of retaliation it focuses on the offender, and is likely to have negative consequences for the survivor. When anger is expressed in a positive way, it involves a validation of feelings and a sense of power which is very therapeutic for the survivor.

For healing from sexual abuse to take place it is sometimes necessary for our clients to express anger towards others in addition to the abuser. These people might include a trusted family member who did not protect them, or someone who did not believe or support them when abuse was disclosed. Sometimes such anger is even more powerful than that expressed towards the abuser. Reasons for this will vary. For some clients, the abuser remains threatening, so it is safer, at least initially, to acknowledge anger towards another. For others, there may have been positive aspects in their relationship with the abuser which were missing in the relationship with the one who did not protect them. Such positive feelings conflict with or inhibit their anger towards the abuser.

It is important that this anger with others is expressed in some way and that such feelings are validated and accepted as a normal response to the circumstances. It may also be necessary to help the client to make a distinction between abuse and failure to protect, as part of placing responsibility where it belongs — with the abuser, regardless of the neglect or mistakes of others.

When the client is ambivalent towards the abuser we help them to make a distinction between the things they liked about the abuser and the things they did not like. We then ask them to set aside the positive things and to address the negative part of the abuser, thus facilitating the expression of anger.

For many survivors the appropriate expression of anger will be a powerful and empowering experience. It may be the first time that they have felt a sense of power since the abuse. It is a sign that they have taken a significant step away from the role of 'victim', that they are beginning to take charge of their lives, and that the abuse is losing some of its power to affect them.

WORKING THROUGH THE DIFFICULTIES CAUSED BY THE ABUSE

As we have noted previously, sexual abuse affects each individual in different ways. Dealing with the effects of abuse is a necessary part of healing, so facilitating this process is an important part of therapy. The more common consequences of abuse include physical, social, emotional, and behavioural problems, as well as the accumulation of unhelpful beliefs about oneself, about abuse, or about life in general. (See also Chapter 1.)

In therapy we help our clients deal with these effects in many different ways. These are described throughout the book, but more particularly in chapters 7 and 11. In our work with children we involve the family in this process, as described in chapters 6 and 9. In therapy with adolescents and adults, we sometimes involve family, partner, or supportive friends.

For some adults, dealing with the effects of abuse takes longer than it does for most children. This is because the effects can become entrenched in habits which take on a life of their own (e.g. drug or alcohol abuse, aggression, lack of trust, poor self-esteem). They can also compound over time as other aspects of the survivor's life are affected by the physical, behavioural, emotional, or cognitive problems caused by the abuse.

Unfortunately the difficulties caused by abuse are not automatically resolved by dealing with the abuse itself. While therapy which reduces the trauma of abuse is likely to also reduce some of its effects, other effects may persist. Unless these unhelpful habits and beliefs are given specific attention, they are likely to cause their own problems, both in the present and over time.

BUILDING A FUTURE

For healing from sexual abuse to occur, some form of acceptance is necessary. This involves acceptance that the abuse has happened and that it is part of the past, combined with a knowledge that it need not destroy the future. It involves the development of self-acceptance and self-respect. For many people it also involves a recognition of the wisdom and strengths they have gained through surviving sexual abuse.

At this stage of healing survivors have left behind many of their feelings of self-blame and guilt. They may still experience times when they feel vulnerable and less confident in themselves, and it is useful for the therapist to predict and normalize these occasions. Generally, however, survivors have developed a different perspective on issues that previously concerned them. They no longer blame themselves, for example, for not being able to prevent the abuse, or for becoming sexually aroused while being abused. They have a better understanding of their reactions to abuse which previously contributed to their poor self-image. Such reactions as outbursts of aggression, failure in school, difficulties in relationships, and alcohol or drug abuse, are regarded less as personal defects and more as behaviours that can be changed.

It is not necessary for the survivor to forgive the abuser, or to have some form of confrontation or disclosure. These are personal matters which are important for some people but not for others. When forgiveness of the offender is important for a particular client, we need to check whether they see it as assisting in their healing, or as something that they owe the offender. It is not usually helpful for a client to feel that it is part of their role to assist or support the offender. On the contrary, it is important for healing that the client recognizes that they are not responsible for the offender's behaviour.

It is necessary, however, for them to have dealt with their anger in some way so that it no longer dominates their emotions and actions. If they are to leave the abuse effectively in the past, they need to let go any desire for revenge and to feel free to put their energy into other pursuits.

The implications of this for therapy are obvious. Right from the beginning we are working towards this stage of healing by respecting and affirming our clients, giving them the chance to express their feelings, and in every way possible conveying our belief that they were not responsible for what happened to them.

Building a future after the abuse also involves dealing with fears. It involves our clients planning ways of taking care of themselves, and devising strategies for safety in a variety of situations, both sexual and nonsexual. It involves setting goals that enable the client to move beyond the abuse and planning the steps needed to achieve them.

This final stage of healing is reached when the survivor is able to experience that there is more to their life beyond the sexual abuse and its effects. While they will probably never forget what happened, they know that the memories have lost their power to draw them back into the pain, emotional trauma, and behavioural responses that they previously experienced. They have a sense of being in control of their experience, rather than being controlled by it.

4

THE THERAPY
PROCESS

A model of the therapy process is basic to our work with both adults and children who have been sexually abused. We need to be clear about the essential steps involved in all therapy for sexual abuse before we can plan for the individual needs of each client.

It must be understood, however, that the steps described here provide guidelines only, and that most therapy moves back and forth between stages as needed. The steps are listed here in their logical order, then described in detail in the following pages:

1 Join with the family/client, i.e. form a relationship and establish a contract for work together;

2 Obtain a brief history of the abuse.
   Make an initial assessment of the degree of trauma and the work to be done:
   (a) with the family
   (b) with the individual;

3 Empower the client to deal with the abuse;

4 Examine the current effects of the abuse in the life of the client;

5 Examine the effects of the abuse over time;

6 Go over the abuse situation in a therapeutic way;

7 Prepare for the future.

It is important that each step in the therapy process is completed before moving on to the next. There will be times however, when it is necessary to go back to an earlier stage, or to repeat a particular step a number of times, perhaps employing different techniques each time.

The time spent on each stage varies between clients, depending on their individual needs and circumstances. We always use a model of brief therapy but this might take three sessions, 30 sessions or more. The model guides the way we work, rather than setting a limit on the number of times we see our clients. We aim to complete therapy in the minimum number of sessions, but not one session less than necessary. Otherwise we contribute to a process of 'secondary victimization' by subjecting our clients to more therapy than they need, pathologizing them personally, and making their problems seem even more difficult to solve.

The therapy process remains essentially the same for all clients, irrespective of age, gender, or intellectual ability. The differences between clients are addressed in the variety of methods used at each stage.

Ideas for working with children and with adults are described in different chapters of this book, but it is advisable to be flexible about this. For example, some adults may respond well to methods more frequently used with children. Work with adolescents may draw on ideas from both the chapter on Tools for Therapy with Children (pp. 104–147), and the chapter on Tools for Therapy with Adults (pp. 202–261).

A number of ideas for working at each stage of therapy are presented throughout this book. Therapists will choose methods which suit their own style, and which are best suited for each client.

JOINING

Joining refers to how we make connections with a client, begin to form a relationship, and establish a contract for our work together.

Both therapist and client need to be clear about the contract between them from the initial contact. For example, when the client first phones for an appointment they may need information about the service we offer, and we may contract at this stage to enter into therapy or to see them once to discuss their needs and the options available to them. By the end of the first session we should be in a position to make a clear statement about what we can offer and to assess with the client whether this is what they want.

A contract may be written or verbal, and may need to be reviewed regularly in the light of progress made and changing circumstances. It should include information about the type of help we offer, the likely costs, who needs to be involved in therapy, what we cannot do, issues of confidentiality, and the number of sessions to be arranged.

Joining begins with the first phone contact and the gathering of basic information about the client's family, such as names, addresses, contact phone numbers, etc. It also includes a social stage at the beginning of the first session where the therapist begins to make connections with the client. It might, for example, include questions about where the client comes from, about the school a child attends, or about an adult's work. This social stage is designed to put clients at ease, and to convey our interest, our respect for them, and our assumption that they have a life outside the problem.

Joining is an absolutely essential part of therapy, because any new perspectives that we offer our clients will be rejected by them unless we have first been able to enter their world. Before we can expect our clients to make changes we need to demonstrate our understanding of their current position and our respect for them as they are.

The joining stage at the beginning of the initial interview will vary in length depending on the client's needs, culture, and personality. It is essential, however, that we acknowledge very early in the interview the client's reason for seeking help. It is important for the therapist to name the problem as sexual abuse early in the interview, otherwise the therapist may signal to the client that they feel uncomfortable or anxious about discussing it. This would make the client feel unsafe in raising the problem in their presence, and can make the abuse seem even more overwhelming and more difficult to talk about.

From the beginning we need to show our clients that we are competent and confident to deal with their concerns. We name the problem and make a statement about our experience in dealing with it. For example, we might say, 'I understand from your phone call that you have been sexually abused. I've done a lot of work with people who have been abused and we have lots of ideas that might help.'

It is also helpful to acknowledge from the start how difficult it might be for the client to come to therapy and to talk about the abuse. We normalize this and allow the client to set the pace for therapy.

The joining process continues throughout therapy and usually will include a social stage at the beginning of each interview, when we catch up on recent events in our clients' lives and gather further relevant information. This might be just two or three questions or it might be ten minutes of conversation. It should not extend, however, into the realms of irrelevant gossip.

HISTORY AND ASSESSMENT

Once a contract has been established and the client is willing to talk about the abuse, we need to get a brief description of the basic facts. We need to establish that abuse occurred, how long ago it happened, who did it, and approximately how many times. At this stage it would be a serious mistake to ask for more than simple statements of fact, because our clients may not be ready or sufficiently empowered to describe the details. This initial discussion should be confined to basic information and maintained at a level where few emotions are unleashed.

When we work with children a lot of the basic information can be obtained from a parent or care-giver. With adults, a simple statement such as 'I was abused by my uncle when I was six' might suffice. Some clients feel able to provide further details at this stage; for others the memories are too vague or too painful. They should not be asked for more details than they can convey in relative comfort.

The development of a theory of post-traumatic stress disorder has major implications for clients who have been sexually abused (Resick & Schnicke 1990), as does the work of Finkelhor and Browne (1985), who developed a model for describing the sources of trauma in child sexual abuse. One of the most obvious implications of this work is that it is essential early in therapy to assess whether our client is traumatized by their abuse, and in what ways. Not all people who have been sexually abused will experience traumatic stress. Therapy varies according to the degree of trauma experienced.

Trauma will be indicated by a wide range of signs, including nightmares, 'flashbacks', regression, anxiety, depression, suicidal behaviour, psychosomatic symptoms, substance abuse, aggression, poor self-esteem, and difficulties with social and sexual relationships.

Assessment is an ongoing part of therapy. It begins with the initial contact and needs to be regularly reviewed until the end of the last session. It is done in co-operation with our clients, rather than imposing our ideas on them. In the case of children, the assessment is also reviewed with parents and other involved adults (e.g. teacher, school counsellor, other care-givers).

For example, after meeting with a child and their family, we may decide early in therapy that the child has not been severely traumatized by abuse. We would then offer a few sessions for the child to express their feelings, regain a sense of power, and to plan for future safety. This could be reinforced with a plan to spend two to three sessions with the parents to help them deal with their own feelings, to discuss options (e.g. prosecution), and to share information about how they can best help their child.

In another example of assessment, an adult may be assessed as severely traumatized, in need of immediate help to prevent suicide, and offered a specified number of sessions, with formal review of progress built in.

With further work these assessments may be modified, and our contract with the client altered accordingly.

EMPOWERING THE CLIENT

Before going over the details of the abuse, we need to help clients feel empowered to deal with the intense and potentially destructive emotions which they may experience. Basically this means enabling them to be aware of their own inner strengths, and ensuring that they have the support they will need when they tackle memories of the abuse.

A sense of powerlessness is inherent in the experience of sexual abuse, and is often compounded by poor self-esteem. Low self-esteem is not uncommon, but is particularly evident in people who have been abused because of the feelings of shame and guilt they often experience. It is likely to be an even greater problem for those who have been told by the abuser, or by others, that they were in some way responsible. As a result they may experience additional feelings of self-blame and worthlessness. The poor self-image is consequently reinforced by the tendency to notice their own failures and to ignore any successes which are inconsistent with this negative view of themselves. The effect of vicious cycles such as this is described more fully in Chapter 2 (pp. 17–18).

A number of ways of helping clients to get in touch with the powerful part of themselves are described later in this book (Chapter 11). The therapist may choose to use more than one method with a particular client. The important element of this process is that the client actually experiences a sense of their own power, rather than just talking about it at a purely intellectual level.

Essentially, clients must feel empowered at this stage of therapy before proceeding to talk about details of the abuse and issues that are potentially more emotive. Helping clients to remain in touch with their strengths through affirmation and questioning is an ongoing part of therapy throughout all stages. At times when our clients are finding feelings or issues raised by therapy particularly difficult, it may be necessary to take time once again to put the client in touch with that powerful part of themselves experienced earlier in therapy.

How this is done is determined by the needs of a particular client at a particular time. Sometimes a reminder about current safety, and about the client's strengths and achievements is sufficient, for example, 'This is a safe place where you can say anything you like', 'You have come through a lot, you must be a very strong person', or 'You're not that little girl any more. You're older now and you know a lot more.' Similarly, questioning can be used to elicit useful information or self-discoveries which help the client to re-experience a sense of their own power.

Another way to help a client feel empowered is to acknowledge that they have different parts, and to facilitate a dialogue between their powerful part and the part that is now feeling distressed or afraid. In this way we put the client in touch with their own inner resources for healing. This method also allows us to address the powerful part of our client directly, checking whether it is safe to continue on the present path of therapy, or asking what their distressed part would need to continue therapy in a positive way. Examples of ways of doing this with an adult client are provided in Chapter 11, under the headings 'Building a Powerful Part of Self', 'Fantasy', and 'Writing Exercises'.

Another way in which we help clients to feel empowered to face the memories of abuse is to ensure that they have the support they need from others. This includes being very clear about how much support we can offer, both in the therapy room and between sessions. It may include putting clients in touch with other resources, such as 24-hour crisis services for those times when we are not available.

We check out in detail how much support is available to our clients from friends, family, and other resources in their social network. When they are involved in therapy, we explain to parents, care-givers, friends, and partners the process of therapy and the needs of our client. We predict and normalize any reactions the client may have to the memories of abuse, and ensure that the support people are available and prepared as much as possible to help. This may involve ongoing contact with the support people to ensure that they, too, have the help they need. (See also 'Normalizing' in Chapter 5.)

EXAMINING THE CURRENT EFFECTS OF THE ABUSE

The effects of abuse may be revealed gradually over several sessions, as the client becomes more aware of its impact and/or more trusting of the therapist. Alternatively, some clients will be able to respond almost immediately with clear and detailed answers to such a simple question as 'What effect do you think the abuse has on your life now?'

This can be a difficult stage for a client who feels overwhelmed by the effects of the abuse. Consequently it is important not to ask questions about the effects of abuse before helping clients to feel empowered with a sense of their own inner resources.

Examining the effects of abuse can arouse powerful emotions such as anger, pain, and grief. The therapist needs to offer a secure place for the client to express these emotions, and as described in the previous section, must always be ready to put the client in touch with their own inner strengths as needed. We also help our clients at this stage by normalizing their experience, and by asking questions which help to show them how strong they have been, at a time when they may be feeling weak and vulnerable, e.g. 'Many people would not have been able to cope with what you have been through. How have you managed to keep your sanity?' (See also 'Normalizing' in Chapter 5.)

As with other stages, information obtained now contributes to our assessment of the client's needs and to our planning with the client for future therapy.

EXAMINING THE EFFECTS
OF THE ABUSE OVER TIME

When we examine the effects of abuse over time similar issues arise as those described above. In addition, however, at this stage we assess the degree to which subsequent events have either reinforced or alleviated the original abuse experience. For example, a positive and sympathetic response from primary care-givers soon after childhood abuse can do much to decrease its long-term impact. Similarly, relevant information given to the client at a crucial time can alleviate fears which otherwise have the potential to hinder development and to affect behaviour for many years. A common example of this is providing information for an adolescent male who has become very anxious about his sexual orientation following abuse by another male.

If helpful information is not provided when needed, or if there is no support at either the time of the abuse or at the time of disclosure, the effects of the abuse can be compounded over time. For example, the abused person may become more anxious or more depressed. They may develop poor self-esteem and, in a vicious cycle, reinforce it by focusing on their own failures and not giving themselves credit for achievements. They may turn to alcohol or drug abuse as a way of coping with their feelings. They may get into situations where they are revictimized because they are more vulnerable or because they feel powerless to prevent it. Unresolved anger can lead to social isolation or trouble with the law.

Over time people can be affected by sexual abuse in many ways and some of these are described in more detail in Chapter 1. At this particular stage in therapy it is important that both therapist and client get a good understanding of the long-term effects of the abuse, and together begin to plan ways of combating its negative effects.

Sometimes the effects of the abuse are not all negative, and although we would never wish abuse on anyone, it can be helpful to acknowledge qualities that the client has developed in order to cope. These might include such strengths as persistence, determination, compassion, sensitivity, caution, and the wisdom to help other people who have been abused.

GOING OVER THE ABUSE SITUATION IN A THERAPEUTIC WAY

A vital part of the therapy process for those traumatized by abuse is to go back over the abuse experience. This requires considerable care and skill because it must be done in a way that differs from the original experience to avoid retraumatization. It must be done in a way that empowers the client to deal with the abuse, and does not reinforce the original feelings of powerlessness.

There is no point in going over the abuse scene just for the sake of reliving the experience and expressing feelings. Unless the client is helped to emerge from this stage of therapy feeling differently about their experience, going over the abuse could itself be abusive. Different ways of helping the client at this stage are described in chapters 7 and 11. Usually these methods involve some form of catharsis and perhaps a symbolic 'rescue' of the person who 'is being abused'.

It is during this stage of therapy that we elicit details of the abuse from our clients. This involves not just a description of the abuse, but also getting in touch with what the client was feeling and thinking, what was said, and the particular memories associated with the abuse. It will include very subjective details, such as the colour of the house or room, the background noise, the way the light fell, the texture of a fabric, and the expression in the abuser's eyes. Unless they are dealt with, such details can trigger memories of the abuse, and emotionally put the client right back into the abuse situation.

Sometimes it is necessary to go over the abuse scene a number of times to desensitize the client to these triggers. We understand this in the language of Cognitive Behaviour Therapy as desensitization (Corsini 1984). Repetition also assists clients to integrate the abuse experience into their life in a different way.

Another reason why it is important to take our clients back over the details of the abuse is that it helps to validate their experience. The opportunity to describe out loud what happened and how it felt for them plays a major role in healing for some people. This assumes of course that their perspective is accepted and valued by the therapist.

When this validation is combined with the expression of anger or some form of imaginary rescue scene, the client has a different experience to place alongside their original experience of the abuse. The new experience provides them with a sense of power and control, and facilitates the learning of new responses. This means that reminders of the abuse are less likely to trigger the old responses. Behaviour therapists refer to this as counter-conditioning (Corsini 1984). It can also be explained in the language of Role Theory (Clayton 1993). With a different understanding of the abuse and of their own strengths and resources, clients are able to develop new roles within themselves (e.g. the role of the courageous person, the role of the self-believer). These roles are particularly effective when practised using action methods (see chapters 7 & 11).

It is not always necessary to go over the details of the abuse scene repeatedly. For some clients once is sufficient. Some clients will have done this work themselves outside therapy. If we go over an abuse scene unnecessarily, we run the risk of pathologizing our clients. With children we need to watch for clues that they are getting bored with catharsis because they may not be able to articulate their feelings. With our adult clients we need to check, and recheck if they 'feel finished' with the abuser. This does not mean that survivors will forget the abuse, rather that it no longer has the same power over their lives.

When there has been more than one abuse experience each occasion may need individual attention. On the other hand, helping a client deal with one experience may facilitate their dealing with other experiences without much further assistance.

PREPARING FOR THE FUTURE

Preparing for the future is the final stage of therapy when our clients are preparing to get on with their lives. By this stage they have put the abuse in its place. It remains part of their history but is no longer a force which rules their emotions and behaviour.

When we are working with children this stage involves at least one final session with the family. Details of the issues to be discussed in this final family session are described in Chapter 6. This final stage also includes at least one session with the child on how to keep themselves safe in the future, as described in Chapter 7. Adolescents and adults may also need help in planning for their future safety.

This is a time when we deal with any dependency issues arising from work with clients who have needed a lot of support through their therapy.

They now may need help to establish their own support systems outside the therapy room, and to learn to have confidence in their own inner resources. Terminating therapy needs to be seen as an achievement, and not as an experience of rejection or an occasion for anxiety. For children this could involve awarding certificates which acknowledge, for example, bravery or beating fears. For adults it involves a lot of affirmation and acknowledgement of their progress. One exercise we have found helpful is for adults to make a list of negative thoughts about themselves which they leave behind them in the therapy room at the end of the last session, and a list of their positive attributes and achievements which they take with them.

Sometimes we need to begin preparing our clients for the end of therapy over a number of sessions, particularly if our contact with them extends over a long period. In other cases the end of therapy is planned from the start. This happens, for example, when we plan a time-limited number of sessions for a client who has not been severely traumatized. Rather than end therapy abruptly, we may choose to have gradually longer periods between sessions, or to build in a session or phone call to review progress several months after therapy is completed.

Planning for the future should always involve some discussion with the client of future times or events which may be difficult, such as the release of the offender from gaol, reaching various trigger stages in the developmental life-cycle (e.g. adolescence, entering a relationship), or having to deal with experiences previously found difficult. We can help by advising our clients about what to expect and by normalizing certain difficulties as part of the process. Any difficulties are then less likely to be experienced as a sign of pathology or failure.

We can also help clients to plan effective ways of dealing with problem areas. When we help them to plan for future difficulties in an active way we are helping them to step outside the victim role and to take charge of their lives.

Preparing for the future also involves putting our clients in touch with other resources which may be useful to them, and advising them about whether or not they could return for further sessions if needed.

For some people preparing for the future also involves building a sense of themselves as active agents of change. Some clients may choose to move beyond surviving sexual abuse to wanting to make their mark on the world in some way, either by direct involvement in the treatment or prevention of abuse, or in the pursuit of other interests. When clients leave therapy believing that they can make a useful contribution to the world, they leave feeling stronger in themselves and more positive about their future.

5

FACILITATING CHANGE:
Tools for Therapy

As we noted in Chapter 2, change becomes possible when we recognize that there are different ways to think, feel, or act in a particular situation. Much of our work with families, children, and adults therefore focuses on presenting them with information which opens up new perspectives and responses. This information may be in the form of words, behaviours, and emotional or physical responses. It always involves the client noticing a difference between one idea or response, and another.

To help our clients notice these differences we use a range of different tools. In this chapter we describe some of the more common techniques which can be used for all age groups, and for individuals, couples, and families. Many of them originated in the various schools of Family Therapy. In later chapters we describe tools more suitable for work with children (chapter 7), and those more suitable for work with adults (Chapter 11).

SEEDING IDEAS

Seeding (Haley 1973) was a method used by Milton Erickson, particularly during hypnotic inductions when he would mention an idea and later develop it. Similarly, in our work we might make an assumption or suggestion almost off-handedly. We then build on it throughout subsequent sessions until it becomes more concrete in the client's mind. For example, we often ask, 'How did he trick you?' Such questions serve to plant or 'seed' ideas that the client was tricked and therefore was not responsible for what happened.

We also take opportunities provided by clients or family members to seed information about abuse and its effects. This is particularly necessary to counter any unhelpful beliefs they may have adopted. They may blame themselves or one another for the abuse. A well-informed therapist can respond to unhelpful comments with facts based on research and experience, and takes opportunities provided by the client or family to seed ideas. That is, the therapist provides information without dwelling on the point. This avoids a situation where the therapist lectures the client, bores them with too much talk, or risks an argument with them. If a family member expresses doubt about whether to believe a disclosure of abuse, the therapist might say, 'We know from research that false allegations are very rare. Probably only about 2 per cent of allegations turn out to be untrue. Usually children don't have the knowledge to lie about these things.'

If the client is ready to hear this sort of information the idea will develop in their mind. More work is needed, however, before a new understanding is reached. This initial seeding is probably the first of many stages in the changing of perceptions.

It is interesting to note that seeding is a technique often used by offenders. They may, for example, seed ideas with the family that the person they abused is somehow bad or dishonest, so that possible disclosures will not be taken seriously. They may seed ideas about blame for the abuse with a child, so the child fears getting into trouble if they disclose. Such ideas are developed over time and eventually lead the abused person to see themselves as guilty and powerless. Seeding therapeutic ideas is therefore a powerful tool to counter the ideas planted by the offender.

REFRAMING

Reframing (Watzlawick *et al.* 1974) refers to redefining the meanings or beliefs associated with a particular behaviour. In work with clients who have been sexually abused we use reframing to help survivors and their families redefine behaviours in a more useful way. For example, parents who are blaming themselves or their son because he was not able to disclose abuse while it was happening could be told, 'Your son must really care about you. He obviously wanted to protect you from the upset and hurt of knowing what was happening to him.'

For many people the use of the word 'abuse' itself can form a new way of understanding the situation. Once survivors can describe themselves as having been abused they can begin to consider the ways that abuse has affected them. They can identify, for example, how the abuse has influenced both their perceptions of themselves and the ways in which they interact with others. They can make sense of previously unexplained feelings. For example, survivors who have defined themselves as neurotic or crazy can begin to see themselves as normal people, responding to abuse in a very normal way. Feelings such as grief, anger, and confusion make a lot more sense in this context. With this new understanding they realize that growth and healing are possible.

Reframing can be used in many situations where a client is focusing on a negative feeling and not noticing their positive achievements. For example, clients who consider themselves to be weak and powerless can be told how strong they are for surviving. They can be told how brave they are for talking about it in therapy, even when only brief details are elicited. Those who see themselves as having been 'bad' for not stopping the abuse can be reminded that they were in fact good children, who were in the habit of obeying their elders.

Reframing is therefore a tool which facilitates another, more useful perspective. To be effective it must be in keeping with the facts and consistent with the beliefs and values of the therapist, who describes the facts in a different way. Responses to the abuse with which the client feels unhappy, could, for example, be reframed as 'coping mechanisms'. We do not use reframing to trick a client, or to convince them of something we do not believe ourselves. We simply find another frame which fits the client's experience, but enables them to construct a different understanding of the abuse.

As with seeding ideas, reframing is also used negatively by offenders to get the person they are abusing to perceive reality in a different way. For example, an offender may reframe the abuse experience by telling the person being abused that they need 'educating' or that they are 'enjoying a special relationship'. This form of indoctrination needs to be effectively countered in therapy, and positive reframing is one way of doing this.

In some situations there is considerable overlap between reframing and seeding. We are doing both at the same time, for example, when we ask such questions as, 'How big were you at age seven, and how big was your stepfather?' or 'Do adults usually do what children tell them? Are children expected to do what adults tell them?' Questioning can help clients to develop their own reframes, and in this way seeds ideas which can be built on during therapy.

NORMALIZING

The concept of normalizing can be traced back to the work of Milton Erickson. More than most therapists of his time, Erickson had in mind the 'normal' or ordinary human processes (Haley 1973). He also believed that all people have a natural desire for growth and health. While they may inadvertently create difficulties for themselves, people do not choose to have problems, and they try in their own ways to deal with their concerns.

From Erickson we have learned the value of understanding many of our clients' 'problem' behaviours as normal or even inevitable responses to the circumstances surrounding them. So normalizing is a way of reframing behaviours, beliefs, emotions, or physical responses which might otherwise have been regarded as pathological. Vicious cycles, for example, can be used to describe a process whereby small beginnings can lead almost inevitably to major problems. These problems can then be regarded as *normal* responses to the preceding events. Times of stress in the natural cycle of life, such as transition points in the family life cycle, can create common difficulties for which no one is to blame. Similarly, problems experienced as a result of sexual abuse can be regarded as *normal responses* to an abnormal and awful situation.

Because it helps to remove blame and pathology, normalizing is essential in sexual abuse therapy. Often, survivors of abuse develop perceptions of themselves as different or abnormal because of what has happened to them, and many of the possible effects of abuse can be pathologized in a way that tells the client that they are sick. Such effects would include anxiety, sexual difficulties, hallucinations, psychosomatic symptoms, difficulty expressing anger, and avoidance of intimate relationships.

It is much more helpful to see these problems as totally normal responses to abuse, than as symptoms of a personal defect or disease. This approach allows therapy to proceed in a way that empowers the client to deal with their problems, rather than feel defeated by them. It allows the client to see themself as a normal person who will be able to move on to leading a normal life once issues relating to their abuse are resolved.

Sometimes an offender still in contact with their victim deliberately distorts their abusive behaviour as being normal. As a result the person being abused develops a confused perception of normality. This occurs, for example, when the abuse evolves from normal affection or game-playing, and it becomes increasingly difficult to define that something 'normal' has gradually developed into something abusive. When we help clients to recognize the nature of abuse we can normalize their responses to it.

EXTERNALIZATION

One of the techniques described by Michael White which we find helpful is 'externalization' (White 1989). This involves separating the client from the problem, so that a problem previously regarded as a personal defect becomes a challenge to be overcome. By taking up a challenge instead of feeling bad about themselves, the client escapes from pathology and is empowered to make changes.

Externalizing a problem often involves turning an adjective or verb into a noun. The noun form gives it an existence of its own which separates it from the individual concerned. For example, we could respond to a client who says, 'I feel ashamed' by asking such questions as:

'What effect does shame have on your life at the moment?'

'How does shame influence the way you feel about yourself?'

'Does shame weaken or strengthen your relationships?'

'Where do you think the shame really belongs?'

Similarly, we might respond to complaints about a child who 'whinges' with such questions as:

'What kinds of problems does the whinging create?'

'Are there times when whinging is not a problem?'

'How would your home be different if the whinging was under control?'

Whenever it seems useful to separate the person from the problem, just about any response to abuse can be externalized, for example, guilt, anger, fear, or anxiety. Such behaviours as hitting, bedwetting, or withdrawing can also be externalized.

Externalization can be particularly useful with children, who often respond well to the challenge to control a 'tricky temper' or a 'hitting habit'. Separating a child from a problem behaviour also helps to unite the parents and the child against the problem, instead of dividing them against one another.

When externalizing we tend to use language that pits the client against their problem. We might talk about 'getting in charge of fears' instead of being scared, 'beating guilt' instead of feeling bad about yourself, or 'becoming boss of those sneaky wees' instead of being a bedwetter. We then help clients to mobilize their resources to deal with the effects of abuse which they previously had no sense of being able to control. When we assist our clients to recognize that they have competence and control over their lives, we assist them to feel good about themselves, and we assist them to make changes.

'UNIQUE OUTCOMES' OR 'EXCEPTIONS'

Another way of helping clients to develop new perceptions of themselves is described by Michael White (1989) as 'unique outcomes', and by Steve de Shazer (1988) as 'exceptions'. 'Unique outcomes' or 'exceptions' are the times when problems do *not* occur. The abuse survivor might, for example, control symptoms of anxiety, make an assertive statement about their own needs instead of feeling powerless, or resist low self-esteem by doing something which makes them feel good about themselves. Drawing their attention to these occasions is one way in which we help clients to develop a different perspective on events in the past. They begin to notice information about themselves which previously they have ignored. By helping clients to shift from an unhelpful and negative perception of themselves and their abuse, we help them to make changes in their behaviour and progress in their healing.

QUESTIONING TO ELICIT NEW PERCEPTIONS

Sometimes it is quite hard to highlight the unique outcomes so that their implications can be appreciated by a client or family. It may not be helpful, for example, just to tell clients about their abilities, because they can easily dismiss information that does not fit with their own world-view. Often it is more effective to help clients to make their own discoveries by asking questions which help them to examine their beliefs. Specifically, we help them to query the meanings they attribute to their abuse experience, and to examine the effects of the abuse on their lives. From their own answers clients are helped to develop a new understanding of themselves and their problems.

For example, a male client who is blaming himself for not being able to prevent childhood abuse might be asked such questions as:

'Do you think your 10-year-old nephew would be frightened if his teacher tried to abuse him?'

'Do you think he'd be really confused about what to do?'

'Do you think a child might believe that he'd get into trouble if he didn't do what he was told?

'What does that tell you about how it might have been for you when you were that age?'

Another example is the woman who feels powerless as a result of her abuse, and who consequently regards herself as ineffectual when dealing with authority figures. Through questioning, details could be elicited about times when she had been able to set clear limits, drawing her attention to facts which she had previously not noticed. She could be helped to recall, for example, times when she had been clear and assertive with a parent, partner, a child's teacher, a shop assistant, or even with the therapist. More questions could then be asked to highlight this information by helping the client to see herself through different eyes, for example:

'What do you think he noticed when you did that?'

'Do you think that would give him the idea that you could not be pushed around?'

'What do you think that tells me about you?'

'Do you think your grandmother would be proud of you if she could see you standing up for yourself like that?'

Such questions provide the client with a different perspective or 'double description' (White 1986), and can be used constructively throughout therapy.

QUESTIONING ABOUT THE CLIENT'S INFLUENCE OVER THE PROBLEM

Another way in which questioning can help clients make discoveries about themselves is by asking them about the effects of the abuse, and the degree of control they exert over any specific problems. These questions are similar to what Michael White (1988, 1989) refers to as 'relative influence' questions. They highlight the fact that a client is likely to feel more in control of their lives at some times, and more overwhelmed by their problems at others. We help them to identify anything they might do to make a difference between the good times and the bad times. Once clients recognize that they can exert some influence over a particular problem, they can begin to plan ways of increasing this influence.

Questions we might ask about the influence of the client over abuse-related problems could be:

'On a scale of one to 10, how much do you think you are in charge of your aggression at the moment?' ... 'How often do you think your aggression is in charge of you?'

'How did you manage to limit your drinking this week, when it was out of control last week?' ... 'What did you do differently?'

'How many times did that temper get the better of you this week?' ... 'How many times did you feel angry but manage to control your temper?' ... 'How did you do that?'

'How come bedwetting is such a problem at home, but not at Nana's place?' ... 'How do you manage to beat the bedwetting at Nana's?'

'What percentage of the time are you in control of depression?' ... 'What are the times that depression takes over?' ... 'What would it take for you to be 10 per cent more in control of depression?'

DEVELOPING NEW STORIES

Application of the ideas of Michael White and David Epston to therapy for sexual abuse is described in more detail by Durrant and White (1990). It often involves a combination of the ideas listed above to create a different story about the client's life. Stories dominated by experiences of power-lessness and failure are replaced by stories that feature strength and achievement. Stories dominated by sexual abuse and its effects, for example, can be replaced by stories of survival and triumph over abuse. By helping the client to notice things about themselves and their experiences which they had previously not noticed, they develop new perceptions and a new aware-ness of their own resources. Therapy is thus seen as a way in which clients 're-author' or 're-story' their experiences (White & Epston 1989).

AFFIRMATION

From Milton Erickson (Haley 1973) we have inherited a belief that people are more likely to change when they feel good about themselves and hope-ful about their future. We therefore frequently take opportunities to notice and comment on any ideas, actions, or changes which are helpful for our clients' healing. In this way we highlight our clients' strengths, successes, and progress in therapy. We help them to notice achievements that might other-wise have been ignored, and to do more of the things that work for them.

Affirmation is a way of showing our respect for the client, and plays a vital part in the joining process (see Chapter 4). It is necessary before effec-tive therapy can proceed, and is important throughout all stages of therapy.

THERAPEUTIC METAPHOR

As with the many other techniques that we use to help our clients develop new perceptions, the use of therapeutic metaphor was pioneered by Mil-ton Erickson. It is described in detail elsewhere, e.g. Gordon (1978), Rosen (1982), and Zeig (1980). Essentially, it involves making connections between two different people, objects, events, or conditions.

One way in which we use metaphor is by describing one thing in terms which are literally applicable to another, as in 'love is blind' or 'life is a battle'. The choice of which two things are compared is obviously crucial. As Antony Williams (1991) points out, it makes an enormous difference whether we think of love as 'magic', 'war', or 'madness'. Williams explains that metaphor is not just a decoration of language, but a way of thinking about something. It implies a particular perspective which both provides information and hides information. Comparing love with war, for example, highlights one perspective on love, but prevents us from seeing other very different perspectives. Metaphors can therefore influence and limit our perspectives and our responses.

By shifting from the use of one metaphor to another, for example, from 'life is a battle' to 'life is a challenge' or 'life is a gift', we open up the possibility of new perspectives and different responses. It is useful therefore for therapists to notice the metaphors used by clients, and where relevant to suggest different metaphors to replace unhelpful comparisons. Using metaphor in our own speech, and finding alternative metaphors for our clients to consider, provides them with more options for thinking about sexual abuse, about themselves, and about their lives. Metaphors in this way provide new information which enables change to occur in the clients' perceptual, emotional and behavioural responses to abuse. Helping a client shift from seeing sexual abuse as 'a life sentence' to considering it as 'part of their story', for example, is helping them to take a major step towards healing.

Another way in which we use metaphor is in telling stories. On the surface a story may be about one person, object, or situation, but it acts as an allegory for another. The story might be drawn from the client's life, from the therapist's life, or from the stories of other clients or family members. It might involve famous people, myths, fables, fantasy, jokes, fiction, or non-fiction. The story chosen usually contains a suggestion about different ways of thinking or behaving. For example, we might tell a story which has some similarity to a client's experience, but which ends differently. Whether the similarities are explicit or implicit, the different ending is likely to be more positive and can suggest new options for the client to consider.

In another variation, metaphorical stories about another person (animal, insect, etc.) may parallel a client's own story, ending in the same way but having a different beginning. An example of this is the young man described in Chapter 11 who felt very anxious about having been sexually aroused while being abused. He was told the story of another male client who ejaculated while being raped at knife-point. Although the first client had previously been told that his body had just reacted normally to stimulation, the use of this story as a metaphor enabled him to separate sexual response and willing participation in a much more effective way. It thereby provided a more powerful antidote for his feelings of guilt and anxiety than providing information directly could have achieved.

Another use of metaphor in therapy is with the client who is unable to talk about their own abuse, but is able to tell their story as if it happened to someone else. This enables the client to talk about what happened from a safe distance.

Clients who have difficulty talking about abuse can also be helped to deal with the offender metaphorically. This applies particularly with children. A story could be told about another child, puppet, soft toy, etc. that was abused, and various dolls, toys, or drawings could be chosen to represent the roles of offender and victim. The 'offender' could be dealt with appropriately, and the 'child' rescued and consoled. In this situation, feelings of grief and anger can be expressed as freely as if the client were referring directly to their own abuse.

Metaphor also can be involved in fantasy rescue scenes, or rescue scenes involving a hero or super-human version of the client. Stories featuring some form of rescue of the person being abused provide a different ending to the real story, and allow the client to develop a sense of power and control not previously experienced.

The use of metaphor by the therapist enables the client to transfer knowledge from one area of ability to another. It can also be an effective way of gaining the client's attention, as the client is invited to make sense of the metaphor chosen. The metaphor used does not confront the client's perceptions and beliefs directly. It allows them to consider other possibilities in their own situation from a less immediate and therefore less stressful viewpoint.

Metaphor provides an indirect way to introduce ideas, when more direct methods may be rejected. It can be used to seed ideas, reframe a problem, or normalize responses. It can suggest solutions, illustrate a point, and capture attention. It can be used to introduce humour and to establish rapport. As with many other therapeutic tools, its use is limited only by the skills, confidence, and imagination of the therapist.

PART 3

THERAPY WITH THE FAMILY

6

WORKING WITH THE
FAMILY

The family's beliefs about sexual abuse and their emotional reactions to it, in fact all the life experiences that contribute to their understanding of an abuse incident, influence the way that the abuse is perceived by the person who was abused. In this chapter we consider the types of information needed by family members to enable them to respond to abuse in helpful ways. We also consider methods of conveying this information effectively, so that it is noticed, and not ignored or rejected.

In our work with children we recognize that family members often will be much more influential than the therapist. It is essential, therefore, that we work with the family while we work with the child, helping family members to develop ideas and skills that will facilitate the child's healing. The most important of these are beliefs that the child is not to blame, and that both child and family can recover from sexual abuse.

Work with the child's family usually involves a minimum of two sessions, at the beginning, and at the end of therapy. Some flexibility in the number of family sessions is obviously required, however, to meet the different needs of our clients.

Family work can also be important with adult survivors. It may be important, for example, to involve the client's partner in therapy, or their parents, siblings, or children. In some cases a friend or friends may take on the roles ascribed to the family in this chapter. Many members of the family will have been affected by the abuse and be in a position to help or hinder our client's recovery.

Even when we work with adults individually, we still ask questions about their relationships and about the reactions of significant friends and family members to the abuse. We assess the influence of the family on our clients' healing, find out where our clients get their support, and help them to deal with any relationship problems.

One of the important tasks of the therapist in the family interview is to ensure that everyone is heard. This can be difficult, particularly when a high degree of stress and/or conflict is present. It is essential that the therapist maintains control of the session, establishing guidelines that allow everyone to speak, to feel respected, and to feel safe.

In this chapter work with the family is described under the following headings:

- The Initial Family Interview
- Framework for the First Meeting with the Family
- The Middle Stages of Therapy
- Finishing Therapy with the Family
- Summarized Examples of Teamwork with the Family.

THE INITIAL FAMILY INTERVIEW

Who should attend?

With children

When a child has been referred for sexual abuse therapy we usually begin with a family interview. We negotiate with the family, and, where relevant, with the referring social worker or health professional about the appropriate people to be present at this first session.

Usually the child concerned is present at least initially. Sometimes, however, it becomes obvious early in the session that there are sensitive issues to be discussed which would be best addressed by seeing the adults and/or child separately.

Often it is not advisable to have the child and the offender in the room together at this stage. The case of abuse by an elder sibling is, however, a common exception to this guideline, assuming that both offender and child live in the same home.

Those present should include the primary care-giver/s of the child, unless of course one is the abuser. If the parents have separated, it might be appropriate for both to attend. This is particularly helpful if both parents are involved with the child, able to co-operate with each other, and able to feel comfortable in the room together. When separated parents are both involved with the child, but cannot come to therapy together without adding to either their own or their child's stress, separate sessions may be necessary.

The family usually decides whether siblings need to be involved in therapy. Generally, those who are old enough to understand what has happened, and who are aware of the abuse, should be asked to attend the initial interview. Older children in particular are often affected by the abuse of a sibling, and it is part of therapy to ensure that they know as much as is appropriate about what happened. We may, for example, help the child who has been abused to tell the siblings about their experience, usually during a family interview with the parents present. This would involve first seeing the child alone to discuss the reasons for doing this, obtaining their permission, and planning with them the details of what the siblings need to be told.

The initial family interview might involve only the child and one parent, or may include a large extended family group. Sometimes, particularly with younger children, a parent or parents are seen first without the child. Some parents prefer to come alone initially so they can discuss their options and investigate the therapy offered. They may also want to provide details of the abuse and background history without the fear of risking further distress to their child by describing details in their presence.

With adults

An adult survivor seeking sexual-abuse counselling may choose to come alone to their first session, or in the company of their partner, family, or friends. Even when contact with family members occurs later in therapy, work with an adult survivor's family can still have many of the functions of the initial family interview listed below.

Assessment

A family interview allows us to collect more detailed information about the history of abuse and its effects. Family members have different perspectives, and particularly in relation to children, may have observed effects not reported by the survivor. This information provides us with an essential tool in the assessment of trauma, which may not be obvious from our observations of the child. For example, without meeting with the family we may not be aware of such child behaviours as nightmares, soiling, or inappropriate sexual play.

The family interview also assists us in our assessment of the social system in which the survivor lives. It provides us with information about the family's influence on the survivor's perceptions of the abuse, and information necessary for planning therapy. We can use the family interview to determine such factors as:

- How have family members been affected by the abuse?
- Who needs further help?
- How do family members feel about the survivor?
- Who is likely to be most supportive?
- What help/information does the family need to facilitate the healing process?
- How have family and survivor coped so far with what has happened?

Assessment of information obtained in the initial family interview plays a major part in planning for therapy. It enables us to establish goals and to plan with the family how therapy should proceed. This includes discussing the type of help needed and who will be involved in future sessions.

Factors to be assessed in work with children are described in more detail in Chapter 8.

Education

Many of the family's fears and anxieties are based on a lack of information or understanding, while some family members may be denying or minimizing the abuse and its effects. By providing information we can give reassurance and ensure that family members are in a better position to help the survivor.

Seeding ideas

While sharing information with the family is an essential part of the initial interview, family sessions should not become a lecture or monologue from the therapist. Rather, we take opportunities to seed facts and ideas, sometimes by making brief statements, at other times by conveying ideas in the questions we ask.

Ideas which we would most frequently want to 'seed' in the initial family interview would include our belief that the person who was abused is not to blame, that the abuse was planned, and that the survivor, and possibly the family, was somehow tricked or 'groomed' by the abuser. An apparently simple question like 'How did he trick you?' can go a long way towards shifting blame and guilt from themselves or one another, especially when asked in the presence of other family members. By implying that the abuse was intentional, and that a child or a family was tricked, we are helping survivors to lay their anger and blame where it belongs. Seeding helps both survivor and family members to gain a different understanding of the abuse, and in so doing helps to facilitate change. The seeding of ideas is explained in more detail in Chapter 5.

Helping the family to help the survivor

During the family session we can provide information and advice about the needs of the survivor — to be believed, to feel safe, to feel supported, and not to be blamed. By doing this we help families to create positive experiences of support and assistance to counter the damaging experiences of the abuse. We are ensuring that the most significant people in our client's life are working together to facilitate their healing.

With preschool children, a parent or care-giver may be the most appropriate 'therapist'. Our role then may be to advise the family on how best to help the child and how to cope with behaviour resulting from the abuse experience. We also provide information and ideas for the families of older children and sometimes for the families of adult clients, but usually in conjunction with individual therapy for the person who was abused.

Establishing guidelines for contact with the offender

In all family interviews it is useful to investigate ongoing contacts with the offender. This not only provides useful information about family relationships and attitudes, but also helps us to ensure the safety of any children involved.

Rules can be established with the family to ensure that the person who was abused always *feels* safe from the offender. They should never be left alone with the offender, or be in a situation where they fear being left alone. Children need to feel safe as well as be safe, and the presence of others will not necessarily protect them from the subtle nuances of comments, actions, or looks which they associate with the abuse. Any of these can create extreme anxiety. For many children a family rule that they have no contact at all with the offender provides the best protection.

An offender should not be allowed in any child's bedroom, or where they are being bathed, nor should they be allowed to have any discussion with them about sexuality. All family members, including children, should be aware of these rules, and should be warned of the danger of underestimating just how little time it can take for abuse to occur.

Guidelines for the offender should apply not just to his (see Introduction p. xviii) contact with the person he abused, but to his contact with any child. In cases where an adult has disclosed childhood abuse by a parent, for example, the abuser's grandchildren can be protected by appropriate guide-lines once they are established in a family meeting. Similarly the family may decide that children are at risk due to an offender's work, or social or sporting activities, and can plan together the most effective ways of dealing with this. It is always important to check on the safety of any children an abuser is known to have contact with.

The primary rule must be that no one — survivor, offender, or anyone else — is left in a high-risk situation. For those families that remain in con-tact with the abuser, this may include doing everything possible to see that the perpetrator accepts responsibility for the abuse, and gets appropriate treatment to prevent further offences. The therapist can provide useful information for the family about the various options available.

Expressing feelings and getting support

Directly or indirectly, everyone in the family is affected by the abuse of one member. Providing them with the opportunity to express their feelings in a family session can be very therapeutic for the individuals concerned and can lead to a greater understanding between family members. Feelings experienced by family members may include distress, confusion, anger, shame, guilt, or torn loyalties. Like the survivor, family members need to have their feelings accepted. They also need the opportunity to work through their feelings to a point where they are not destructive to themselves or others. They may require the support of a therapist to do this, as well as encouragement to tap into their own personal resources and support net-works.

Guilt

Guilt is one of the feelings which many family members experience relating to both child and adult survivors. It is not uncommon for us to see family members who feel tremendous guilt because they did not realize that their child, sibling, or partner was being abused, or because they failed to offer protection in some way. This can be particularly distressing when they acknowledge that the survivor previously tried to tell them what was hap-pening, but was not believed or understood at the time.

In the case of a child, sometimes it is useful to explore with the family any reasons that made the child more vulnerable to abuse. Perhaps the child felt unloved, or thought that they would not be believed if they dis-closed. Perhaps they did not have adequate supervision, or a parent lacked discrimination in their choice of care-givers. In such cases it is not helpful to pretend that mistakes were not made, but neither is it helpful to focus on events in the past which cannot be changed. Nor is it useful to be critical or judgemental. We assume that these parents want to do the right thing for their children, and we try to help them make constructive plans for the future. Guilt is only useful to the extent that it motivates these plans.

Guilt is debilitating when it gets in the way of parenting. It can disempower parents at a time when their children need support and security. Children who have been abused need to know that a parent is strong enough to take care of them. This includes setting the normal limits on their behaviour, and not letting them get away with behaviour generally considered to be unacceptable.

Therapists can acknowledge any guilt that family members may be feeling, and help them to deal with it. When appropriate we can reassure the parent/care-giver that they did the best they could in the circumstances.

When we work with children, we concentrate on helping parents to provide the kind of parenting the child needs *now*. This is essential for their recovery from abuse, their future safety, and their general development. When a parent is unable to provide the help their child needs due to unresolved guilt, issues from their own past, or lack of resources, providing help for the adult becomes an important part of therapy for the child.

Hurt, anger, and self-doubt

In work with children who have been abused, family members, and particularly parents, may experience a variety of feelings when they discover that a child has not confided in them about sexual abuse. They may find it difficult to understand, or they may feel angry with the survivor and imply that the child colluded in the abuse by not seeking help to stop it. They may question their relationship with the child, doubting levels of communication and trust which they had previously believed to be good.

In these situations it is often helpful to provide family members with a different perspective on what is happening. Therapists can assist both the family and the survivor by providing information about how difficult it is for children to tell, and by seeding such ideas as:

'Your daughter must care a lot about you: she must have really worried about upsetting you because she found it so hard to say anything.'

When they realize that a child in their care has been abused, family members may also lose confidence in themselves and question their judgement (e.g. 'Why did I trust him?') or even their self-worth (e.g. 'I failed her ... I'm not fit to be a parent.'). An adult whose partner has abused a child may worry about their sexual performance and appeal. Therapy needs to acknowledge their pain, affirm them for their good intentions, plan for the future, and shift blame for the abuse onto the offender.

In work with adults, feelings of hurt and anger are common problems for the partners of abuse survivors. Difficulties with trust, intimacy, or their sexual relationship can be experienced by the partner as personal rejection. It is helpful to provide a chance for the partner to express their feelings, and to offer a new perspective. We do this by normalizing the problem as a response to abuse, rather than attributing it to personal defects in either partner. (See 'Normalizing' in Chapter 5.) Counselling to help the couple resolve their difficulties is often important for both the survivor and their partner. Individual therapy for the partner may also be helpful.

Helping family members to discuss their fears

Fears about abuse can have a crippling effect on family members. They may worry unnecessarily about the effects of the abuse on the survivor, or may pathologize everything the survivor does, perhaps misinterpreting normal behaviour as a product of abuse. Consequently family members can exacerbate the effects of abuse with implicit messages to the survivor that they are damaged and unable to live a normal life.

In the family interview we provide a forum for family members to express their fears, and counter these with information and strategies for coping.

Providing reassurance that the survivor can lead a normal life

These days people are more aware of sexual abuse and its possible effects. Consequently some of the family's fears may include worst-case scenarios. They might not be aware that some people are not traumatized by sexual abuse. They may not know that therapy, combined with a positive family response, can assist survivors to lead normal, healthy, and well-adjusted lives. Providing appropriate reassurance helps both family and survivor to develop a more useful understanding of sexual abuse and its effects.

Normalizing

Sometimes the family's fears about the effects of abuse on the survivor arise from their observations of changes in their behaviour. When we normalize these changes as a 'normal response to an abnormal situation' we provide a more positive perspective for all concerned. This can be reassuring and therapeutic in itself. Normalizing, therefore, plays an important part in the initial family interview. It requires a sound knowledge of the issues and possible effects of abuse, and an awareness of the need to share relevant information with the family.

Further information about normalizing can be found in Chapter 5, while Chapter 1 contains useful information for sharing with families.

Dealing with conflict between family members about blame

The stress of discovering sexual abuse in a family, and all the strong emotions associated with this discovery, can often lead to family members directing their feelings of anger, blame, and guilt at themselves, at the survivor, or at one another. When this happens we stress in the initial family interview that the person responsible for the abuse is the abuser. We might do this directly with statements about how unfortunate it is that people often get angry with one another, instead of with the person who caused all the trouble. Normalizing such responses is a way of making these observations without conveying criticism or blame. Or we might be more indirect, asking questions which allow the family to discover for themselves what is happening, for example:

'How did this guy manage to get you fighting amongst yourselves, instead of putting the blame on him where it belongs?'

Often just getting family members to observe their own reactions helps them to consider more helpful options.

Lack of support from the non-abusing parent

One of the most difficult situations, for both survivor and therapist, occurs when one parent abuses a child, and the other parent either blames the child or refuses to believe their disclosures. This situation can arise in work with children, and with adults who were abused as children.

Sometimes it is just a temporary problem, a stage in the difficult process of coming to terms with sexual abuse. Sometimes it becomes entrenched over time in firmly held beliefs. The response of the therapist can help or hinder the parents' ability to reconsider their position.

In these circumstances it is a mistake for the therapist to become so angry with the non-abusing parent that they cannot work with them effectively. An angry therapist is likely to make such a parent even more defensive about their beliefs and to push them even further into an alliance with the abuser. Information that is rejected does not facilitate change, so we first need to communicate effectively with the non-abusing parent. This does not imply that we must agree with the non-abusing parent, but we must try to understand them.

To avoid a conflict of roles, it is always preferable for a non-supportive parent to be seen separately from the person who was abused, and by a different therapist. Otherwise the survivor may feel betrayed by the therapist's apparent division of loyalty.

Therapy for the non-abusing parent explores the experiences and beliefs which guide their responses. It might focus on their family history for a non-blaming explanation of current attitudes. It could also be useful to examine the consequences for the parent of believing what had happened. These might include loss of a valued relationship, concern for the abuser, fears about financial security, fear of the abuser, anxiety about parenting alone, and/or a history of antagonism towards the abused child.

Any of these factors may make it difficult for a parent to consider the possibility of abuse. Any of them can be exacerbated by an angry, non-compliant child, who is distressed by the abuse and perhaps even blaming the parent for not protecting them. In order to facilitate change it is essential to understand the parent's viewpoint rather than criticize it. The only thing we have a right to insist on is that a child is safe within this family.

Helping family members whose own lives have been torn apart by the abuse

Discovery of abuse can be devastating for the family, particularly when the abuser is a member of the family or a close family friend. Often family members experience a sense of crisis in their lives, in which their view of the world and of themselves is radically altered. They are faced with major decisions about where their loyalties lie, and they may have to cope with the break-up of the family unit. For the partner of an abuser there may be enormous pressure to leave a relationship which has been very important to them. They may lose confidence in themselves and question their own integrity, asking, for example:

'What sort of person am I to love someone who abuses children?'

Different family members may need ongoing help for themselves or referral to other agencies. Ensuring that they get the help they need puts them in a better position to help the person who has been abused.

Family members with a history of sexual abuse

It is not uncommon during the initial interview that some family members reveal that they, too, have been sexually abused. The discovery of abuse within their family can trigger memories and feelings of their own abuse experiences which have not been dealt with. This situation is not surprising given the prevalence of sexual abuse in our society. Sometimes this information has never been disclosed before, which is also not surprising, given what we know about reporting rates. Family members who themselves have been abused may need help either within the agency or through referral elsewhere.

When a parent has not dealt effectively with their own history of sexual abuse, they may need encouragement to get help for themselves before they are in a position to meet the needs of their child. The therapist can also play a useful role by making explicit what is happening, encouraging the parents to take time to care for themselves, and helping them to plan ways to ensure that their child's needs are met until they can be more available.

The parent with a history of abuse may also lack the experience and skills to protect the sexual safety of their child. They may not always recognize the risks inherent in allowing their child to be in certain situations or with particular individuals. They may not be good at setting limits on their child or on others. It is helpful if they can be provided with information which will help them to keep their child safe in future. This should be done in a way that is non-blaming, and which acknowledges the influence of their past abuse on their present difficulties.

Sometimes we suspect a history of abuse which has not been disclosed by a family member. In such a situation it is often helpful to make an opportunity to ask them, either alone or in the group, if anything like this has ever happened to them.

Apart from ensuring that family members get the help they need, we can also help them to use their own experience of abuse in a positive way to help our client. We do this by asking questions like:

'From the wisdom you have gained from your experience, what do you think your daughter needs most now?' or

'What were the things that didn't happen for you then which you think would most help your son now?'

Such questions help to empower family members by putting them in touch with their own strengths at a time when they may be feeling overwhelmed and vulnerable.

Affirming the family

Family members whose lives have been torn apart by sexual abuse often feel uncertain or confused about how to respond to a disclosure. It is helpful if we affirm all the positive steps they have taken. For example, when a child discloses abuse we can congratulate the family for believing the child, laying responsibility with the offender, getting appropriate help, and ensuring the safety of all concerned. By affirming the way the family has coped we put them in touch with their strengths, and thus begin to address any doubts, confusion, self-blame, and fears. This enables family members to act with more confidence in helping the child.

The family of an adult survivor may also need affirmation for the various ways in which they have supported the client. By drawing attention to those actions that are helpful, we encourage them to maintain their supportive role.

Coping with the effects of abuse

With children

When the family is not sure about how to respond to the effects of abuse, it is important that they get appropriate information and advice. Parents of young children may need help in dealing with such symptoms as nightmares, soiling, or inappropriate sexual play. They could benefit from the information that these responses are normal in the circumstances. They could also use support to cope with problems while they last, and practical ideas for dealing with the problem behaviours (see Chapter 9). They may need permission to take a firm stand if their child is inappropriately touching other children, and to know that they should not excuse such behaviour because their child has been abused.

We make a distinction between understanding why a behaviour may be occurring, and allowing children to persist with it. This can be a great relief for parents distressed by unacceptable behaviour, but afraid to set normal limits for fear of being unjust or doing further damage.

Issues about parenting an abused child can be particularly difficult for a mother whose partner was the abuser. The abuser is likely to be out of the home and allowed little or no access to the children, so she may need support to cope with increased responsibility for parenting and discipline. The mother will also need help in getting a break for herself and meeting her own needs. Similar issues would exist for a male parent in the unlikely event that a mother was the abuser.

With adults

Adult partners of survivors of abuse may need help to understand and deal with other effects of sexual abuse. Difficulties in a sexual relationship is a common example of a problem which could benefit from joint sessions with both partners. Information about dealing with sexual difficulties is provided in Chapter 11, and includes a list of references for clients, partners, and therapists.

Childhood abuse can impact on the development of trust and intimacy in the client's adult relationships, as well as on their own parenting. Difficulties in these areas might also be addressed by working with their partners, and/or with other family members.

Informing family members about options

It is empowering for survivors and family members to have information about the options available to them. This includes information about therapy and the resources available, as well as information about relevant but potentially confusing official procedures involving other agencies. It could include knowing where to go for a medical examination and what this involves, how to lay a complaint with the police and the likely outcome of this, how to put in a claim for any insurance or compensation they may be entitled to, how the legal system works, or how an agency such as a statutory child-welfare service is likely to respond to a disclosure.

We can help family members to clarify their options, and can support them through any difficulties. We may need to put them in touch with people known to be helpful in other services or make direct contact ourselves with the other agencies, by phone call or referring letter. We ensure that they have the support they need when they face a particularly difficult situation in another agency.

When our clients know about their options they are in a much better position to make good choices and to get the help they need. Particularly in the case of children, it is important that those family members responsible for the child get this information through a family interview.

Helping the family to talk about abuse

Talking about sexual abuse can be very difficult for families. It will often arouse intense emotions and is likely to be stressful or embarrassing. In the initial family interview, we frequently see family members who know little of what has happened, but enough to feel distressed and anxious. Although it is a major event in the life of the family, sexual abuse can take on the powerful status of a taboo subject and not be discussed.

When we help family members to talk about sexual abuse, we take away some of its power. When they are better informed about what has happened, they are in a better position to deal with it and to help one another. Sometimes this involves a separate discussion with the survivor to support them in giving the family as much information as they choose. It may even involve coming back to the family with the survivor and speaking on their behalf, if they find it too difficult to speak for themselves about what has happened.

It is important that the family can tolerate some reference to the abuse, as the survivor may need to talk about it from time to time. We encourage the family to help at such times, by framing it as an opportunity for them to carry some of the burden for the person who has been abused. It is also a way that they can provide support, assistance, and relief. For any family member who is so upset about discussing the abuse that they are unable to help, some form of individual assistance is indicated, such as support and/or therapy.

Explaining the therapy process

The family interview is an opportunity to explain the therapy process to all concerned. We can give families information about what is involved in therapy, who needs to be seen, and the likely length of therapy. In doing this we empower the family, establish a clear contract with them, and are more likely to get their co-operation. This increases the likelihood that the survivor will keep regular appointments, that therapist and family are working together to help the survivor, and that therapy will be more effective. It is particularly important to have family co-operation when we are working with children who are dependent on others to get them to therapy sessions.

Ensuring safety

Finally, the initial family interview is an opportunity to ensure that both the survivor and others are safe.

When we are working with children we need to know that their primary care-giver is able to provide adequate protection and support. If a parent is overwhelmed, unsupportive, or even abusive we need to consider the possibility of alternative care for the child. Ideally this situation is temporary, and can be arranged with the agreement of the family while therapy for both child and family continues. When the therapist is not successful in getting the family's co-operation, concern for the child's welfare and safety must take precedence. This may involve reporting the situation to an agency with formal authority to arrange alternative care.

In work with children and with adults, we sometimes find that the perpetrator continues to present a risk to the client or to others. It is then our responsibility to do everything possible to ensure that all concerned are safe, and to get treatment for the offender. Ideally this is be done with the co-operation of the family, but it may also require reporting to a statutory agency such as police or welfare authorities.

FRAMEWORK FOR THE FIRST MEETING WITH THE FAMILY, FOLLOWING DISCLOSURE OF SEXUAL ABUSE OF A CHILD

The initial family interview that follows a disclosure of sexual abuse of a child is potentially a very difficult meeting for both family and therapist/s. To make this primary and most critical stage easier to understand and manage we provide here some suggestions about the structure of this session, the statements to be made, and the questions to be asked.

The primary tasks of the therapist during the initial family interview are to:

- Join with each family member;
- Obtain a history of the disclosure;
- Obtain a brief history of the abuse;
- Assess the effects of the abuse — on the child;
                                         — on the family;
- Ensure that blame is attributed to the perpetrator;
- Address any of the family's fears for the future;
- Address the needs of any family members who have a history of abuse;
- Ensure the safety of all concerned;
- Affirm all positive action and highlight any reasons for optimism;
- Establish a contract for future sessions.

Joining

Interviews generally begin in a very structured way, with specific tasks carried out in the following order:

1 Introduce yourself and any other team members. Provide relevant information about the agency and about the interview format. If a one-way screen is to be used, explain its function and obtain the family's consent for its use. Similarly, consult with the family about note-taking and the use of any audio- or video-recording equipment.

2 Obtain the names and ages of each family member. Find out where they come from, and gather relevant information about occupations, schools, and children's interests. Whenever possible, involve every family member by asking each person for the information which applies specifically to them.

A genogram may be drawn at this stage to show the relationships between the various family members, and to determine who the significant people are in the family.

How this introductory stage is carried out depends partly on the cultural background of the clients. It may be helpful, for example, for families with a strong spiritual focus, to commence with a prayer. For families from cultures with strong links to the extended family, it is important to take time obtaining information about the individuals involved. Our aim is to help the family feel as comfortable as possible, but usually it is helpful if this stage is not prolonged, as this may heighten anxiety about the purpose of the interview by making sexual abuse seem unmentionable.

3   Acknowledge very early in the session why the family has come to see you, and name the problem 'sexual abuse' for example:

'I understand from your phone call Mrs Thompson that Lucy has been sexually abused, and that you are wanting help to deal with this.'

If you have not already done so, establish your own credentials as some-one who is competent to help the family, for example:

'We have worked with many children and families at this agency after sexual abuse has occurred. We have a lot of experience and good ideas that you may find helpful.'

4   Acknowledge the difficulties for the family in coming to this meeting, for example:

'I understand that it is really hard for a family to come to a place like this to talk about sexual abuse. It's really normal for people to feel anxious about being here, because it's not an easy situation to be in.'

5   Acknowledge the difficulty of talking about sexual abuse, and offer appropriate reassurance, for example:

'Everybody in a family gets affected when somebody is abused. That's why we asked the whole family to come here. You might have been affected in different ways, so we want to make sure that everyone gets a chance to talk today. Even though it might be difficult to talk about, it's really good that this has come out in the open.'

'There may be things that some of you do not feel comfortable talking about in front of the whole family. If I ask you any questions that you don't want to answer, or if there are things that you need to see me about alone, please let me know.'

Children and adolescents often need particular acknowledgement of the difficulty they may experience, for example:

'Are you finding it difficult to be here today? … That's really normal. Lots of kids I see find it really hard to talk about sexual abuse. You've been very brave to come here today.'

Obtain a history of the disclosure

When we meet with a family, it helps to start with a subject that is not too threatening, and which provides a useful background to events which led immediately to this meeting. So we often begin with the disclosure, and the response which has already been made to it. At this stage we affirm the courage of a child who has disclosed, and any positive responses made by family members, for example:

'It must have taken a lot of courage to tell your Mum what had happened.'

'That was a really hard position for you to be in, knowing that your sister was being abused. It's really good that you decided not to keep it a secret because now she can get some help.'

'It's great that you believed Julie, that you've already told her it wasn't her fault, and you're making sure she's safe. Do you know, that's the best way a family can help someone to get over abuse.'

We also find out who else is involved in a professional or support capacity, and establish some guidelines for contact with them, for example:

'The social worker whom you first contacted may ask me for a report. They don't need to know the details of what we talk about, just that you are coming here and getting help. Most of what we talk about is confidential, but I'd have to say if I think someone may be at risk. We can talk about what information I hand on to your social worker, and I'll show you a copy of any reports I write.'

When a parent is upset that their child did not disclose earlier, or made their disclosure to a friend, teacher or statutory agency, this needs to be addressed. They need information about the difficulties children face in making a disclosure, both from the therapist and the child. The therapist provides information directly, and also asks questions which help the child or the family member to explain, for example:

'Did you think that your Mum might not believe you because she really liked Uncle Hector?'

'Some children think that they might get into trouble, or that their parents will be really angry or upset. Was that what made it difficult for you to tell your parents?'

'I can see that you were very angry and upset when you first found out about it. Do you think Jenny might have got the wrong idea that it was her you were angry with?"

'There are lots of reasons why children find it hard to tell someone when they've been abused. That's really normal. Sometimes it's most difficult to tell the people they love the most, because they don't want to upset them. It doesn't mean that there is anything wrong with your relationship — it can mean quite the opposite.'

The parent who is finding it difficult to believe a disclosure, and/or whose own life has been thrown into disarray by the disclosure, will need particular attention. It is important to acknowledge the difficulty of their position at the beginning, rather than get into an argument with them, for example:

'It looks like you're really torn. If you believe your kids, you have to face some really hard decisions about your marriage. And if you believe John,˚ your children will feel angry and unsupported. Do you feel caught in the middle — like you can't win, whatever you do?'

When a parent is not sure whether they should believe a disclosure, or when they believe that the child is partly responsible, we need to be ready to respond with brief statements of fact. Once again we try to avoid an argument or long discussion at this stage, but take opportunities to seed information, for example:

'Children very rarely lie about abuse. The research tells us that only about two out of every hundred disclosures turn out to be false.'

'Children don't ever ask to be abused. But for lots of reasons it's very difficult for them to stop it from happening. It's not their fault — abuse is always the responsibility of the abuser.'

Obtain a brief history of the abuse

During the discussion of the disclosure, or immediately after, we begin to ask about the abuse itself. We need to find out who has been abused, who the abuser is, and any other information that the family feels comfortable about sharing at this stage.

It is important that the family is not pushed to talk about the abuse details now, as this is best done later within individual sessions. We need to watch each family member carefully, and to be sensitive about how much information we request. This varies enormously between families. Some families will already have discussed the abuse openly, and will talk relatively freely as a family group for the whole meeting. In other families, various individuals need to be seen separately very early in the session, when they are clearly uncomfortable or unwilling to speak in the family group. The availability of therapy team members to see the various family members separately is invaluable in this situation.

The therapist working alone may have to make separate appointments for individual family members to return at other times, if they want to ensure that everyone feels heard and no one is subjected to long delays in the waiting-room.

In most families, it is best to address the first questions about the nature of the abuse to the adults, rather than placing this pressure on the child who has been abused, for example:

> 'I don't want you to tell me in detail about the abuse, but can you tell me generally about what happened?'

It is important to get each person's understanding of what has happened. We use discretion, however, in talking with younger children, and check with parents how much various siblings have been told, for example:

> 'Have you been able to discuss this as a family?'

> 'Do you all know why you are here today?'

Sometimes parents and/or siblings have very little knowledge of what has happened. Talking about sexual abuse within a family meeting can serve to challenge unhelpful beliefs, and break the silence which often feeds the power of abuse. When family members do not know much about what has happened, it may be important to empower the survivor to tell them more about it. It is very important that the therapist's questions do not force or rush a child in this process, for example:

> 'Would you be willing to talk to your Mum and Dad about what happened to you? I think they need to hear more about it so they can understand. I don't want you to go into details — just what you can manage to say.'

> 'Would you be brave enough and willing enough to say what happened?'

It is important to respect the child's wishes if they are not ready to speak about the abuse at this stage.

Before a child discloses information about the abuse, they need to know that their parents will listen and be supportive. We can ask questions which help to create a positive context for a disclosure by addressing specific questions to the parents, in the presence of the child, for example:

> 'Do you think there's any way you might blame Rhonda when you hear more about what happened?'

'What Joseph has to tell you might be very upsetting. Do you think you can cope with it? How will you take care of yourself if you need help to deal with it?'

When a child does disclose any information about their abuse during a family meeting, both child and family need affirmation and encouragement, for example:

'It must have been really hard for you to talk about this. You've done something very strong and brave today.'

'It must be very painful for you to hear this, because you love your son/daughter and care about what happens to them.'

When the offender is a family member, it can be particularly difficult for children to disclose details of abuse. They may be caught between two people they love, and may also be very aware of the impact the disclosure is likely to have on other family members. This needs to be acknowledged by the therapist, for example:

'You really needed to tell someone so you could stop what was happening, but you didn't want to upset your mother. That must have been a terrible position to be in.'

Parents can also be encouraged to understand and acknowledge the difficulty their child has had in disclosing, for example:

'Do you think it would have been easy for your son/daughter to tell, or do you think it would have been difficult?'

When it is clearly too difficult for a child or adolescent to speak to the family about the abuse, this needs to be respected. Usually we see them alone, either during this first meeting or at a future session. We work with them to help them feel prepared and empowered to come back to the family to share any information which would be helpful. Alternatively, we can offer to act as spokesperson for a child, sharing with the family any information they have been able to tell us when seen alone. This, of course, is done only with the child's consent, and usually in their presence, for example:

'Neil has been very brave today, and managed to tell me some things that are very difficult to talk about. He has asked me to tell you about it too, so you will know what has happened to him. I will keep checking with you Neil, as I talk, just to make sure I've got it right.'

Once we have ensured that the adults in the family have adequate information about the abuse, we check on their response. This is particularly important when we are working with parents who were initially unsure about what to believe, for example:

'So when you hear your daughter/son say that, does it make it easier or more difficult to believe what has happened?'

'Maybe I'm wrong, but I wonder if it might almost be a relief to hear what they say. Because now you know what's happened, and you've got something tangible you can begin to deal with.'

Enquire about the effects of the abuse

We enquire about the effects of the abuse on the child, and on the family, for example:

'Now that you know when the abuse started, can you think of any changes you might have noticed in Jenny around that time?'

'How do you think Michael has been affected by the abuse?'

It can be helpful at these times to have in mind a checklist of ways that children are commonly affected by abuse, and to enquire specifically about them. We ask about possible responses such as regression, nightmares, sleeping and eating problems, moods, clinging, aggression, non-compliance, and sexualized play, for example:

'Has he had any problems with nightmares?'

'Has she gone backwards in any areas, such as toilet training or speech development?'

'Has her behaviour changed in any way?'

We also start to check on how other family members have been affected, and what help they may need for themselves, for example:

'What's it been like for you since you found out?'

'It seems like its triggered off a whole lot of feelings for you about your own past. Have you had any help for that? Is that something you'd like to talk about?'

'Has the worry about this brought you closer together as a family, or pushed you further apart?'

It is important to enquire specifically about the family's response to the abuse, and also to behaviour changes they may have noticed in the child, for example:

'How did you feel when you first found out?'

'What did you do when David told you?'

'What do you do when she has a nightmare?'

'How have you been dealing with the bedwetting?'

Shifting blame

Throughout the interview it is important to seed information and dispel unhelpful beliefs. We should not fail to respond to statements by the family which indicate blame of the child or one another, disbelief about a disclosure, or a tendency to pathologize the child as 'damaged' forever. (See 'Seeding Ideas' in Chapter 5, pp. 54–55.)

It is not unusual for family members to blame themselves when abuse occurs. We respond with such comments as:

'From my experience, when abuse happens in a family people often feel terribly upset, and think it's their fault because they trusted someone or didn't realize what was happening. They blame themselves when really they need to put responsibility where it belongs, and that is definitely with the offender.'

We help to shift blame from the survivor by talking about how they may have been tricked or 'groomed' prior to the abuse. In order to do this we use details already provided. These can be drawn out by asking 'leading questions', which would not be acceptable in a context where there was any doubt that the child had been abused by a particular person. These questions can be illuminating for both child and family, for example:

'It sounds like he made a friend of you, he was nice to you and gave you things. Probably in some ways you liked him. And then once he'd got you to be his friend he tricked you into doing things you hated and which made you feel really bad. Is that right? Some of the time he would have been nice, but a part of him would also be conning you.'

'Abuse doesn't happen by accident. These guys plan what they're going to do, and they use tricks or bribes or threats so you won't tell anyone.'

Often other family members also feel betrayed, and this, too, needs to be addressed, for example:

'Sometimes offenders not only groom their victims, but they groom the whole family. In some ways you've all been affected, and you've all been abused.'

'You were abused too, because he got your trust and tricked you, like he tricked your children.'

In some families, adults blame one another for a bad choice of friends or for failure to provide adequate supervision. While there may be some truth in their accusations, they are often unhelpful. During this initial session we need to help the family to focus responsibility onto the offender, for example:

'It's really normal for people to feel very stressed in these circumstances, and sometimes the stress gets them arguing and blaming one another. The person who really deserves the blame is the offender.'

Addressing fears

During this primary session family members spontaneously may express their fears for the future, and we need to be ready to respond to these with appropriate information. Common fears include concern that their child has been damaged permanently, that they will be afraid of sexual relationships, that they will grow up to be an abuser, or that they will become homosexual. It helps if we can quote relevant research (see Chapter 1), and if we make our responses to these fears clear and confident. With some of these more common fears, it sometimes helps to refer to them yourself rather than risk that family members may be worrying unnecessarily about something they dare not mention, for example:

'These days people know a lot more about the possible effects of sexual abuse, but they don't always know that children can be perfectly OK if they get the help they need.'

'There's no reason why your daughter/son shouldn't live a normal healthy life. Research shows that children do best when they are believed and supported by their families, so you've already made a really good start.'

'Most children who are abused don't grow up to be abusers. Abuse is a choice people make.'

When families do not mention their fears, we can enquire directly about them, for example:

'People often have lots of worries about sexual abuse. What are your concerns for your daughter's future?'

'Do you have any fears about how this might have affected him?'

Family members with a history of abuse

When a family member reveals that they have also been abused, we may need to make a clear statement that their child's experience does not need to be the same as theirs. We can also help them to see themselves as an expert with something valuable to contribute to their child's healing, for example:

'From the wisdom of your experience, what do you think your child needs now?'

'It sounds like you didn't get the help you needed then, but you're providing a very different experience for your son. Because you're making sure he gets help he doesn't have to go through everything you've been through.'

We must also ensure that family members with a history of abuse have had the help they need to deal with their own abuse. If appropriate they could be offered therapy for themselves or referred elsewhere.

Safety

Ensuring the safety of any child at risk needs to be a priority during the first interview. We ask about the child who has been abused, and others who may have contact with the offender, for example:

'It's very important that Jane feels safe. Can you make sure that she and her father are never alone together?'

'Does he have contact with any other children?'

'Paul shouldn't have any contact with the offender that he doesn't want.'

Other issues

Sometimes the family's response to abuse is coloured by other issues within their history. An abused child may have a reputation for lying, or the parent who always disliked the abuser now blames the other parent for trusting him. It is important that we acknowledge these issues, but not accept invitations to get involved in old family arguments at this stage. The focus of the interview must be kept on the abuse, and on the responsibility of the abuser, for example:

'I understand that this has been a big issue in your family, but we need to put it aside at the moment so we can work out what's best for your daughter.'

'You two have had some big differences in the past, but the main thing now is that we agree about who is responsible for this abuse, and that's the abuser.'

Concluding the session

Usually we conclude the first interview with a summary of our meeting and arrangements for future sessions. This includes our acknowledgement of the difficulties faced by the survivor and the family, and affirmation of the family's strengths. A message of hope for the future should be part of our closing comments, together with a clear statement of what the agency can offer. The concluding statement might sound something like this:

'It's been a very difficult session today, and I want to acknowledge your strength as a family in coming here and supporting Margaret.

'You've been brave, too, Margaret, in telling us about the abuse, because I know it wasn't easy for you.

'You've all been through a lot in the last few weeks, and you've had to deal with some really strong feelings like guilt, and anger, and fear. It's hard for you as a family to face this, but now it's out in the open and that's the best thing that could happen. Now you can start to deal with it, and we can help you with that.

'We know that Margaret can be helped to feel OK again, and we have some ideas to help you as a family to help her. We think that Margaret needs a chance to see someone by herself to get rid of some of those 'yucky' feelings she talked about. So we suggest that we make some more appointments for the whole family, and some separate times to see Margaret by herself.

'We could start off with three appointments each and then review where we've got to. How does that sound?'

Policy about confidentiality needs to be explained at this closing stage, particularly when children are being seen separately from parents. Both child and parents need to know how much of what they say will be kept in confidence, and how much will be reported back to the family or to relevant social agencies.

Information about payment of fees also needs to be made very clear, and the family should be provided with any information about resources available to assist in this. Appointment times should be written down along with the therapist's name and phone number. Both child and family should know how to contact us if they need to.

The family should also know when we are *not* available, and, when relevant, they should be given suggested contact numbers for alternative sources of assistance, such as crisis services or 24-hour telephone counselling.

The middle stages of therapy

By the end of the initial family interview we will have assessed how much work needs to be done with the family. We will have discussed this with the family and established a contract for any further sessions required.

With some clients, particularly adults, a lot of our work will now be on an individual basis, and there may be little or no family work required at this stage. However, some adults bring a friend or family member with them for support. For others we may arrange for couple or family counselling to complement their individual therapy, with the goal of ensuring that the client has the support they need while dealing with the abuse. This complementary assistance can also be helpful when the consequences of the abuse impinge on their adult relationships, such as when there are unresolved issues with a parent or sibling, or when loss of trust or difficulties with intimacy affect a couple relationship.

Adult clients may also seek help in parenting their children, particularly if their own childhood has not prepared them with good role models. In such cases the adult client might be seen by the therapist or another team member for several sessions, which may include the children, to plan more effective ways of parenting.

Keeping parents informed about their child's therapy

When working with a child, it is useful to spend a few minutes with the parents at the beginning and end of each session, to catch up on how things are going at home and to keep them as fully informed as possible about the progress of their child's therapy. This helps them to trust the therapist and to be prepared for any reactions they may experience at home. Before we finish a session we usually talk with children in the playroom about what we could tell their parents about our time together. This way we ensure that we do not breach their trust and confidentiality.

Information shared with a child's family might be very general, for example:

'We've had a really good session and Jane has been very brave talking about the bad things that happened to her.'

Other children are happy to share very specific information about therapy with their parents. They may like the opportunity at the end of the session to invite parents into the playroom to see what they've been doing. They may like to show parents their drawings, for example, or to explain or demonstrate their different activities.

The issue of client confidentiality with children is a sensitive one. We must be careful not to make false promises about keeping confidences, as we may need to share some information with parents or make reports to other authorities. Children should always know what they can tell us in confidence and what we may need to discuss with others. It is best to be clear about this and to give them as much power as possible in the circumstances. For example, we might say:

'Your Mum really needs to know about this. What do you think would be the best way to tell her?' or

'We have to stop that man from hurting other kids. Let's plan how we could do that.'

Usually we advise parents not to question their child about what happens during therapy, but to be available if the child wants to talk about it. This is easier for parents if they know that they can direct any queries to the therapist.

Therapy for the child's family

Some parents need a lot more from the therapist than a few minutes before and after their child's sessions. Sometimes the therapist also wants a lot more time with the parents. This might be necessary for the therapist to keep informed about what is happening at home, to help the parents deal with their own issues, or to help the parents to help the child. Any of the issues referred to in the previous section about the initial interview may warrant further attention during the middle stages of therapy. One or more sessions with the family might be involved, scheduled as frequently as their needs require.

Teamwork

When ongoing family work is required a team of (at least) two therapists is ideal whenever possible. This enables child and parents to be seen separately or together, as required. For the family it allows for concurrent appointments, and therefore reduces the time involved in transport, time off work, etc. It also provides adult family members with the support of their own therapist. It enables one therapist to build up a relationship with the child, while the other may be supporting the parents in limit-setting and child management, thus avoiding a possible conflict of roles.

Similarly, in work with adults it can be helpful to have one therapist for the individual work, and another for work with the family. The second therapist may be more free to challenge the client when necessary in a joint family session, while the first can maintain a supportive role with the client which does not confuse the therapeutic relationship.

Clear communication between team members is obviously essential. Team members should meet before and after each session to share information and co-ordinate plans. It may be helpful to have a meeting of the team during a break in the session, feeding back to the family any conclusions reached before they leave.

Teamwork has the added advantage of providing each therapist with a different perspective, and with inbuilt support for what can be very stressful work. It is described in more detail in Chapter 13.

Family work with adult clients

As in our work with children, family work with adult survivors depends on the needs of the client during these middle stages of therapy. We might, for example, involve partners in counselling for sexual difficulty, or invite family members to discuss issues relating to the abuse, as when the client needs help in making a disclosure or confrontation. We can involve the family in providing more effective support when the client is feeling isolated, misunderstood, or suicidal.

There are numerous ways in which family sessions can play a constructive role in therapy for adults, providing, of course, that the client is willing to have the family involved.

FINISHING THERAPY WITH THE FAMILY

Therapy with a child or adolescent usually finishes with a family session incorporating the functions described below. Many of these functions are not appropriate for work with adult survivors, but when our adult clients have involved family members in their therapy, a concluding session with relevant family members may be useful. Such a session would probably cover specific issues raised in therapy, but may also include some of the functions listed here.

Explaining what has happened in therapy

With children

Particularly in therapy with children, a summary and explanation of what has happened is helpful for family members. As mentioned previously, this might be quite general to ensure that we do not breach the confidence of our client, for example:

> 'Tracey has talked about what happened and how she felt about it. She has been helped to feel OK again and has lots of good ideas about keeping herself safe in future.'

With our client's permission, feedback to the family might be much more specific. It might involve detailing the activities in therapy and possibly showing family members some of the work completed, such as drawings or writing.

With adults

An adult client may choose to involve a partner, other family members, or friends in a final session, so they have a better understanding of the therapy process and the gains made. This can help to demystify therapy for the relevant support people, and can help the client to provide them with guidelines for any ongoing help and support she or he may need.

Checking behaviours at home and school

With children

While we will have been maintaining contact with care-givers and possibly teachers during the course of therapy with a child, the final family session is a chance to ask in detail about current behaviour. We check in particular for signs of unresolved trauma or indications that further therapy is required.

This is a meeting of those people working together to help the child. It is a chance to compare our perceptions of progress made, and to decide with the client and family if therapy is completed. It is necessary to get information from the family at this stage, to check this against information from our own limited contact with the child. This can lead to a decision that more help is needed for either the child or the family, or it can confirm our belief that no further work is needed at this stage.

With adults

Similarly, in work with adults, the final family or couple session is an opportunity to check on problems previously identified by the survivor and/or fam-

ily as joint concerns, such as difficulties with trust, intimacy, or sexual relationships. It is helpful for the therapist to have more than one perspective
on whether these problems have been resolved, in order to fully assess the
extent of any remaining difficulties.

Ensuring that family members have had all the help they need

The final family session is also an opportunity to review the needs of the
various family members, and to assess with them whether they have had all
the help they need for themselves. Some will have been in therapy themselves, some will have needed information, support, or referral to other
agencies. Some will have had to cope with major changes, such as leaving
a marriage, or the imprisonment of a husband or son. Regardless of how
they have been affected by the abuse, family members can benefit from a session which takes the time to review their own situation, to assess whether
any further help is required, and to provide information about any counselling
resources they may need in the future.

Checking for any remaining fears

During the final family session we check with the family members about any
fears they may now hold about the effects of the abuse. It can be a time to
reinforce information previously given, or to discuss fears for the future.
We help the client and family to make their fears explicit so they can be dealt
with.

Concerns about a child's future

One of the fears commonly held by parents of abused children is that further difficulties will be experienced by their child as they grow older. We
advise parents that children are likely to reach a different understanding of
the abuse experience as they reach different stages in their development,
and reassure them that questions at these times are normal.

It is important that parents see their child's questions about the abuse as part
of the process of healing, and not as a sign of pathology or unresolved trauma.
When they answer the questions calmly and honestly they help to develop their
child's understanding of what has happened. This helps the child to integrate
the abuse and the healing as part of their history as they grow up.

Sometimes children do need more help when new issues arise at different stages in their development. During the final family session we can
mention this as a possibility, without making it seem like it is inevitable,

abnormal, or serious. Parents can be advised of the help available, and reassured that children are less likely to have serious problems later if they have already had the help provided by good therapy and a supportive family.

Acknowledging change and reassuring the family

With children

The important message to convey to the family in a final family interview is that the sexual abuse survivor is normal. In work with children this should be clearly stated in front of the child. This way they hear it themselves, and also know that their parents have been told. By highlighting the healing which has already taken place, we draw it to the attention of those involved. This helps to prevent the very real danger that children may be treated differently because of their abuse, and consequently receive ongoing messages, either implicit or explicit, that they are damaged in some way.

We give parents reassurance that they can treat their child's unacceptable behaviours in the usual ways, as described in Chapter 9. This empowers them in their parenting, and hopefully prevents them from pathologizing behaviours likely to have occurred in the usual course of development.

With adults

We also need to acknowledge positive changes made by adults in therapy. By making explicit a list of their achievements, we help them to incorporate new information about themselves into their self-image. When family members have attended therapy with an adult survivor, we ensure that they too have noticed these changes and this helps them to avoid the risk of pathologizing the client in any way.

Like children, adults need the support of people who appreciate their strengths and acknowledge their healing. Family members who continue to see our clients as weak or damaged will almost inevitably have a debilitating influence. Such attitudes indicate the need for more work with the family. It also may be useful to do more work with the adult client to help them establish protective boundaries around their contact with the family.

Ensuring that children are safe

Children need to *feel* safe as well as *be* safe. In the final session with the family we check on this once again by determining whether there is likely to be ongoing contact with the abuser, and whether there are any situations in which the survivor feels vulnerable. Depending on the circumstances, parents may be advised to ensure that there is no contact with a particular person, that a particular place is avoided, or that the child should not be left alone in a particular situation.

This advice applies to any situation where the abuser still has contact with children — with the child who was abused, and with any other children, such as grandchildren, neighbours, nieces, and nephews. It is therefore a relevant concern in our work with both adults and children who have been abused.

Safety education

With children

The final interview with the family is an opportunity to explain to parents the details of any safety education undertaken during therapy with a child. This ensures that parents have the necessary information and skills to implement ongoing awareness of sexual safety. Often we refer them to useful videos or books (e.g. Elliott 1985). We usually suggest that they reinforce safety education by raising the subject in a non-threatening way every few months when natural opportunities arise.

Safety education is, of course, also advisable for children who have not been abused. Whenever possible we involve siblings as well as parents in this part of therapy.

Details of safety education provided for children and parents are described in Chapter 7.

With adults

Adults, too, may need help in planning for their future safety. Sometimes it is useful to involve family, friends, or neighbours in this process. Some clients live in potentially dangerous situations and may need help to develop strategies for keeping themselves safe. They may need to ensure that their home is secure, that they can contact someone who will come immediately if phoned, that they are never left alone with a particular person, or that their home telephone number is unlisted.

We encourage adult clients to use support people and to take sensible precautions in the spirit of being strong, proactive and self-nurturing. It is more positive for them to regard themselves as taking initiatives to care for their own safety, than to consider themselves as reacting defensively to fear and victimization.

Affirming the family

It is important in this final session to affirm the family for the help that they have provided for the survivor, and for their own strength in dealing with the issues raised. Ensuring that people are in touch with their own strengths and resources is an important part of a therapy process which has often had to deal with anxiety, fears, and self-doubts.

This final session is therefore a bit like a graduation ceremony. We acknowledge that the need to focus on problems is over, and that the family can now move into the future, confident that they have the resources to cope. In effect, we mark the shift from a world-view dominated by the abuse, to a view of the world in which they have triumphed over abuse. We might even reinforce this message with some sort of celebration or ritual to mark the end of therapy, or by giving the child or family a letter or certificate highlighting their successes.

Dealing with dependency

Affirmation of the family's resources is also a way of helping them to move away from any dependency on either therapy or the therapist. We provide affirmation, of course, throughout therapy, but as we approach the end of our work it is particularly important to seed ideas that focus on the family's strengths and on their ability to cope without further help.

When we have been working with a client or family for a significant period, it is helpful to prepare for this final session over several interviews. Often we incorporate gradually longer intervals between sessions. In this way the family builds up confidence that they can cope, while not feeling rejected. They are still free to seek help if needed, but in a position to develop skills and self-reliance.

Preparing for the future

The final family session should leave the client and family with information about resources available, should further help be required. It helps to dispel anxiety about terminating therapy if the client and family are prepared for any problems that may arise, and know that resources exist to deal with them. The family might like to know, for example, if they could return to the same agency, or if they could benefit from a different therapy experience, such as group work, marital counselling, etc. They would probably like to know if they are welcome to contact the same therapist for further advice or counselling. We can reassure them that help would be available (if necessary) in a way that empowers them to use appropriate resources, but does not imply ongoing dependency or pathology.

SUMMARIZED EXAMPLES OF TEAMWORK WITH THE FAMILY

1. The child client: family needing ongoing assistance and support

Initial interview

Two therapists meet with the family and the child. They may stay together or separate for part of the session if either the parents or the child need to be seen separately.

Middle stages of therapy

One therapist meets with the child, another with the parents. At the beginning and end of each session both therapists meet together with the family and the child to review events at home and progress in therapy.

Final interview

The family and child meet together with both therapists to conclude therapy.

2. The child client: family needing minimal assistance

Initial interview

One or two therapists meet with the family and child together.

Middle stages of therapy

Individual therapy is provided for the child. The parents may be seen with the child at the beginning and end of each session.

Final interview

The therapist meets with both the parent/s and the child to conclude therapy.

3. The child client: sibling abuse — both offender and survivor remain in the home

Initial interview

Ideally there is a team of at least three therapists available. We usually start with the whole family in the room, with the option of using individual team members to see the survivor, offender, and parents separately during the session.

It is helpful if one or two therapists are in the room with the family, and the rest of the team behind a one-way screen. Team members behind the screen are in a better position to monitor progress and to determine when/whether it would be helpful to see family members separately during the session.

Middle stages of therapy

Individual therapy is provided for the survivor. The parents and other family members are seen as necessary, separately and/or within family meetings. The offender is usually required to attend an individual treatment programme.

Final session

The team meets with the family to review progress and conclude therapy.

4. The adult client: no family involvement wanted

Initial interview

The client meets alone with the therapist.

Middle stages of therapy

Individual sessions are provided for the client. Issues relating to the family or other relationships are discussed, but any interventions relating to them are made by the client outside the therapy room. If it seems useful, the client could be offered the option of inviting any relevant family members to join them in therapy.

Final session

The client and therapist conclude therapy. Where appropriate, future options for involvement of the family or others in therapy may be discussed.

5. The adult client: assistance with couple issues is requested

Initial interview

Depending on the client's wishes, initially they may be seen alone by one therapist, or they may attend the first session with their partner. The therapist should be the same gender as the client, and when a heterosexual couple is seen, ideally both a male and female therapist should be present.

Middle stages of therapy

Most adult survivors need individual sessions relating to their abuse and its effects. During this period appointments for the couple can be scheduled as appropriate. The client's partner may also like some individual sessions, ideally with their own therapist. When different therapists are working with each partner, both therapists should attend the joint sessions with the couple.

Final interview

This can be a review of progress at a meeting with both partners, or can be a conclusion of therapy with the adult survivor who is seen alone.

6. The adult client with unresolved family issues

Initial interview

The client is seen alone by one therapist.

Middle stages of therapy

Individual therapy sessions are scheduled for the client. These may be interspersed as appropriate with sessions involving relevant family members. For example, family members may be invited to attend when support is needed, or when a confrontation or disclosure is to be made. Ideally a second therapist can be involved whenever family members require individual assistance.

Final interview

In most cases therapy concludes with a session alone with the client.

PART 4

THERAPY WITH CHILDREN AND ADOLESCENTS

7

TOOLS FOR THERAPY
WITH CHILDREN

Children usually do not have the verbal skills of adolescents and adults. Their therapy therefore cannot rely so much on spoken language, but needs to incorporate other means of expression and communication, such as artwork, writing, playing with dolls and puppets, using playdough, sand, clay, and water, role-playing, and making a video film. Outdoor activity beyond the therapy room and safety education are also useful therapeutic tools.

In working with children it is important to be prepared to use a variety of therapeutic tools for a number of reasons. Some children will respond more to one approach than another, so providing them with choices and the skills to reject approaches they do not like is one way that we help them to feel empowered during therapy. Therapists, too, have different preferences for the various ways of working, and find that some fit more naturally with their personal style. Some approaches are more appropriate for use at a specific stage in the therapy process, so others are needed to complement them at different stages.

A review of the research on the effectiveness of different types of therapy (Resick & Schnicke 1990) concludes that techniques which take the client back over the memories and emotions associated with the abuse, combined with techniques that address their reasoning and belief systems, are likely to be more effective than either type of therapy alone. By using a variety of tools for therapy we are able to address the various effects of sexual abuse relating to perceptions, emotions, physical symptoms, and behavioural responses.

Ideally the therapist working with children has the use of an attractively decorated playroom equipped with the necessary tools of therapy. Where this is not possible, a large, colourful bag containing the required materials can be carried by the therapist to various venues. The bag can be used to facilitate the joining process as the child is involved in the intriguing game of examining its contents.

Having a variety of materials for use in therapy is particularly useful for children who tend to be action-oriented and who have a limited concentration span for any one activity. When words fail them children may be able to express themselves more clearly using drawings or dolls. This might be useful, for example, when the subject matter is too threatening, or when they lack the necessary verbal skills.

When children get bored with one activity they can shift to another, while still working on the same therapeutic task. For example, they may begin to describe their abuse verbally, shift to drawing it, and complete the task by demonstrating with dolls. When they are not ready to deal with a particular issue, they can give us a clear message by changing the subject or choosing another activity.

During their time in the playroom, children may be allowed to do things that are not normally acceptable outside. It is important to make clear this distinction between what children may do in the playroom and what they may do in real life. Children are told that the playroom is a safe place to express angry feelings, but that aggression and violence outside the playroom are unacceptable.

We also set clear limits on what is allowed in the playroom. For example, a rule that no one is allowed to hurt themselves or anyone else provides security for both child and therapist. Such limits also reassure parents, who may be concerned that lack of rules in the playroom will encourage out-of-control behaviour at home. We advise parents that their child's angry feelings are a normal response to abuse, but also encourage them to deal firmly with any aggressive behaviour at home.

GAMES

Games and artwork are relatively non-threatening for children, and provide a relaxed format for obtaining information. They allow children to exhibit skill and competence at a time when they may be feeling anxious or low in self-esteem. They also aid in the joining process, as the therapist demonstrates a willingness and ability to reach the child's level. The therapist does this by joining in games, sitting on the floor and 'playing' with blocks, dolls, etc.

It is useful to start and end each therapy session with a game. This helps to orient the child to the playroom, to relax with the therapist in a non-threatening activity, and as far as possible, to leave the room feeling good about the time spent there. Suitable games are of relatively short duration (less than five minutes) and need to be appropriate for the age and skill of the child. A well-stocked playroom will include games currently in fashion (e.g. hand-held electronic games, draughts, 'Connect 4') as well as old favourites such as blocks, model cars, dolls'-house, and tea-set.

Toy telephones are useful for playing games, and can be put to more serious use. Sometimes children find it easier to talk to the therapist about some of the more difficult aspects of their abuse while pretending to be having a telephone conversation. The pretence of talking on the phone can help to engage the child, and can help to empower them by providing a sense of fun, distance, and safety not always evident in normal conversation.

DOLLS

Male and female dolls of various sizes, shapes, and colours are invaluable for therapy with children. Children need a variety of dolls to choose from, in order to represent different people and to perform various functions. Soft or 'rag' dolls, for example, are useful for cuddling, or for beating up and throwing about the room when venting of emotion is appropriate. Dolls of different appearances can help children to act out what has happened to them as we ask such questions as:

'Which one looks like Daddy?'

'Which one shall we choose to be you?'

'Show me what happened next.'

'What would you like to do to him now?'

Anatomically detailed dolls help us to discover the child's words for various parts of the anatomy, their knowledge of sexual behaviour, and their reaction to genitalia. They also help the child to demonstrate what happened to them in a way that can be clearer and less-threatening than words. The child may believe that 'showing' what happened is all right when they have been threatened or cajoled into not 'telling'.

Anatomically detailed dolls are also used in official evidential and assessment interviews, but when we use them in therapy we do not have quite the same restraints on making suggestions or asking leading questions. We therefore need to be aware of any incomplete investigations or court proceedings before we begin therapy. When we are seeing a child who may still be required to provide evidence for the court we must be particularly careful about how we use the dolls and about the style of our therapy generally. This includes specifically the avoidance of leading questions. While the needs of the child may dictate that therapy should not wait for the completion of protracted court proceedings, some compromises may be required.

When we use anatomically detailed dolls it is important that we present them to the child fully dressed. The child can then choose to undress them, or to look only at those parts with which they feel comfortable. Otherwise these dolls can create fear or anxiety for a child who has been sexually abused.

Dolls of all types have many uses in therapy. When the child is having difficulty talking about what happened, the dolls can be introduced as friends of the therapist, for example:

'I've got these special friends here … would you like to meet them? … perhaps they could help.'

Similarly, the dolls can be introduced as friends or supporters of the child:

'What name shall we give this doll?'

'Would you like her to be your friend?'

'How do you think she could help you?'

'Do you think she could whisper some things to me when it's too hard for you to talk?'

Once we have gone over the abuse situation with the child, dolls can be used to act out the rescue of a person who is being sexually abused. In this scenario we use dolls to represent the roles of the offender and his victim, while the child is empowered to take on the role of the rescuer. Dealing with the doll who represents the offender provides a useful forum for the expression of anger and grief.

PUPPETS

Puppets can also be used by both child and therapist to talk about things which may be too threatening to disclose directly. A puppet talking to a child, to a therapist, or to another puppet can help to put a safe distance between the child and the issue, so that it can be dealt with in a less-threatening manner.

As with dolls, a variety of puppets allows the child to choose those that fit their purpose, and allows for the interaction of a variety of 'personalities'.

In a 'conversation between puppets' a child may describe the abuse, and the feelings they have about it. They may express feelings and act out rescue scenes which enable them to feel powerful and in control. Puppets can be useful tools at all stages of the therapy process. An example of the use of puppets in therapy is given in the case-study at the end of this chapter.

DRAWING

Another method which can be invaluable throughout the process of therapy with children is the use of various art materials. Drawing is particularly useful because it requires only basic equipment. A lot can be achieved with just felt-tip pens, crayons, and newsprint. A whiteboard with coloured markers can also be useful for work which need not be kept.

Children can draw pictures themselves or can be asked to tell the therapist how to draw something, for example:

'What sort of a face shall we give him?'

'Do you look happy or sad?'

'What sort of things make you happy/sad?'

Children's drawings can be very revealing. They may, for example, distort the size of any body part which generates anxiety. For children who have been abused most commonly this is fingers, arms, tongue, or genitals. Children may want to exclude themselves or someone else from a drawing of the family, or to draw themselves quite differently from other family members.

Miriam Saphira (1987) suggests that we notice these things but the therapist should be wary of over-interpretation. They need to be seen in the context of other information before we jump to conclusions. Long (1986) agrees that interpretation should be kept to a minimum, and that children need shared, positive experiences, rather than insight. Allowing children to express themselves freely in their art is a way of validating their experiences and helps to pave the way for more sharing of feelings within therapy.

While they are drawing, children can be questioned about people, events, and feelings related to the picture. Drawing allows these questions to arise naturally, and the activity gives the child space to answer at their own pace and without the pressure of eye-contact. Sitting beside a child when working on a task together can make it easier for them to share confidences, while the more threatening position of sitting opposite can make the child feel more vulnerable to being observed. Drawing provides a relaxed format for child and therapist particularly when they work together on the floor, or at a low table in a setting conducive to trust and rapport.

Drawing the family

Drawing a picture of the family at the beginning of therapy can provide an enormous amount of information about each individual, about family relationships, and about the child's feelings for each family member. It provides the opportunity to ask a lot of questions important in the assessment process, for example:

'What do you like about Jenny?'

'What are the things you don't like about Jenny?'

'Who would you go to if you were upset?'

'How do Mum and Dad get on?'

'Who's angriest with (the offender)?'

'Whom do you like playing with most?'

It is possible that the child may see people outside the immediate family as most supportive. Questions should be asked to include this possibility. Questions should also be asked about pets, because pets can represent strong attachments or significant sources of comfort.

Drawing the child

Drawings can also be used to assess children's feelings about themselves. For example, one child may love to draw a self-portrait, while another with low self-esteem may hate it, and want to screw up the drawing or damage it in some way. Either way, the therapist has useful information. In the latter case the child has provided an opening for work on a problem area.

A child whose drawing reveals a poor self-image needs to have their feelings acknowledged, and then needs to be helped to move on to a more positive perception. For example, the therapist might ask:

'What do you feel like when you look like that?'

and then ask questions about the child's self-perception, such as:

'How do you know that?'

'Where did you get that idea from?'

'Who told you that?'

A supportive person or fantasy hero could be used to elicit a more positive image:

'What would Captain Planet say your strengths are?'

'What are the things your Nana loves about you?'

'What good things has your teacher noticed you doing?'

These positive attributes can be listed and the picture then redrawn in the light of this new information.

Drawing the offender

Drawing the offender provides an opportunity to assess the child's relationship with him, and their current sense of safety in relation to him. Therapists can use this drawing to reinforce the message that abuse is wrong and that the offender is totally responsible. This can be done by drawing attention to how much bigger, older, and more powerful the offender is.

Ambivalent feelings about the offender can be acknowledged verbally and reinforced by encouraging the child to make separate lists of the things they like and the things they do not like about the offender. The 'good parts', the list of positive attributes and feelings, may then be set aside in a safe place, while feelings may be vented on a drawing representing the 'bad parts'.

It is important, however, to stay with the client's feelings. It would be a mistake, for example, to emphasize the negative aspects of a person about whom the child feels mostly positive. Similarly, we do not want to imply that the child should feel positive about someone whom they dislike.

Feelings can be expressed by encouraging the child to tell 'the offender', as portrayed in the drawing, what they think of him. They may also be allowed to punish the abuser by tearing the drawing, stamping on it, and/or burning it.

Drawing the offender on a whiteboard rather than on paper is a useful variation on this theme, as they can be effectively 'wiped off' by the child when the discussion is finished.

Drawing feelings

Encouraging a child to draw their feelings can be useful for gathering information, venting feelings, and facilitating change. They might like to draw a picture of their sad feelings, for example, and then deal with them in some sort of symbolic way, like ripping them up, putting them in a safe place, or hanging them out in the sunshine. Such drawings can lead to useful discussion with questions like:

'Who else is in the picture when you feel sad?'

'Who do you go to when the bad feelings come?'

'What can you do when you feel like that?'

Children can be helped to plan strategies for dealing with the sad feelings, and can then be directed towards drawing another picture of themselves feeling powerful and good.

When they are unable to identify or acknowledge their feelings, children can sometimes be helped to describe feelings by drawing a picture of somebody else. We might suggest that they 'draw a sad person' and then elicit feelings with such questions as:

'What do you think might have happened to them?'

'What advice would you give them to get over their sadness?'

'What colour will we give that feeling?'

'Which parts of the body do they feel it in?'

'Where are they when they feel like that?'

Children can also be encouraged to draw pictures of themselves feeling happy. This provides a different perspective, and a source of optimism. Once again we use questions to maximize the effects of this exercise, for example:

'What makes you happy?'

'Who might be with you when you feel happy?'

'What do you need to change from a sad person to a happy person?'

'When was the last time you felt like this?'

Drawing what happened

Drawing the abuse scene is another way of helping the child to describe what happened. Drawing can be used when children do not want to talk about the abuse, to explain something for which they lack the words, or as a way of taking time over the difficult task of describing what happened. Older children sometimes like to draw a plan of the house to explain where and how various incidents occurred.

Drawing the abuse scene can also be a way of helping children to access memories of the abuse and the emotions it engenders. It helps them to enter fully into the details required for going over the abuse experience. The therapist may facilitate this process by asking such questions as:

'Who's in your picture?'

'What's happening to you?'

'What are you thinking?'

'What does he look like?'

'Has he got a beard?'

'Was this what you wanted?'

'What did you want?'

This is also a time when we can seed ideas, normalize, and reframe, for example:

'A lot of people would have felt really scared — how did you feel?'

'He shouldn't have done that, should he?'

'He's a lot bigger than you, isn't he?'

When the drawing of the abuse scene is complete, children can be helped to deal with it in a way that empowers them to take control of the situation. They may, for example, 'rescue themselves' by cutting themselves out of the picture and placing that rescued self in a safe place. This may be accompanied by comforting words of reassurance to the drawing of their rescued self. They may want to destroy the abuse scene in some way, by tearing, burying, or burning it. If a whiteboard is used they can experience the relief of wiping the scene away when the session is over.

Drawing the rescuer

Another way of helping the child feel powerful is to draw an abuse scene, in which a child in similar circumstances to their own is being rescued. The child can be helped to enter into a fantasy in which the victim is rescued and comforted, and the offender dealt with effectively. It is more powerful if the child is encouraged to draw themselves as the rescuer, and to experience the rescue at an emotional level. This is aided by questioning them about what they are doing and reinforcing the action portrayed with comments about their strength and bravery.

This drawing of the rescue scene may be one that the child would like to keep as a reminder of their strength, so it's best for it to be on paper rather than on the whiteboard.

Drawing a hero or imaginary helper

A child who is having difficulty describing what happened or dealing with the effects of abuse sometimes may be helped by being asked to draw a hero or fantasy helper who would give them strength. They may choose to draw a character from a favourite story or television programme, or they may draw an imaginary friend. This is a picture children might like to keep beside them in the therapy room, to give them strength to talk about difficult things. They can be encouraged to consult it when in need of advice or reminders about their achievements and resources. They may also like to take it home with them to keep in some prominent place.

Drawing nightmares

Sometimes it helps children suffering from nightmares to draw the dream and dispose of it as they would dispose of the bad feelings previously described. They could do this by burning, locking away, burying, or ripping up the drawing, or perhaps by hanging it out in the sunshine where, metaphorically, it loses its power. They can also draw a happy ending to the dream, or draw a hero who later can be suspended over their bed to keep the bad dreams away. The message of the drawing is reinforced in the discussion between child and therapist as the child is drawing.

Drawing body parts

It is an essential part of the safety education described later in this chapter that a child is able to name the various human body parts. Being able to name these is an important part of being able to communicate clearly if they are ever in an abusive situation again.

A body outline is first drawn by either the therapist or the child, and the therapist then checks that the child can name the different parts. They should start with the parts likely to be least threatening, such as nose and eyes, and conclude with both male and female genitalia.

As with the anatomically detailed dolls, body drawings provide the therapist with another way of understanding exactly what the child means when they use particular words to name their body parts. They therefore help to clarify the child's description of what has happened to them. Similarly, body drawings also help to determine the child's reaction to various body parts and to assess levels of anxiety associated with them.

Drawing success at the end of therapy

At the end of therapy the child's experience of healing can be reinforced with drawings of how their life is now. We can help to elicit details for the drawing by asking such questions as:

'What good things do you do with your family?'

'Whom do you see?'

'Who are your friends?'

A drawing of 'how life is now' can also be part of a final check that the child is no longer traumatized and is successfully getting on with their life after the experience of abuse.

CLAY AND PLAYDOUGH

Playdough or clay can be used in several ways in therapy. They may be used to make anatomically detailed human figures to check on names for body parts, instead of using dolls or drawings. They may also be used when a child needs to express anger, and they may be used to make models of the offender, who can then be stabbed with pins, squeezed, or dismembered.

When the playroom is in premises which allow for the making — and cleaning up — of mess, wet clay can be used to throw at pictures of the offender. The offender might be drawn, for example, on a large whiteboard, or on a wall with acrylic paint that can easily be cleaned. The energy involved in hurling clay and the pleasure of being allowed to deal with the offender in such an active and anarchic way contribute to a very effective form of catharsis. Wiping the offender off the wall when cleaning up afterwards can add to the power of this exercise.

For those premises not suitable for hurling clay, wads of wet paper may provide a satisfactory substitute.

WRITING

As with drawing, writing exercises can be useful at any stage of therapy with children. They can be used by themselves, or in conjunction with drawing.

When it's too hard to talk

When children find it difficult to talk about abuse we need to validate their caution, normalize the reasons why it is so difficult to talk, and try to find other ways of communicating. Older children and adolescents may be encouraged to write down things they find too difficult to talk about, while in the therapy room. The therapist may even leave the room for a short time, to enable them to be more in touch with their memories and feelings. In this way many children and adolescents have managed to communicate what has happened and how they felt about it, when they were too fearful, anxious, or embarrassed to discuss it directly while in the therapy room.

If writing about what happened to them is still too difficult, children could write a story about someone else to whom something similar happened. We help them to do this by asking such questions as:

'What happened to this person?'

'How did it affect them?'

'Did it change anything about their relationships?'

'What advice would you give them?'

Lists

Writing lists can be a very effective exercise for children of all ages. Older children can write for themselves, but some younger children also enjoy having the therapist write lists which they dictate. Lists may cover a wide range of topics, such as 'Good things' and 'Bad things' about the offender, 'Things I like/don't like about my family', 'Things I'm good at', 'What to do if someone tries to hurt me', 'Whom to talk to when I'm worried', 'Progress made in therapy', or 'Things I still need to achieve'.

Lists can be made on big sheets of paper spread across the playroom floor, or on small sheets which the child can easily carry around with them. The smaller more portable lists are especially useful to remind children of their strengths, because they can be kept in pockets where they are accessible at all times. Children may enjoy the novelty of writing their lists on a blackboard or whiteboard, or they may like to write lists beside an appropriate drawing (see 'Drawing' pp. 108–114). For children who can read, the therapist can record a list elicited verbally from the child, and have it typed up after the session and sent out in letter form.

Rating scales

A variation on the use of lists is a rating scale where children can place themselves on a continuum, represented perhaps by a line marked at intervals with the numbers one to 10. We can ask children to score themselves on this line for any of the concerns for which they are needing help. For example, the scale could represent strength, honesty, making friends, progress at school, control over anger, or involvement with hobbies. Comparing scores over several sessions allows them to mark their progress, and provides a context for discussing the steps needed to attain their goals.

Journals

For older children, keeping journals can be a way of communicating with the therapist, expressing feelings too difficult to talk about, recording ideas before they are forgotten, or maintaining progress between therapy sessions. Journals provide a vehicle for writing about anything which has meaning for the child. When journals are used to focus on issues relating to sexual abuse, children may record any incident that triggers memories of what happened. They may also write about the thoughts or feelings they have in response to these triggers. They might write, for example, about their response to something they have seen, to a particular smell, a photograph, a news item, or a song title. This provides useful information for both child and therapist, and may be part of a process of dealing with their feelings.

Writing about a rescue

Older children may benefit from writing a story about the abuse, concluding with a fantasy in which they are rescued and the offender dealt with appropriately. This has an effect much like the rescue scene previously mentioned as a drawing exercise (pp. 112). When children are encouraged to place themselves in the role of hero or rescuer, they feel stronger and more powerful. The satisfaction they get from devising this alternative story can also help to alleviate anxiety associated with the memories of what actually happened.

ACTION METHODS

Action methods appeal to children and can be combined with dressing-up to create a particularly effective form of therapy. By acting out their angry feelings towards an offender, or by taking on the role of rescuer, children can make major shifts in their emotional response to the abuse.

Action methods are a dramatic way of empowering the child and so decreasing the sense of powerlessness inherent in the abuse experience. By *doing* something different about the abuse, children incorporate different emotional responses more associated with strength and success. These can very effectively replace previous responses associated with shame, fear, and defeat. According to Role Theory (Clayton 1993) they learn new roles by practising them with action methods.

Perhaps more than other methods of therapy, action methods can be fun for child and therapist alike. Despite the pain involved in confronting sexual abuse, there is no reason why therapy should always be dreary. When children are having fun they are more likely to be engaged in therapy, and to remember what happened in the therapy room. Providing pleasurable experiences for these children can be therapeutic in itself.

Dressing-up

Dressing-up can facilitate action methods, and often very basic equipment will suffice. A simple cloak adapts to various roles, a few masks can be useful (e.g. ferocious animal, 'Ninja-turtle', hero figure), and hats such as a magician's hat, or a pretend police helmet or royal crown help to create effective roles.

Sometimes children are encouraged to bring their favourite costumes from home, or to make something themselves which will help them to feel the part. This might be a very simple mask, a cardboard hat, an adaptation of clothes from home, or bits of old fabric. Asking children to bring things from home can help to engage them and their families in the exercise. It can also help to build up their anticipation, and so enhances the impact of the exercise.

Catharsis

The most effective use of action methods with abused children is probably in the cathartic expression of anger. Once children have described the details of their abuse we encourage them to freely express the feelings that relate to it. In this active release of emotion we have a method which comes easily and naturally to most children.

Moreover, this release allows children to go beyond catharsis to the practice of new and more powerful roles. Catharsis may involve acting out anger and so help the child to feel more powerful. Play and fantasy are often used for this purpose because they are familiar to children and tend to come to them easily and naturally. By using action methods in the playroom, children can deal with the offender in ways that may not be possible or desirable in the real world. They can understand readily the difference between behaviours which are allowed in the playroom, and those that are unacceptable outside. Nevertheless the therapist is careful to make this distinction explicit, and should never be seen by the child or family to be encouraging aggression or retaliation in real life.

Action methods can be combined with other methods for the expression of anger. Drawings, for example, can be ripped up, stomped on, or beaten.

A tube of rolled up newspaper or a length of plastic hose can become a weapon for striking at a doll.

Soft dolls and puppets can be thrown about the room. Children can be supported in shouting, stamping their feet, or throwing missiles at a target. Providing they have the abuser represented in some form, they can use action methods to deal with him.

The rescue scene

For some children it is sufficient to express their anger towards the offender, and then move on to dealing with the effects of the abuse and/or planning for the future. For others, acting out a version of their abuse which includes a fantasized rescue scene can be a useful adjunct to catharsis.

When action methods are used to create a rescue scene, the child is coached into a role which symbolizes strength and authority. Preferably it is a role they choose themselves. The process is very similar to the way in which we created hero roles in drawing and writing. We might ask them, for example:

'Who would you like to be?'

'Think of someone (or something) really strong and brave who could help you.'

We then draw out the description:

'What do you think he/she would do if they found someone being hurt like you were?'

'What would you like to do to that guy?'

'What would you like to say to him?'

Together we develop a picture of a powerful person and help the child to take on that role. Usually this person combines physical strength with clear firm statements about abuse and comfort for the child. We plan things they could say, things to do, and what they could wear to help them feel the part.

Specific dialogue is worked out with the child and can be written out for them to learn or to read. It is usually just a few basic lines, for example:

'I'm Policewoman Wendy! Leave that child alone! You don't touch children in their private parts — it hurts them and they don't like it! You are going to gaol!'

This would be followed by words of reassurance and comfort for the child such as:

'You're safe now.'

'That was a bad thing he tried to do to you.'

'I'll look after you and no one is going to hurt you again.'

The scene is set up by the therapist, manipulating the dolls or puppets which take on the parts of victim and abuser. The primary therapist remains available to the child as a coach or support person, reinforcing the message of the 'play' with encouraging comments or cheers. When available, a second therapist could be enlisted to hold the dolls and to speak for the 'offender' and the 'victim'.

The essential part of the scene is that a doll or puppet is abused in much the same way as the child in therapy was abused. The child takes on the role of rescuer, saving and comforting the victim and dealing with the offender. In doing this the child takes a significant step in their healing. They shift from the role of victim and experience a new and more powerful role. They also provide the comfort they needed at the time of the abuse.

Dealing with sexualized play

A common response to abuse is that the child learns to behave in a sexual way, and engages in inappropriate sexualized play with other children. The assessment and treatment of sexualized children is described in considerable detail by Gil and Johnson (1993).

Acting out the rescue scene very much as described above is an effective way of dealing with this, so long as it is combined with advice to parents about taking a strong stand against inappropriately sexualized behaviour at home.

The child who is put in the role of rescuer is helped to shift from the role of abuser, just as they were helped to shift from the role of the victim in the rescue scene. Developing a powerful dialogue which has the child speaking out against abuse helps to reinforce the message that abuse is wrong. They integrate the role of rescuer through their actions, and are consequently less likely to repeat abusive behaviour. (See also Chapter 3.)

By combining action methods with video recordings, a very powerful and effective way of dealing with sexualized behaviour can be developed. This is described in detail below.

Action methods and video recordings combine to deal with sexualized behaviour

Access to a video camera enables the therapist to record the drama of action methods more vividly. The added dimension of 'making a movie' or 'being a film-star' helps to make the occasion more significant for the child, while watching the film several times, seeing themselves in the powerful role of rescuer, reinforces the message. The film can be stopped at various key places to maximize its impact by asking the child such questions as, 'Why shouldn't he do that?' and making such affirmative comments as, 'Wow, that was really great! I bet he's sorry now!'

Finally, the film can be shown to a larger audience comprising the child and significant family members. Involving the family helps to keep them in touch with the progress of therapy, and to support the development of the child's new role at home. Family members also act as witnesses to the new role taken on by the child and so make it more difficult for the child to regress to the role of either victim or abuser.

There are nine steps in this powerful method for dealing with sexualized behaviour:

1 Help the child to identify a hero who would stop the abuse.

2 Develop with the child a brief script about someone who is about to abuse a child — a situation similar to their own abusive behaviour, for example: The therapist holds two dolls, one to represent the victim, one to represent the child abuser. The therapist creates the scene by moving the dolls and speaking for them. The abuse scene depicted parallels the abuse perpetrated by this child. The essential difference is that in this case the rescuer intervenes before the abuse occurs.

Victim (Therapist):   'Help, help. Somebody please help me.' The child bursts into the room, dressed as Batman.

Batman (Child):   'Don't touch that boy! How dare you try to hurt him like that! That's a bad thing to do! You are in serious trouble! I'm taking you to the Police Station immediately!'

The doll representing the offender is removed from the room by the hero.

3 Maximize the impact of the film by talking to both child and family about how they are going to 'star' in a film. Send them home to prepare costumes between sessions.

4 In the next session the child takes on the hero role, dressing appropriately to facilitate the change in role.

5 With video camera operating, the therapist acts out the prepared script about events leading up to abuse, perhaps using dolls or puppets. The child–'hero' observes from outside the room (through the door, or from behind a one-way screen). Whenever possible, the child is accompanied, supported, and prompted by a co-therapist.

6 The child–hero intervenes to save the victim *before they are abused*. They read from the prepared script. The abuser is dealt with using powerful

action and dialogue. This will include a statement about the injury he is about to perpetrate and the punishment he will incur.

7   The child watches the video recording several times with the therapist, then with the family. The message is reinforced by stopping the film at various points for discussion, for example:

'What's Captain Planet doing here?'

8   Questions are asked of the child while watching the film to test their understanding of the abuse situation, for example:

'What is happening here?' ... 'Is that a good thing or a bad thing to do?' ... 'Do you think the little girl likes that?' ... 'What should happen to that bigger boy?'

9   The family is asked to reinforce the message at home with comments about how well the hero saved the child.

GETTING OUT OF THE PLAYROOM

Therapy does not need to be confined within four walls. Particularly with older children and adolescents, it can be helpful at times to get outside and go for a walk together.

Walking side by side with the therapist can release the pressure for those children who are daunted by the relative intensity of being in a confined space with someone who is watching their every response. They may feel safer in a more public setting, provided that it is still possible to talk confidentially. They may also feel more relaxed because they can avoid eye contact, can distract if the pressure gets too great, and are engaged in a familiar physical activity.

Going for a walk can also provide useful opportunities for therapy. For example, children who blame themselves for being abused at an earlier age can identify other children in the street who are about that age, and can be helped to acknowledge their relative powerlessness. Seeing another small child who seems innocent and carefree can bring home the enormity of the betrayal of abuse and the possible extent of its effects.

Sometimes, particularly with children who have special needs, rescue scenes enacted in the playroom need to be reinforced by practising the same skills within the child's usual environment. A visit to the home, or to wherever the child is either vulnerable to abuse or likely to behave in an inappropriate sexualized way, could ensure that the role of rescuer is integrated where it really counts.

Care must be taken, however, to ensure that the child feels comfortable and that confidentiality is maintained. When we take a child outside the playroom, consideration should always be given to the possibility that the child may be overheard or seen by someone they know. It is best to plan beforehand with both the child and the family some explanation of who you are and what you are doing together.

The potential for other difficulties also needs to be considered. Taking a child out of the playroom can be threatening for a child who feels unsafe in unfamiliar surroundings, or unsure of the therapist's motives. Also it can be unsafe for a therapist, who may be accused of various forms of malpractice, including sexual abuse, without the usual protection of agency guidelines and the close proximity of other staff and clients. Children should never be taken from the agency without the agreement of both child and parent, and without clear agency guidelines for such occasions.

Whenever we take a child out of the therapy room we need to ensure that the circumstances are very different from those associated with their abuse. We should be very open about where we are going and what we are doing, with both the child and the parents. We should not take them where they cannot be seen by others, and we should be particularly careful not to touch them.

Of course, some of the potential difficulties involved in taking a child outside of the playroom are also inherent in the privacy of the therapy room itself. Wherever we conduct our therapy, priority must be given to providing a setting which helps the child to feel safe, and which facilitates communication.

SAFETY EDUCATION

Teaching children ways of keeping themselves safe from future abuse is one of the last tasks of therapy. This must be done in a way that does not imply any blame for not putting these ideas into practice at the time of their abuse. There should be explicit acknowledgement that this is new information, which will be useful for keeping them safe in future.

Safety education should be carried out with both the child and their family. We go over this information with the child alone, but also with parents and siblings. Parents can be given ideas for reinforcing safety education at regular intervals, and if appropriate, older siblings can be encouraged to take care of younger ones.

Naming body parts

Basic to safety education is ensuring that children can name body parts. They must be able to explain anything that might happen to them, so colloquial terms used only within their family may not be the most useful. Such commonly used terms as 'titty', 'willy', and 'fanny' may suffice, but wherever possible families are encouraged to teach their children clear, unambiguous words such as 'penis' and 'vagina'. It is respectful to discuss with the family which words are to be used, as they may have strong feelings on this subject.

As previously described we can check the child's names for various body parts using drawings or anatomically detailed dolls (see 'Dolls', pp. 106–107 and 'Drawing body parts', p. 113). For children who feel comfortable with this, we can make a game of it by getting the child to lie down on a big sheet of newsprint while we draw a rough outline around their body. We then get them to name the various body parts. We usually start with the less threatening body parts before asking them to name the genitals.

Good and bad touching

The next concept children need to understand for their future safety is the difference between 'good' or 'OK' touching, and touching that is 'bad' or 'not OK'. We engage their interest in this learning by asking questions (e.g. 'What sort of touching would be OK?') and perhaps by making lists or demonstrating with dolls or drawings, asking, for example, 'Would it be all right if I touched him here?'

Good touching might include hugs from someone they like, Mummy taking their hand, Daddy carrying them on his back, Nana holding them on her lap. It might include patting the head and tickling. But any of these activities might also be classed as 'not OK' if done in a particular way or by a particular person. Children are encouraged to trust their own instincts about what feels 'OK' and 'not OK'.

Children are also helped to make a list of 'bad' touching, which generally includes various forms of aggression (pinching, kicking, punching) as well as inappropriate sexual touching. To avoid confusion it is useful to talk about having a wash or visits to the doctor as times when it may be OK for someone else to touch their genitals in specified circumstances.

'Good' and 'bad' secrets

Children need permission to reveal secrets if they are going to talk about sexual abuse. To avoid confusion, 'good' secrets are perhaps more usefully labelled 'surprises'. Surprises may be defined as time-limited secrets that will make someone happy when they are revealed, such as birthday presents or planning a special treat for someone. Secrets that are *not* OK might include doing something naughty while your parents were not looking, not saying anything when you see someone hurting another person, or not getting help when someone is threatening you. A clear distinction needs to be made here between 'getting help' and 'telling tales'.

The right to say 'No'

One of the reasons that children are vulnerable to abuse is that they have been taught to obey their elders. They need to know that they have choices in some things, ranging from relatively minor issues, such as whether to wear the blue or the green socks, to major issues, such as being able to say 'No' to abuse. Parents can be encouraged to give reasons for any instructions they give a child, rather than teaching 'blind' obedience in all situations.

In the playroom we can reinforce this message by giving children permission to break some rules. They don't have to be polite to abusers and they can yell, kick, and bite if someone is trying to hurt them.

We can coach children in such skills as shouting 'No!' loudly or pushing away a doll made to represent an offender. When they are in a situation where they feel unsure, they can be given ideas for coping without being rude. We might suggest, for example, that they say, 'I'll have to ask my mother first.'

Encouraging children to tell

Children need to know that they will be believed and supported if they report any incidents of sexual abuse. This message can be conveyed in the playroom, and in conjunction with the family. A list should be made of people to tell, including telephone numbers and addresses for older children. This could be a list they remember or, if there are too many names, one that is written down for them to carry in their pocket or pin to their bedroom wall. It could include supportive family members, teachers, parents of friends, school counsellor, social worker, or police.

We need to check that those on the child's list are supportive and accessible. We also need to check that the child knows what to do if they don't get the help they need from the first person they tell, or if a particular person they want to tell is not available. An important part of this is checking that they know how to use both public and private telephones.

It is useful for people who have been identified as 'safe to tell' to know that they are on the child's list. This particularly applies to parents and close family members. They might even be presented with certificates by the child and/or therapist, as a way of reinforcing the message for both the child and their support people. Certificates can also be awarded to the child, once they have grasped essential safety concepts.

'What if ... ' games

We use 'What if ... ' games to help children recognize and cope with a variety of dangerous situations, including potentially abusive situations. This needs to be done in a way that empowers children rather than frightens them.

Potential hazards that children can be prepared for might include:

'What if you see the baby crawling near the heater?'

'What if there's a fire in the kitchen?'

'What if there's an accident and someone you're walking with gets hurt on the way home from school?'

We help children to recognize the early danger signals of sexual abuse:

'What if somebody wants you to play rude games?'

'What if somebody does something you don't like and tells you not to tell anyone?'

'What if someone offers you money or sweeties if you'll go into a private place with them?'

Or more directly:

'What if someone tries to touch your bottom?'

Where necessary we can make suggestions and discuss the ideas proposed by children to ensure that they are realistic.

Consolidating plans for keeping safe

When children have not grasped the essential ideas about keeping themselves safe, it may be necessary to spend more than one session on the topic. Local counselling services can also recommend a number of useful videos which are available in most major cities.

Parents should be advised to go over safety education with both abused and non-abused children approximately every two to three months as opportunities arise. Talking about body parts and touching might occur reasonably naturally, for example, around bath time, or when having a relaxed cuddle together. Care should be taken to prepare children rather than alarm them with frightening details, and they may become fearful, or bored and uninterested, if the subject of safety is raised too frequently.

The kind of message we suggest parents convey to their children is that children's bodies are their own, and should be respected by other people.

As soon as they are old enough children should be encouraged to take care of themselves, for example, when washing or going to the toilet.

Safety education should be seen as part of normal parenting rather than as a response to abuse. Parents can be provided with information, pamphlets, and booklists to help them in this task. Amongst the books which we have found useful are *Katy's Yukky Problem* (Morgan 1986) and *Megan's Secret* (Morgan 1987), but it is worth checking with local bookstores for up-to-date information on what is available. Michele Elliott's (1985) guide to talking with children about sexual abuse is another useful reference to which parents can be directed.

Case Example
Working with Puppets

To demonstrate the way that puppets can be used to facilitate communication with children, we include the following extracts from two interviews with a 10-year-old boy. They are included with the permission of both the boy and his parents.

In this example we demonstrate not just the use of puppets, but the way that any therapy with a child might proceed. If we had used other methods such as dolls, artwork, or action methods, the same issues would have been dealt with and similar questions asked.

James (not his real name) was abused extensively over a 12-month period by an uncle. Although the abuse left James significantly traumatized, he managed to deal with it in a relatively short time. Therapy comprised three family sessions and three individual interviews.

The extracts recorded here are from the first and second sessions when James was seen alone by the therapist, Les Simmonds. They had previously met during an initial interview with the family.

THE FIRST INTERVIEW WITH THE CHILD

The first session starts with an introduction to the therapy room, and a game which helps James to relax and to feel more comfortable with his therapist.

After about 10 minutes Les asks James to draw his family, while Les sits beside him on the floor drawing his own family. Both use felt-tip pens and large sheets of newsprint. This activity is non-threatening, and allows Les to begin gathering information about the various family members from James's perspective. It also helps to orient James to the therapy process while developing the relationship between therapist and child. The goal of this activity is an assessment of family sub-systems, so we know in particular where James gets his support. We learn that James feels secure within his family and is well supported by them in coming to therapy.

As James becomes comfortable in this activity, he is asked to draw the family member who abused him, his Uncle Garry. While they work on the drawing Les begins an assessment of James's attitude to the offender in the following interchange:

LES	Do you like him?
JAMES	No.
LES	You dislike him?
JAMES	I liked him until he started abusing me.
LES	What do you think of him now?
JAMES	If he comes near me his nose will be through the ground!
LES	You'd like to hit him?
JAMES	Yep!

James clearly has a lot of anger towards Garry that he is ready to express. Les takes this opportunity to get out the puppets, asking 'Does he look like any of these puppets?' James responds to the puppets with interest, but does not take up the invitation to talk about Garry immediately. The activity proceeds at the pace James dictates. Both Les and James select a puppet from the collection, and place them on their hands. The puppets begin to talk to each other:

PUPPET 1 (LES)	Hello.
PUPPET 2 (JAMES)	Hello.
PUPPET 1 (LES)	Who are you?
PUPPET 2 (JAMES)	Harry. Who are you?
PUPPET 1 (LES)	I'm, Oh let me see, I'm Fred.
HARRY (JAMES)	Hello Fred.
FRED (LES)	Hello Harry.
HARRY (JAMES)	What shall we do today?
FRED (LES)	I don't know. What do you want to do today?
HARRY (JAMES)	Keep away from that dog that's looking at us.

	[He indicates another puppet lying amongst the collection on the floor]
FRED (LES)	That dog?
HARRY (JAMES)	Yeah, that dog.
FRED (LES)	Oh, what's the dog's name?
HARRY (JAMES)	Peter.
FRED (LES)	Peter?
HARRY (JAMES)	[James puts the dog puppet on his other hand] Here he comes. [a scuffle ensues between the two puppets on the boy's hands, Harry and the dog. The dog is defeated and cast off]
FRED (LES)	That's it — Is he dead?
HARRY (JAMES)	Yeah [uncertainly]
FRED (LES)	Or is he alive?
HARRY (JAMES)	He's dead.

James's choice of activity with the puppets can be seen as a metaphorical way of beginning to deal with the abuse situation. It illustrates how close to the surface his fears and anger lie because it follows immediately after reference is made to the abuser. There is a good character Harry, who is fearful of the dog but also very ready for a fight. When attacked by the dog Harry fights back and emerges victorious. While not addressing the abuse directly, it acts as a good warm-up exercise and encourages Les to proceed with an invitation for James to deal with Garry in a more direct manner. The session proceeds as follows:

FRED (LES)	I'll tell you what, Harry. What are we going to do about Garry?
HARRY (JAMES)	Dunno.
FRED (LES)	What do *you* think we should do about Garry?
HARRY (JAMES)	Beat his head in!
FRED (LES)	Beat his head in? Oh, how're we going to do that? Is there any puppet around here that looks like Garry? [James chooses a puppet to be Garry] What about we ask Les to be Garry — to put Garry on his hand.
HARRY (JAMES)	Put Garry on your hand, Les.
GARRY (LES)	[snarling] Aarrgh, I'm Garry.
HARRY (JAMES)	[defiant] So, I'm Harry!

GARRY (LES)	I'm Garry and I'm big! [James selects another puppet for himself. Perhaps he is feeling a little anxious and needs a puppet that looks stronger] Who are you?
HARRY (JAMES)	[defiantly!] Perpendicular.
Garry (Les)	You're Perpendicular! So what! I'm Garry and I'm sneaky and quick!
PERP. (JAMES)	I'm hungry! [James uses the puppet he has named Perpendicular to attack 'Garry' and another scuffle ensues]
GARRY (LES)	What are you going to do to me?
PERP. (JAMES)	Eat you!
GARRY (LES)	Eat me? Go on then, do that. [James uses 'Perpendicular' to catch the puppet representing Garry and to 'eat him'. He tosses 'Garry' across the room]
PERP. (JAMES)	Throw that away!
LES	What shall we do to it now?
JAMES	Get Perpendicular here to give him a couple of nose punches!
LES	Go on then! [using the puppet James attacks Garry once again. He is a bit tentative, however, and Les encourages him to express his anger] Could we hit him or beat him and bury him? Do you want to do that? [James uses 'Perpendicular' to hit the Garry puppet with more energy and conviction]
JAMES	It's your turn.

Les and James continue to beat up the Garry puppet. This provides a good example of using puppets for catharsis. It enables James to express his feelings in a safe place, because it gives him permission to act in ways not normally available to children. Action methods within therapy are particularly effective for children to deal with anger, and must be distinguished from any form of encouragement of aggression.

JAMES	Let's throw this guy into the Tasman Sea!
LES	Into the Tasman Sea?
JAMES	Yeah, that's it.
LES	Oh, right. Do you think that's enough?
JAMES	Yeah, I think he's learned his lesson. Pig's coming for a visit. [he selects another puppet which represents a pig]
LES	Are you sure he's learned his lesson?
JAMES	Pig's coming for a visit. Hello Piggy. [James uses another voice] Hello. What's your name?

By changing the subject, James has signalled that he is finished with catharsis for the present time. In the next session Les will get James to go over the abuse in detail and to express more of his anger towards Garry, but now he respects that James is ready to move on to another activity. Les takes the pig puppet, and a conversation develops during which Pink Pig, Harry, and Perpendicular introduce themselves to one another. Harry feeds Pink Pig some vegetables. Les and James now both have two puppets each, one on each hand. James has Harry and Perpendicular, and Les has Pink Pig and Fred, whom he has renamed 'The Changer'.

James is obviously enjoying the game, so Les uses the opportunity to help James express some of his fears:

CHANGER (LES)	Do you know Harry, that Pink Pig over there — he can help people. He can help people feel better about themselves. Pink Pig wants to know if James needs any help. How can James be helped?
HARRY (JAMES)	Well, for one thing he can be helped in not worrying about other people — not worrying about Garry.
CHANGER (LES)	Oh, what does he need to know, so he doesn't worry so much about Garry?
HARRY (JAMES)	Well, if he worries about Garry any more, when he comes to be 12 or 13 the problem might still be there.
CHANGER (LES)	Oh, what problem?
HARRY (JAMES)	James might go around abusing people. [James indicates that he is a bit agitated about disclosing this fear by picking up another puppet and making a diversionary statement about it]. This isn't a rabbit, it's a cat.
CHANGER (LES)	[gently] Do you think, Harry, that James is going to go around abusing people?
HARRY (JAMES)	No, but that's what he might do if he doesn't forget about it, Change.
CHANGER (LES)	Mmm, how do you think, Harry …
HARRY (JAMES)	[eagerly] Yes?
CHANGER (LES)	How do you think we can help him not worry about it?

With this question Les is assessing James's own resources, checking to see what ideas he can elicit. Any good strategies which James comes up with on his own can be affirmed and developed, and are likely to be more effective than suggestions from the therapist.

The opportunity to acknowledge James's good ideas also provides a forum for putting him in touch with the strength he will need to deal with the abuse. If, however, James does not have any useful ideas, we are then aware that he needs more help from the therapist:

HARRY (JAMES)   Talk to him and encourage him not to worry about it?

CHANGER (LES)   Oh, talk to him and tell him not to worry, OK? [Les acknowledges this idea, but knows that it will not be sufficient. He goes on to develop it further] Now the Pink Pig, he's a real healer — he's a bit like a wizard.

HARRY (JAMES)   Can I make a statement, Changer? Umm, I was just thinking — James should have enough advice from us so he won't be scared of Garry, and if Garry comes near him again he should tell him to go away, and run away from him.

CHANGER (LES)   Right, shall we tell him that?

HARRY (JAMES)   Yes!

CHANGER (LES)   Good, let's tell him then! [Les now slows the pace to maximize the effect of the message] Hang on, we all better calm down so we can tell him really slowly, OK? And we'll tell him separately, all of us. [addressing James] My name is Changer.

PERP. (JAMES)   My name is Perpendicular.

HARRY (JAMES)   My name is Harry.

PINK PIG (LES)   And my name is Pink Pig.

HARRY (JAMES)   You're a wizard, aren't you?

PINK PIG (LES)   Yes, I'm a Pink Pig Wizard.

CHANGER (LES)   And I'm Changer, and I want to tell James something.

JAMES   [James leans forward and listens intently] Yes?

CHANGER (LES)   [Les drops his voice to a whisper and speaks slowly and emphatically] I want to tell you James, that you don't have to worry, you don't have to worry at all, so long as you know what's right and wrong. And so long as you know how to do that — how to be right instead of wrong, things are going to be fine for you.

                  [louder and more confident] And the Pink Pig has some ideas, about what is right and what is wrong.

JAMES   I'll try to forget about it, Changer.

CHANGER (LES)   Oh, I don't know whether you're going to forget about it … you don't have to forget about it. But it will be good when you don't worry about it so much.

At this stage James indicates that he is uncomfortable with the intensity of the conversation by becoming distracted by two other puppets. He selects a dog and a lamb from the collection, which he puts on his hands. After a brief diversion he indicates that he is ready to continue the discussion:

LAMB (JAMES)	Now I heard about James's problem.
CHANGER (LES)	Did you?
LAMB (JAMES)	Yes.
CHANGER (LES)	And we were just telling him that he might not ever forget about it. But that doesn't matter, so long as he knows what is right and what is wrong. And Pink Pig knows what is right and what is wrong.
LAMB (JAMES)	We live on the same farm, don't we Pink Pig.
PINK PIG (LES)	Oink, oink.
JAMES	[holds up his two puppets] This is White Sheep and Brown Doggie.
CHANGER (LES)	White Sheep and Brown Doggie? OK? Do you think Brown Dog, that James wants to hear anything from Pink Pig?
BROWN DOG (JAMES)	[eagerly] Yes!
CHANGER (LES)	What does he want to hear from Pink Pig?
BROWN DOG (JAMES)	Good news!
CHANGER (LES)	Good news! OK, we'll have some good news from Pink Pig.

James is fully engaged in this activity and listening intently. Les uses the Pink Pig to ask James some questions, directing the Pig to the Lamb and Dog puppets. The questions help to clear up some misunderstandings that James has about sex, and to lay responsibility for abuse clearly with the abuser. There is much cheering and encouragement from the Changer and the Pink Pig when James gets the correct answers, and a seeding of information when James is not so clear, for example:

PINK PIG (LES)	I, James, want to know — do you know about sex?
JAMES	Yeah … er … Yes and no.
PINK PIG (LES)	Now, who should a man have sex with?
JAMES	A woman.
PINK PIG (LES)	And should he have sex with a very, very young woman?
JAMES	No.
PINK PIG (LES)	When should a man have sex with a woman?
JAMES	Oh, when they're about over 20.
PINK PIG (LES)	What about 16 or 17?
JAMES	No. Oh, they could have it when they're 16 but um …

PINK PIG (LES)	Should they have it when they're younger than 16?
JAMES	No.
CHANGER (LES)	Hooray!
PINK PIG (LES)	Wow, that's really good, James! You've got that right! Correct! Why shouldn't they have sex with really young girls?
JAMES	Because they could hurt them.

This discussion continues in a similar manner, dealing with issues of consent, equal relationships, and adults having sex with young boys. When the subject of sexual abuse of boys is raised, James acknowledges that it has happened to him. He had made an attempt to tell his parents what was happening, but was not believed at the time. The interchange between the puppets allows James to begin to express some feelings about this, backing off to the safer distance of pretending that it was actually Harry who had the problem. It also allows Les to begin some safety education:

BROWN DOG (JAMES)	It's bad for the boy, it might hurt him or make him unhappy. It's happened to me.
CHANGER (LES)	Oh, and how are you unhappy?
BROWN DOG (JAMES)	I'm unhappy because my Mum doesn't believe that my brother's done it to me.
CHANGER (LES)	Doesn't believe that your brother has done it to you?
BROWN DOG (JAMES)	No.
CHANGER (LES)	Which brother has done it to you?
BROWN DOG (JAMES)	My older one.
CHANGER (LES)	Have you got an older brother?
BROWN DOG (JAMES)	No, not me, Harry has.
CHANGER (LES)	So Harry's mother doesn't believe him?
BROWN DOG (JAMES)	No.
CHANGER (LES)	What should Harry do if he's not believed?
BROWN DOG (JAMES)	Make sure he's believed.
CHANGER (LES)	How can Harry make sure?
BROWN DOG (JAMES)	Get advice from somebody else that's had it done to them.
CHANGER (LES)	And who could that be?
JAMES	Me!
CHANGER (LES)	Oh, right. So you're going to look after Harry. What sort of advice have you got for Harry?

JAMES	Just forget about it — try to forget about it — like me.
CHANGER (LES)	What other advice have you got for Harry?
JAMES	That he should keep well away from his brother.
CHANGER (LES)	Oh, that's a good idea. And what happens if his brother ever wants to come near him again?
	[James now allows the pretence about Harry to slip]
JAMES	I'm going to run away and never come back to him again.
CHANGER (LES)	Is there anyone you can tell?
JAMES	Yeah, my Dad believes me.
CHANGER (LES)	Oh, your Dad believes you! So you can tell your Dad if you ever have some worries. And will your Dad protect you?
JAMES	Yes.
CHANGER (LES)	Oh, that's really good, that's really good. And should anybody ever force anybody to do it — to have sex with them?
JAMES	Only if you're over 16, and only if you love the girl.
CHANGER (LES)	It's good if you do that. But should you force the girl to do it?
JAMES	No.
CHANGER (LES)	Oh Hooray! That was really good. And Pink Pig has some questions:
PERP. (JAMES)	Can I ask you a question?
PINK PIG (LES)	Yes you can.
PERP. (JAMES)	I was walking home from school with Harry and Brown Dog a couple of weeks ago, and they were walking a couple of metres ahead of me, and I got taken behind a bush and I got abused.
PINK PIG (LES)	Who was that by?
PERP. (JAMES)	Oh this stranger, he was about in his thirties.
PINK PIG (LES)	Gee, and what did you do?
PERP. (JAMES)	I took a short cut, came up and headed them off, and yelled 'Help, I've been abused.'
PINK PIG (LES)	Right, and who listened?
PERP. (JAMES)	Both of them.
PINK PIG (LES)	Right. If someone asks you to go behind the bushes with them, what could you do?
PERP. (JAMES)	Run ahead and keep up with my mates.

PINK PIG (LES)	Right. And what if people offer you lots of money to do it?
PERP. (JAMES)	I wouldn't do it.
PINK PIG (LES)	And what could you do then?
PERP. (JAMES)	Just turn my back.
PINK PIG (LES)	And what?
PERP. (JAMES)	And walk away.

The discussion between the puppets continues and Les takes an opportunity to enquire a bit more about James's response to the abuse, and to offer some reassurance:

PINK PIG (LES)	Does James still feel sad?
PERP. (JAMES)	A little bit.
PINK PIG (LES)	What does James feel sad about?
PERP. (JAMES)	Oh, I don't know.
PINK PIG (LES)	James won't always feel sad, but he might feel sad for a while. How can we help him when he feels sad?
BROWN DOG (JAMES)	Give him advice.
PINK PIG (LES)	OK.
BROWN DOG (JAMES)	I've been abused as well!
PINK PIG (LES)	Oh, and do you know, that's what Les is there for?
BROWN DOG (JAMES)	Yes.
PINK PIG (LES)	And does James know Les's 'phone number?
BROWN DOG (JAMES)	No.
PINK PIG (LES)	Well, I will ask Les if he can make sure that he gives James his phone number.
LES	Pink Pig has just asked me, James …
JAMES	… if you could give me your 'phone number!
LES	Right, OK and I'll do that when we go.
JAMES	So I can ring you when I'm troubled a bit.
LES	You can always ring me when you're troubled. Is that helpful?
JAMES	Yes.

At this stage James appears to be reassured, and reverts to a discussion of the abuse, using the puppets again. He describes a situation which illustrates some of his fears, and Les takes the opportunity to help James to deal with them. Once again James is given information and helped to devise strategies to keep himself safe:

BROWN DOG (JAMES)	Umm, when I was abused a little bit, this guy offered me money, and said he didn't do it and he'd blow my head off if I told anyone.
PINK PIG (LES)	Who said that?
BROWN DOG (JAMES)	Oh, this stranger, he's about in his thirties.
PINK PIG (LES)	Right. And did that happen to James?
BROWN DOG (JAMES)	I don't think the guy made threats to him — I think James has just been abused.
PINK PIG (LES)	Oh. That must have been pretty awful for James. What could James do if anyone ever tries to do something like that again?
BROWN DOG (JAMES)	Tell the person to stop. But what if you get abused and you don't have a voice?
PINK PIG (LES)	You write it down.
JAMES	But what will happen if you don't have a pen and a piece of paper?
PINK PIG (LES)	You have to run away.
JAMES	What would happen if you run but the guy takes a short cut and trips you up? And you fall over a barbed wire fence?
PINK PIG (LES)	Then you'd be hurt.
JAMES	And then he'll do it to you.
PINK PIG (LES)	And then afterwards you must go and tell the police.
JAMES	Or a family member.
PINK PIG (LES)	Or a family member and they'll tell the police.

This session concludes with a discussion between the puppets about arrangements for the next appointment:

PINK PIG (LES)	I'll tell you what, shall we ask James if he wants to come back to see me again.
LAMB (JAMES)	Yes.
PINK PIG (LES)	OK, you ask him, White Lamb.
LAMB (JAMES)	James, do you want to come back and see Les and Pink Pig and all of us again?
JAMES	Yes I do!
LES	OK, we'll make an appointment with your Mum. Shall we put these [puppets] away, so we can make sure they're here when we come back?

Summary of session one

While there is much work to be done, therapy with James has begun in a very positive way. The puppets have played a major role in the joining process. They have engaged James's attention at a relatively intense level. In so doing they have made it easier for him to raise difficult subjects, and to hear and accept the information he needs for his healing.

In this first session, puppets have been used in various ways:

- They represent a playful activity in which the therapist can communicate at the child's level;
- They help to gather information about the abuse and its effects in a way that is relatively non-threatening;
- They provide a safe context for James to express his fears, and an opportunity for him to begin to deal with the worries he has about the abuse;
- They are used to seed ideas, to offer reassurance and affirmation, and to educate about future safety; and
- They are used for catharsis when they attack the offender and emerge victorious.

Work with the puppets has also been useful for assessment because it has clearly revealed areas needing further attention. During future interviews Les will need to return to most of the issues raised at this meeting, to check on progress made, and to determine what more needs to be done.

THE SECOND INTERVIEW WITH THE CHILD

During the second interview with James, the puppets are used to go over the abuse situation in a different way. James uses the puppets to describe some of the details of the abuse, and to deal with the offender. The puppets are also used to provide James with a lot of affirmation, and to introduce the notion of 'trickery' by the abuser.

The session begins with a brief game with some toy cars. This helps to orient James to the playroom, and back to the therapy process.

After several minutes Les raises the subject of Garry, and asks James how Garry got to see him. James explains that Garry visited the family regularly, and would take James to visit his farm. James says he doesn't like Garry now. As the conversation develops Les takes out the puppets, which he gets James to name. James recalls the names they used previously: Brown Dog, White Sheep, Changer, Perpendicular, Pink Pig, Garry, and Harry.

LES   Who do you think wants to talk to whom today?

JAMES   I know! [he selects the white rabbit which has previously been called The Changer, and puts it on his hand. Les selects the Pink Pig]

RABBIT (JAMES)	I was just thinking … when I came home from the disco last night, I was driving on the motorway and this silly mug ran into the back of me — my car that is.
PINK PIG (LES)	Not into the back of you, yourself?
RABBIT (JAMES)	No.
PINK PIG (LES)	Did you get hurt?
RABBIT (JAMES)	A little bit — see? I bruised myself there.
LES	Where did you bruise yourself?
RABBIT (JAMES)	Just down there. [James indicates his elbow]
LES	Oh, right. Is it still sore?
RABBIT (JAMES)	A little bit.
LES	Mmm, a little bit sore, eh?

James had in fact been involved in a minor car accident since his last session with Les. As he goes on to talk about it, however, it becomes a metaphor for the abuse.

PINK PIG (LES)	What do you think James wants to talk about today?
RABBIT (JAMES)	Beats me!
PINK PIG (LES)	Beats you! Oh, I've got some questions.

Before the Pink Pig can continue, James picks up the Garry puppet and puts it on his other hand.

GARRY (JAMES)	[evil tone] Oh, I was the one that rammed into the back of your car!
PINK PIG (LES)	Did he run into the back of your car?

The Rabbit and Garry puppets on each of James's hands begin to fight. James throws off the Rabbit and picks up Perpendicular.

PERP. (JAMES)	You two, you two, break it up now! Break it up!
GARRY (JAMES)	Oh, I'm hungry!
PINK PIG (LES)	Who wants to break it up?
PERP. (JAMES)	These two have to break it up — they're fighting.
PINK PIG (LES)	Oh right. Why are they fighting?
PERP. (JAMES)	I know! Garry was driving his car …
PINK PIG (LES)	Yeah …
PERP. (JAMES)	… and Rabbit was driving his car, and Garry pulls out, and Rabbit's brakes weren't working, right? And he goes straight into the back of Garry's car!

PINK PIG (LES)   Mmm ... and what does Perpendicular think of that?

PERP. (JAMES)   I think Garry shouldn't have been in the road!

PINK PIG (LES)   Garry shouldn't have been in the road? Where do you think Garry should have been, Perpendicular?

PERP. (JAMES)   In gaol!

PINK PIG (LES)   In gaol! That's a good place for Garry to be! And it's really good, it's really good, Perpendicular. One thing that's really good, is that James told the police, and he's managed to help put Garry in gaol. And that is really good!

PERP. (JAMES)   Yes it is!

With this affirmation, James feels empowered to express his continuing fear of Garry, and his lack of a sense of safety even though he knows Garry is in gaol. James now has discarded the Garry puppet and has Perpendicular and Brown Dog on his hands.

PERP. (JAMES)   Umm, I was walking along the footpath last night when I was coming home from school ...

PINK PIG (LES)   [encouraging] Really!

PERP. (JAMES)   ... with Brown Dog and White Sheep, and we were all walking along the side of the road, and we thought we saw Garry come out of .. we thought we saw Garry ... running along ... running ... running along a fence ... running along another paddock.

As he describes this scene, James becomes more hesitant and anxious. Les helps him to continue by making a purposeful shift from addressing Perpendicular to questioning the other puppet now on James's hand:

PINK PIG (LES)   What happened when you thought you saw Garry?

                  [no answer]

PINK PIG (LES)   Brown Dog?

BROWN DOG (JAMES)   Yes?

PINK PIG (LES)   What happened to James when he thought he saw Garry?

BROWN DOG (JAMES)   Dunno. I guess he saw him.

PINK PIG (LES)   Yeah? Was he scared?

BROWN DOG (JAMES)   Yes!

PINK PIG (LES)   Wow! What sort of things made him scared?

BROWN DOG (JAMES)   The things ... he thought that Garry was doing it to him.

PINK PIG (LES)	Wow, that must have been really, really horrible to feel like that.
BROWN DOG (JAMES)	Yes it must.
PINK PIG (LES)	What sort of things ...
BROWN DOG (JAMES)	Do you think ...
PINK PIG (LES)	Do you think what?
BROWN DOG (JAMES)	I think that James must have felt upset that Garry was doing it to him.

James is so totally engaged in this conversation that he is even beginning to help Les ask the questions. He is taking the opportunity to express his feelings about the abuse and to have these validated by the therapist. This is an important part of the therapy.

PINK PIG (LES)	Can I ask James that, do you think?
BROWN DOG (JAMES)	Yes!
PINK PIG (LES)	James ...
JAMES	Yes!
PINK PIG (LES)	Were you upset that Garry was doing it to you?
JAMES	[adamant] Yes I was!
PINK PIG (LES)	And what sort of things did Garry manage to do to keep you quiet?
JAMES	Once he sang about a beautiful day.
PINK PIG (LES)	Did he?
JAMES	Yeah, and he told me it was a beautiful day and not to worry about what he was doing to me, and stuff.
PINK PIG (LES)	Did he? He told you not to worry about it?
JAMES	Yeah.
PINK PIG (LES)	How else did he manage to keep you quiet? Did he tell you not to tell ... or what sort of things did he say?
JAMES	Yeah, he told me not to tell.

At this stage Les decides to ask James about the details of the abuse. While this is an essential part of James's therapy, it is obviously not easy and James first needs to feel empowered to cope with it. A lot of preparatory work has already been done through affirmation and building trust. It is the use of the puppets, however, which finally enables James to go over the details of the abuse. Note how Les facilitates the disclosure by offering limited choices, again suggesting a change of puppets when it becomes too difficult for James to continue:

PINK PIG (LES)	What sort of things did he do to you?
	[no reply]
	Shall we ask Brown Dog what sort of things Garry did to James?
	[no reply]
	Whom do you think I should best ask? I'm Pink Pig, and you know I'm a bit of a wizard! Who do you think I should talk to about it? [James puts a puppet on each hand: Harry and Brown Dog]
JAMES	Harry's quite nice, but Brown Dog ... let me see ... these are the two guys ... you have to decide out of these two.
PINK PIG (LES)	Oh.
JAMES	Harry or Brown Dog?
PINK PIG (LES)	OK. What about ...
JAMES	You could talk to both!
PINK PIG (LES)	Can I talk to both of them? That's great! What sort of things, Harry, happened to James?
HARRY (JAMES)	Um ... let me think now ... He felt sad about Garry. Garry was his favourite uncle and he felt sad that Garry was doing it to him.
PINK PIG (LES)	Oh, so did Garry become all friendly with James first?
HARRY (JAMES)	Yes.
PINK PIG (LES)	And did James begin to trust Garry?
HARRY (JAMES)	Yes. Until he started ... oh ... kind of abusing him — or whatever you call the stupid word.
PINK PIG (LES)	Mmm ... So did he trick James?
HARRY (JAMES)	Yes.
PINK PIG (LES)	That was really bad of Garry.
HARRY (JAMES)	Yes it was, wasn't it, Pink Pig?
PINK PIG (LES)	That was terrible of Garry to trick James.
HARRY (JAMES)	[defiantly] Yes it was!

Reframing Garry's actions as 'trickery' is part of the empowering process, because it helps to remove any notions of guilt which James may be harbouring. Use of the work 'trick' helps to shift responsibility onto the offender.

| PINK PIG (LES) | And what sort of things did he do when he tricked him? |
| HARRY (JAMES) | He started rubbing his penis and ... started rubbing his penis...started rubbing James's penis and ummm... |

PINK PIG (LES)	Maybe Brown Dog could help. What else did he do, Brown Dog?
BROWN DOG (JAMES)	Oh, sucking James's penis.
PINK PIG (LES)	Did he really do bad things like that to James?
BROWN DOG (JAMES)	Yes!
PINK PIG (LES)	What other sorts of things did he do to James?
BROWN DOG (JAMES)	Rubbed his hands up his backside.
PINK PIG (LES)	Did he! Did he do anything else with his penis to James?
JAMES	He started itching my penis for one thing.
PINK PIG (LES)	He started itching it?
HARRY (JAMES)	He started itching it, yeah.
PINK PIG (LES)	And how did he manage to keep James quiet, so he didn't tell some adults?
BROWN DOG (JAMES)	He probably said if he didn't keep quiet he'd probably get a blood nose.
PINK PIG (LES)	Did he say that? Is that how he managed to keep James quiet?
BROWN DOG (JAMES)	Kind of. I think so, anyway. If it wasn't like that, well, how else would it have been?
PINK PIG (LES)	Well, I think you must be right, if that's what you think, because you're pretty close, Brown Dog — you know James quite well.
BROWN DOG (JAMES)	Yes I do!

James puts on the Perpendicular puppet. He indicates a need for a break from the intensity of the conversation by changing the topic at this stage. Les respects this and allows the brief distraction, although he is aware of the need to deal further with Garry before this topic can be successfully concluded.

PERP. (JAMES)	I've just been out to see if it was raining or not.
PINK PIG (LES)	Have you! And was it raining?
PERP. (JAMES)	Yes. And I've just got soaking wet!

The diversion continues for about another minute, with a discussion that involves several puppets. Interestingly, it is James who knows by instinct what needs to happen next. He spontaneously picks up the Garry puppet and hurls it across the room.

JAMES	One, two, three! Boom!
LES	Wow! Is he still around do you think? Do you think you've got rid of Garry enough?

JAMES	I hope so.
LES	Do you want him over there, or do you want to put him somewhere even further away? Or somewhere where he can't get out?
	[James picks up the Garry puppet and throws it out the door]
LES	Yeah! Great! You threw him out! Yeah, that's great! And shut the door!
JAMES	[excited] I threw him down the corridor!
LES	Great!
JAMES	I don't know how far I threw him! I just biffed him out the door!

This brief incident was performed with great gusto and was clearly a very effective form of catharsis for James. The obvious pleasure he had in disposing of Garry helps James to renounce the role of victim, and thus takes away some of the power of the abuse.

James has just described the abuse and got in touch with some of the feelings of fear and anxiety associated with it. He then quickly moves on to dealing with the abuser. He is left feeling exhilarated and in control.

The session continues with a great deal of affirmation for James, designed to reinforce this sense of personal strength. Les is now using two puppets — the Pink Pig puppet and the White Sheep. By involving several puppets in the following discussion, Les ensures that James is extremely responsive, and the message he wishes to convey has maximum impact. Once again, James shows how involved he is in the process by helping to direct the proceedings:

SHEEP (LES)	Hey!
JAMES	Hey, what?
SHEEP (LES)	I've got something to tell James.
JAMES	Well, tell me then!
SHEEP (LES)	Right! I've been dying to tell you this.
	[he waits to get James's full attention]
	I think that you are a pretty fantastic boy!
JAMES	Why?
SHEEP (LES)	Why?
JAMES	Why do you think that I'm a pretty fantastic boy?
SHEEP (LES)	Are you ready? Pink Pig, I don't know whether James is ready to hear this. Do you think he's ready to hear it — why he's fantastic?
	[James is nodding energetically]
PINK PIG (LES)	Oh, I think he's ready to hear it now!

James puts on the puppets Perpendicular and Brown Dog, and picks up the White Rabbit (Changer) and Harry which he holds between his two hands, forming a row of four puppets.

RABBIT (JAMES)	I do!
BROWN DOG (JAMES)	I do!
PERP. (JAMES)	And I especially do!
SHEEP (LES)	Oh Perpendicular, do you think he's ready to hear it?
PERP. (JAMES)	Yeah!
SHEEP (LES)	And Brown Dog, do you think he's ready to hear it?
BROWN DOG (JAMES)	Yeah!
SHEEP (LES)	And Changer, do you think he's ready to hear it?
CHANGER (JAMES)	Yeah
SHEEP (LES)	And Harry, do you think he's ready to hear it?
HARRY (JAMES)	Yes!
SHEEP (LES)	OK! Shall we tell him?
ALL IN SEQUENCE (JAMES)	[eagerly and enthusiastically] Yes!
SHEEP (LES)	What I want to tell James is … Shall I tell you lot as well?
ALL IN SEQUENCE (JAMES)	Yes!
SHEEP (LES)	I think he is so brave …
JAMES	Whisper it!
SHEEP (LES)	Oh [whispers] I think James is so brave and so fantastic because he made some really good statements to the police, and he's got Garry locked away! And I think that's *really* fantastic! And I think he's so good and so brave! That's what I think! I think he's amazing!
JAMES	Now say it out loud!
SHEEP (LES)	Say it out loud?
JAMES	Yeah, to me!
SHEEP (LES)	Do you want me to say it, do you want Les to say it, do you want the Changer to say it, or …
JAMES	White Sheep to say it!
SHEEP (LES)	White Sheep to say it. James …
JAMES	[almost shouting with excitement] Yes!

SHEEP (LES)	[loudly] There's something I must tell you!
JAMES	There's no need to yell!
SHEEP (LES)	I thought you wanted me to tell you loudly!
JAMES	Not very loud! I didn't mean yell!
SHEEP (LES)	How loud — about this loud?
JAMES	Yeah.
SHEEP (LES)	I want to say that you are really, really, amazing, and a really fantastic boy!
JAMES	But how can I be amazing and fantastic?
SHEEP (LES)	Well, you're amazing and fantastic because you told the police, and told your parents, and helped put Garry behind bars. And that is really, really brave! And what I want to know, is how can we help James a little bit more to feel good about that? That's what I want to know! Does James believe what I've told him? What do you think, Brown Dog?
BROWN DOG (JAMES)	Maybe if you made it simpler, he might understand it easier then. I mean, he might understand more.
SHEEP (LES)	Brown Dog, can you tell James in a simpler way what I've been saying?
BROWN DOG (JAMES)	Well, what he's been saying is that you were real good because you told the police, and now you've got nothing to worry about.
SHEEP (LES)	That's really good, Brown Dog That's really, really good. And I'm wondering, if I gave James some homework — fun homework — do you think he'd do it for me?
BROWN DOG (JAMES)	Depends what sort of homework it is.
SHEEP (LES)	Oh! He's not sure that he can tell you yet. Shall we tell him?
BROWN DOG (JAMES)	Yes!
SHEEP (LES)	I want James to draw me three people, whom, if he ever felt he was in danger, he could go and tell — other than his Mum and Dad.
JAMES	Can I do it now?
SHEEP (LES)	Shall we let him do it now?
JAMES	Yes! [gets out paper and felt-tip pens]

With the change in activity, the puppets are left aside for the rest of the session. The focus of therapy shifts to planning for James's future safety.

This is not only a practical component of all good therapy with children, but in James's case helps him to deal with the fears that he still has about his safety.

Summary of the second session

Once again the use of the puppets has helped to maximize the effect of therapy. The puppets have enabled James to express his fears, to go over the abuse, and to deal with the offender. They have provided him with considerable affirmation, and so helped to put him in touch with his strengths. The puppets have facilitated James's involvement at all stages of the therapy process.

It still may be necessary to take James over the abuse again, in another session. We would have to check whether he feels finished with Garry at our next meeting. We would also need to check again how fearful James is feeling, and to question his family about any signs of continuing trauma they have noticed at home. Undoubtedly, however, significant progress was made during this session.

Therapy involved one more session with James by himself, and a total of three meetings with the family. When therapy was completed, contact with James's family continued over several years. All reports indicated that James had successfully dealt with his abuse and was getting on with his life. The fact that this was achieved with relatively brief therapy was due largely to the support provided by the family and to the intensity of James's involvement in these sessions.

8

THE PROCESS OF THERAPY WITH CHILDREN

In Chapter 4 we described in detail the various stages of therapy with clients who have been sexually abused. We listed these stages in logical order through which therapy must proceed, but also noted that the various stages overlapped and that frequently it was necessary to go back to an earlier stage before moving forward.

Here we present a summary of how progress through each stage might be effected specifically in work with children and their families. The stages are described under the following headings:

General guidelines

- Safety first.
- Have a purpose and provide some direction.
- Make the most of opportunities.
- Phrase questions carefully.

Joining

- Making connections with the child.
- Orienting the child to the therapy process.
- Confidentiality.
- Communicating at the child's level.
- Humour.
- Encouraging the child's progress.

History and assessment

Assessment of the child

- The personal resources of the child.
- Reactions to the abuse.
- The social system.
- The child's relationship with the offender.
- The progress of therapy.

Assessment of the family

- How the family perceives the abuse.
- The effects of the abuse on the family.
- Relationships within the family system.
- The family's relationship with the offender.
- The family's resourcefulness.
- Indicators for termination of therapy.

Empowering the child

- Putting the child in touch with their strengths.
- Creating a safe haven.
- Identifying a hero.
- Fighting fears.
- Creative use of therapeutic tools.
- Dealing with guilt and shame.
- Respecting the child's pace.

Examining the effects of abuse

- Current effects and effects over time.

Going over the abuse in a therapeutic way

- Describing the abuse.
- Catharsis.
- The rescue scene.
- Checking for remaining trauma.

Preparing for the future

- Highlighting changes made.
- Safety education.

GENERAL GUIDELINES

In addition to the therapeutic goals associated with each stage of therapy, there are a number of important guidelines which we follow throughout any counselling with children who have been sexually abused.

Safety first

Before we engage in therapy with a child it is essential to ensure that they are living in a safe environment. Appropriate precautions need to be taken so the child is not in contact with the abuser, or at least feels confident that they are suitably protected. Ideally, this protection will be provided from within the child's natural environment, by the family, school, or other social contacts.

When a family is unable or unwilling to provide protection, consideration must be given to removing the child from the family home. With its implications of punishing the child, obviously this is not an ideal course of action, but it is preferable to leaving a child vulnerable to further abuse. Whenever possible we encourage the abuser to leave the home, rather than have the child experience the added difficulties of being removed from a familiar environment.

Have a purpose and provide some direction

It is important that we maintain a clear vision of the purpose of each session, and that play therapy is directed towards specific goals required for healing. It is not enough that a child enjoys coming to see us, because children do not get the help they need if they are given total control in the playroom. The therapist sets the agenda, always reassessing this as work progresses, but allows the child to set the pace.

One way in which we may do this is by offering limited choices. This can be particularly effective with children who have experienced blurred boundaries and few choices. Long (1986), for example, gives the child a choice of talking about the abuse whenever they want within the first three appointments. Long reports that no child she has seen has ever refused to share the details and emotional side-effects of the abuse within this three-appointment time frame.

We offer limited choices in different ways, for example:

'Your Mum needs to know about this. Do you want to tell her yourself, or do you want me to tell her?'

'When shall we talk about it, this week or next week?'

'Would it be easier to explain using the dolls or making a drawing?'

To help ensure that we are clear about our purpose it can be useful to make notes after each session, reviewing briefly what has happened, and specifically listing goals for the next session.

Make the most of opportunities

At all stages of therapy we take opportunities to offer reassurance, seed ideas, reframe unhelpful beliefs, and normalize responses, for example:

'You're not to blame — it was the adult's fault.'

'You're very brave to talk about this.'

'Other kids come here with worries like yours.'

'You're really scared but I've met a brave part of you here today.'

'It was quite normal for your body to react in that way — it just means everything is working properly.'

'It's not surprising that you have mixed-up feelings — there were lots of things you liked about Uncle Tom.'

Phrase questions carefully

It is often more useful to ask 'open' rather than 'closed' questions. Closed questions require only a 'Yes' or 'No' answer. They are likely to start with verbs like 'Do' or 'Have' or 'Are', and provide limited information. Open questions require a longer answer and usually provide more information. They start with such words as 'How' or 'What', for example: 'What happened next?', 'How do you feel about that?'

Particularly in cases where a child is finding it difficult to talk, closed questions can make therapy slow and stressful for child and therapist alike. Open questions can guide the child into what needs to be discussed and are helpful to get communication flowing. They have the added benefit of being value-free, because there is less suggestion of there being a 'right' or 'wrong' answer which might be implied by some closed questions.

In some situations it is useful to provide specific reassurance that there are no right or wrong answers, particularly with a child who is anxious to please or uncertain about the function of therapy. On the other hand, there are also times when we query a particular answer. For example, when a child answers a question with 'I don't know', it may be useful to ask, 'Is that a real "don't know" or does it just mean that it's too hard to say?'

Whenever possible, we try to avoid asking questions that start with the word 'Why'. 'Why' may sound accusing, and is best replaced by a gentler 'How come ... ' if this type of question is needed.

JOINING

The first contact with a child is likely to happen within a family interview. This ensures that the child comes supported to therapy, and has the security of being with familiar people in an unfamiliar setting.

Making connections with the child

A social stage at the beginning of the family session helps to put everyone at ease, while providing useful background information. Attempts to engage the child should be made as soon as possible. Younger children might be shown some toys they could play with during the session, and praised regularly for playing well, demonstrating skills, or answering hard questions. An item of clothing or a favourite doll they have brought with them might be admired. They can be involved in the session by being asked questions which relate specifically to themselves:

'How old are you?'

'Do you know when your birthday is?'

'What's your baby sister's name?'

'Do you go to afternoon kindy or morning kindy?'

'What's the name of your teacher?'

It is important to make some connections with the child and to establish rapport before discussing the abuse. This might include some general discussion about family, school, or special interests.

Developing trust and rapport is easier with some children than with others, and depends on the skills and temperament of the therapist as well as on the nature of the child and their particular situation. It may involve a few minutes' conversation or may develop over several sessions.

Joining is an ongoing process that occurs at different levels during different stages of therapy. Joining may occur initially at an intellectual level, before developing into a deeper connection at a more emotional level. It is important to make this emotional connection if we are to provide the support a child needs to face intense feelings about abuse. So we need to assess how well we have joined with a child before taking them over details of abuse which could trigger strong emotional responses.

Orienting the child to the therapy process

While the child is with the family some discussion should occur about the reasons why they have come and an explanation of what therapy will involve. Some children come to therapy well informed about its purpose; others have no idea why they are there. Answers to such questions as:

'Do you know why you are here today?' and

'What has Mummy told you about coming here?'

can indicate how comfortable family members are about discussing the abuse and how effectively they communicate generally. Such questions also help to clarify the purpose of therapy and to clarify any misunderstandings.

One of the initial tasks in individual therapy with a child is to provide them with as much understanding as possible of the therapy process. This involves explaining who you are and why you are seeing them, and being open and honest in response to any queries they have. Failure to do this properly can create confusion and anxiety, and block the progress of therapy.

The process of joining with a child begins in the family interview and continues when the child is seen alone. Explaining to the child about the playroom and what happens there is an important part of this. When the playroom is first introduced family members may be invited to accompany the child, to see the playroom, and to see where the child will be. This helps to engage the family and to reassure the child that their family knows where they are.

We introduce the child to the playroom, and describe it as a safe place where they can say anything they like. We might say, for example, that 'Lots of kids come here to talk about their worries, and to get help to feel better.'

Confidentiality

Establishing rules about confidentiality is really important at this stage. Children need to know that it is safe to say anything they like in the playroom. They also need an age-appropriate explanation of any limits to confidentiality.

We do not, for example, keep secrets when anyone is at risk, be it our client or someone else. On the rare occasions when we need to deal with such a situation (e.g. risk of suicide, risk of further abuse by the perpetrator, information about abuse of other children) usually we can give the child prior notice that we have to tell someone and why this is necessary. We may even be able to negotiate with them the details of how the information is to be revealed.

Unless we have been clear initially about the limits to confidentiality this could be experienced by the child as yet another abuse of trust, and seriously affect the progress of healing and therapy.

Communicating at the child's level

The process of joining with a child continues throughout therapy, as therapist and child engage in various therapeutic activities together, such as acting out various situations. It is helpful to get down on the floor with a child, or to sit at small tables and chairs. A willingness to be playful, and to participate in 'childish' activities such as drawing, modelling clay, using games, dolls, puppets, blocks, and other play equipment, is also important.

Beginning each therapy session with a game helps to gain the child's interest and can act as a warm-up for more difficult tasks. Similarly it is helpful to complete each session with a game. This is a way of relieving tension and provides a bridge back to life outside the therapy room.

Knowledge of and enthusiasm for the latest games, films, and popular television programmes are also useful tools in establishing rapport and communication with children.

It is important that we use language familiar to the child and that we do not 'talk down' to them. Where appropriate we use the child's language as a means of communicating and establishing rapport, but not in a way that seems false or unnatural. If we are to gain a child's trust we need to be honest about who we are, while demonstrating our respect for the way they are.

Humour

The appropriate use of humour can play a valuable role in the joining process. Laughter helps children to relax. It introduces an element of fun to therapy, and ensures that children are more likely to be engaged and ready to participate.

Encouraging the child's progress

Joining is also facilitated by using lots of encouragement and praise. We do this by acknowledging skills, commending the child's bravery for sharing something difficult, empathizing with their pain, and noting their strengths and achievements. It can be further strengthened at the end of each session with a positive report back to the parent about the child's activities in the playroom and their progress in therapy.

HISTORY AND ASSESSMENT

Assessment is an ongoing process throughout therapy that involves comprehensive assessment of both the child and family. We therefore ask about the abuse, the child, the family, and the offender.

The tools we use to complement questions and to generally facilitate assessment include drawing, dolls, puppets, games, writing exercises and role playing. The use of these tools during assessment is described in detail in Chapter 7.

Because of the family's pivotal role in the child's healing, it is essential that assessment covers both child and family.

Assessment of the child

The primary goals of assessment are to determine the degree of trauma experienced by the child and family, the needs of the child, how much therapy is needed, where it should focus, and which methods will be most effective. To do this we investigate five main areas:

1 The personal resources of the child.
2 The child's reaction to the abuse.
3 The social system of the child.
4 The relationship between the child and the offender.
5 The progress of therapy.

The personal resources of the child

Identifying the child's personal resources involves assessment of the child's verbal and social skills, their ability to relate to others, and the appropriateness of their emotional responses. Assessment also occurs when we observe the various skills the child uses to play games.

It is important to have a knowledge of normal child development as a guide to what can be expected of a child at each stage. This is used to check their understanding of language, their interests, and their various abilities.

We ask the family how well the child is doing at school, and perhaps also check this with the teacher. Before contacting anyone else, however, a parent's informed consent should always be obtained. It is wise to have some record of this agreement on file, preferably in the parent's own writing.

When we have gathered all this information we have a clearer idea of the child's level of functioning, and which techniques will be most appropriate for therapy.

Reactions to the abuse

Clearly, different people are affected by abuse in different ways. To some extent it is the child's perception of the abuse and their response to it, rather than the facts of what happened, that determine how damaging the abuse will be. The child's response determines the type of therapy required and indicates the degree of trauma. It is important, therefore, to assess the child's perception of the abuse, their emotional reaction at the time, their current behavioural responses, and their current feelings about it, (e.g. guilt, anxiety, fear).

In order to assess the child's reaction to abuse we ask about what happened, and watch their emotional or behavioural reactions as they talk about it. We note, for example, if they become anxious, if they withdraw, if they become agitated and rush about the room. One child may change the subject abruptly or find other ways to avoid the discussion. Another may be able to describe the abuse in a relatively matter-of-fact way, or even seem bored and uninterested. This is all useful information, although we would need to check any conclusions we draw with the family, and again with the child during a subsequent session.

It has been estimated that between a quarter and a third of children abused do not experience any serious trauma (Finkelhor 1990). If the child has not been traumatized it is not usually necessary to go over the abuse again, other than to answer any questions the child may have. The focus of therapy would then be on affirmation of action taken by the child and family, and on the provision of information and support for them to cope with any legal and medical interventions. Therapy for children who have not been traumatized is likely to be brief (approximately three sessions) and crisis-oriented. After one or two sessions it is likely to concentrate on planning for future safety. Safety education is described in Chapter 7.

Sometimes children show no signs of trauma immediately after sexual abuse, but develop symptoms later. It is wise to alert parents to this possibility, without unduly alarming them. Parents should be advised of the times when problems are most likely to occur, of the signs of trauma they might observe, and of the help available. Care should be taken not to convey the idea that the child will inevitably have problems, and to minimize the risk that normal behaviour problems might be regarded as evidence of pathology.

When the child has been traumatized, assessment includes listing the 'triggers' that remind the child of the abuse and set off panic or anxiety reactions. This might include panic at the sight of someone or something that reminds them of the offender (e.g. a man with a beard, a particular model of car). A traumatic response indicates a need to go over the abuse in detail in order to desensitize the child to these triggers. In going over the abuse, however, we do not repeat the abuse experience in ways that just add to the child's distress, but provide an empowering experience that helps them to deal with it. Various ways of doing this are described later in this chapter.

As well as assessing the degree of trauma, we also look at other emotional and behavioural responses to the abuse. For example, does the child feel guilty or responsible? What has been the effect on their self-esteem? How has their behaviour been affected? Are there any signs of inappropriate sexual behaviour? Have there been any changes in their school performance? Are there any indications of regression, sleep disturbance, or eating disorders? What has been the effect on their relationships with other family members? These and many other questions are part of assessment, and the answers are checked with both the child and the family.

The social system

Another major factor which impinges on the child's recovery is the degree of support within their social system, and the response to the abuse from those people significant to the child. It is essential that we assess this before we go over the abuse experience, so we can ensure that the child has the necessary support to cope. We need to know, for example, whether it is necessary to introduce extra support people, whether we need to do more work with the family, whether we need to help the child to tap more into their own strengths, or to enlist the strengths of their heroes (real or imaginary) in order to deal with their abuse.

To assess the social system, and more particularly the child's perception of this system, we ask questions to elicit information about relationships, support, and communication, for example:

'What do you like about being in this family?'

'Who do you spend the most time with?'

'Who do you play games with the most?'

'Who would you go to if you had a worry?'

'Who helps you when you're upset?'

'Is there anything you don't like about this family?'

The degree of support for the child available within the family circle has major implications for the type of therapy required. The greater the degree of support, the more likely that some form of brief therapy will suffice, for example, several sessions over one to six months.

When the child has no experience of bonding, when they live with punitive parents or with a family that blames them for the abuse, denies that it happened, or allows the abuser to remain within the family circle, longer-term therapy is indicated (Long 1986). This would include establishing a trusting relationship with the child, developing relationships outside the family, and/or work with the family or with social service agencies to improve the home environment.

The child's relationship with the offender

The child's relationship with the offender is another key factor to be assessed because it helps to determine the child's response to abuse. In general the closer the relationship and the more dependent the child is on the abuser, the more traumatized the child is likely to be.

We ask questions designed to check on the nature and quality of the relationship between survivor and offender. We might ask, 'What was he like?', or we might get a child to list the things they liked and the things they did not like about an offender. Sometimes it helps to get the child to draw a picture of the offender, and to ask questions while they are engaged in this activity. (See also Chapter 7.)

Whatever the child's response to the offender, be it love, hate, ambivalence, fear, anger, etc., it is important to accept their feelings and to normalize their reaction. It is a mistake, for example, to label an offender as a 'bad person' if the child still cares about them. We can, however, label the abusive behaviour as 'bad' and 'wrong' In all cases we need to be sensitive to the child's relationship with the offender and not impose our own assumptions or judgements on them. Children tend to be particularly alert to adult responses, and are likely to be quick to notice any signs of disgust or dislike on our part.

If a child does have mixed feelings about an offender, it is useful to talk about how difficult and confusing this can be. Before addressing the negative effects of the abuse, it may be necessary to acknowledge the good things about the abuser. Once acknowledged, these positive features can be written down and set aside. This frees the child to deal with the things they did not like by making a separate negative list. They can then express their feelings of anger, hurt, etc. to the part of the offender represented by the second list.

We are also interested in whether the child has any ongoing contact with the abuser, and if so how they feel about that. Do they still worry about the offender? Do they feel guilty if the offender is in gaol? Do they blame themselves for any breakdown in the family?

Part of what we are assessing here is whether the child feels safe, and whether they feel supported by the family. We also ask, therefore, whether other family members remain in contact with the offender, and how that affects the child. Safety by itself is not sufficient. It is also important that the child *feels* safe.

The progress of therapy

As therapy proceeds, it is important to assess progress towards our goals. Long (1986) lists a number of useful indicators for assessing whether therapy can be successfully completed. Our own version of guidelines for determining when the goals of therapy have been achieved include:

- Feelings of guilt, fear, anger, confusion, shame, embarrassment, and depression have been dealt with.
- The child does not feel responsible for the sexual abuse, or for any family disruption which followed disclosure.
- A useful understanding has been reached about the nature of the abuse, the grooming process/methods of coercion, and the positive (if any) and negative feelings experienced.
- The child has some ideas about keeping safe in future, and knows how to seek help if necessary.
- Feelings about lack of protection from other adults have been dealt with.
- The child does not confuse sex with affection.
- The child has increased social skills and has developed (or is developing) age-appropriate social contacts and activities.
- Increased self-esteem.
- Ability to trust others as appropriate and to feel safe in a protective relationship.
- Symptoms (e.g. regression, nightmares, sexualized behaviour, aggression, withdrawal) are no longer causing significant difficulties.

Assessment of the family

In addition to assessing the child, we assess the family. We examine here six key factors which influence the child's progress and the healing of the various family members affected by the abuse.

1 How the family perceives the abuse.
2 The effects of the abuse on the family.
3 Relationships within the family system.
4 The family's relationship with the offender.
5 The family's resourcefulness.
6 Indicators for termination of therapy.

1 How the family perceives the abuse

It is important to check out the family's beliefs and fears about the abuse. They may, for example, be blaming the child, themselves, or one another. They may have fears for the future which are not grounded on fact, for example, the fear that 'She will be unable to have intimate relationships' or that 'He will be homosexual'. Unless we deal with these beliefs and fears they will continue to hinder recovery of both the child and the family in a very powerful way. Ways in which we deal with such fears include seeding information, reframing, and normalizing, all of which are described in Chapter 5.

2 The effects of the abuse on the family

There are many ways in which a family can be affected by the sexual abuse of one of its members. Most likely, individuals within the family are affected in different ways. They may be shocked or angry. They may have to deal with such major losses as the break-up of a marriage. They may feel stigmatized, blamed, and isolated. Their different responses may divide them against one another, or unite them against the offender or even against the child who has been abused.

The ways in which family members respond to abuse have major implications for themselves and for the child. Therefore it is important to assess this fully so we know which issues need to be addressed and can plan our therapy accordingly.

3 Relationships within the family system

An assessment of relationships within the family gives us information about the strengths and weaknesses of the child's support system. We assess this from the child's perspective, as previously described (p. 157), and from the perspectives of the different family members. We aim to find out who is closest to the child, who is likely to be most helpful, and who may be unhelpful. We look specifically at the relationship between the child and each parent, and between the child and each sibling. We also look at the relationship between the parents, and between the parents and siblings.

It is relevant to know if the abuse has created a shift in any of these relationships, either bringing people closer together or creating tensions which have driven them further apart. The history of these relationships is also important. We need to know, for example, if a significant care-giver has never felt close to the child, and to take into account this important information.

Having assessed relationships within the family system it may become necessary for therapy to focus on strengthening bonds, empowering parents, or establishing clearer boundaries. An obvious example of the need for clearer boundaries is where inappropriate sexual behaviour occurs between family members.

In any family, an assessment of subsystems plays an important part in planning therapy.

4 The family's relationship with the offender

The relationship between the family and the offender has major implications for therapy. We need to know, for example, if family members are closer to the offender than they are to the child, or if their loyalties to both cause division and tension. Any indication that family members support the offender and blame the child presents serious obstacles to healing unless dealt with effectively. The child's safety also may be jeopardized if the family fails to take responsibility for protecting them from the offender.

As we noted previously (Chapter 1, p. 9), the more distant the relationship between family and offender, the more likely they are to report the abuse to the authorities. Family members are much more likely to protect one of their own than they are to protect a stranger. If the family fails to take a clear stand against abuse by one of its own members, the child may feel confused, invalidated, or unsafe.

When some family members continue to have contact with the offender, this can create tension and conflict, and it is not uncommon for serious rifts to develop within the immediate or extended family. We therefore need to know about the family's relationship with the offender before and after the abuse, and the implications of this for the child.

5 The family's resourcefulness

We assess the various strengths of the family members to determine how they themselves are coping with the abuse, how they can help the victim, and what assistance they need.

Family members may need help in developing parenting skills or in learning how to resolve conflict. They may have a good support system or be socially isolated. They may be good at communicating with each other and confident in dealing with the relevant authority figures (e.g. doctors, police, social workers), or they may express their feelings in unhelpful ways and need support to cope with other agencies. They may have a good understanding of the effects of abuse or need a lot of information and explanation.

Our assessment takes into account the skills and resources the family brings to therapy, so we can support them to tap into the strengths they have, while offering assistance in those areas where they have difficulties. This enables us to be more effective in helping the family, and in empowering family members to help the child.

6 Indicators for termination of therapy

As in the case of the child, it is important that work with the family includes ongoing assessment of progress towards therapeutic goals. Indicators that work with the family may be completed successfully include:

- The child is not held responsible for the abuse by the family.
- The child has been told by significant family members that the offender is totally responsible for the abuse.
- The family is able to protect the child as much as possible from future abuse.
- The family is able to provide the child with emotional support while setting effective limits on unacceptable behaviour.
- Feelings of anger and guilt about the abuse, and feelings of anxiety about the future have been dealt with.
- Family members know what to expect in future, and what help is available if needed.
- Pathological labels or expectations are not placed on the child by the family.
- Support systems are in place to help a family disrupted by abuse, or to help a family member who may need individual help.

EMPOWERING THE CHILD

Therapy is about helping our clients feel empowered to deal with sexual abuse, not about discussing it in ways that add to their pain and distress. While some children may cry in the playroom, tears are not an essential part of good therapy. Children always should be able to leave each therapy session emotionally intact.

Putting the child in touch with their strengths

Before we discuss the details of the abuse, children must feel empowered to deal with it. We help them with this in a variety of ways, but methods used generally include making the most of opportunities to give praise and encouragement. We notice the child's strengths and achievements both inside and outside therapy, and draw their attention to their positive characteristics. Lists can be made of the child's strengths, preferably by eliciting the relevant information from the child so they are less likely to dispute it.

A list might include personal characteristics or behaviour associated with specific situations: 'I do what the teacher says', 'I ride my bike well', 'I help with my little brother', or 'I'm brave/kind/honest', etc.

Creating a safe haven

In order to deal with the abuse the child must feel safe in the therapy room. The joining process must have been successful to the point where the child has confidence in the therapist and is clear about the purpose of therapy. The therapy room must be a place where they feel comfortable, secure, and supported, and where they can say whatever they like, confident that they will be respected and that their trust will not be abused.

Identifying a hero

Sometimes the child can feel empowered by drawing on the strengths of others. They may, for example, identify a hero who could help them to talk about the abuse. This hero may be a real person, a character from a book or film, or a fantasy figure. The child can be encouraged to imagine their hero with them in the room, or to consult with their hero for advice or affirmation, for example:

'Do you think your Grandmother would be proud of your bravery today?'

'What do you think Superman would advise you to do in this situation?'

The child may feel stronger if they draw a picture of their hero to keep by them during therapy, and/or to take away with them when they go home at the end of the session.

Fighting fears

Eliciting information about fears is also important, so that suitable strategies for dealing with them can be devised with the child, and, where relevant, with the family. Plans can be written down, and a sense of power can be consolidated by getting the child to draw pictures which illustrate their positive attributes.

For example, a child who is afraid of sleeping alone can be helped to develop a plan to feel more secure. They might enlist the help of a favourite toy, pet, or photograph of a hero figure to act as a guard, or draw a picture of themselves looking strong and brave, which they hang by their bed. They might take on the role of night-watchman before bedtime, checking all the doors, windows, and cupboards. The family, too, might assist by providing rewards and encouragement for any signs of progress.

Creative use of therapeutic tools

Another way in which we help children to feel empowered is to make it as easy as possible for them to express themselves. This requires us to be flexible about the tools we use, and prepared to change as necessary from one method to another.

A child who finds it difficult to talk might like to draw a picture or demonstrate with dolls. A child who is reluctant to use action methods or artwork can be taught new words so they can communicate verbally more effectively. Chapter 7 discusses the use of a variety of therapeutic tools in detail.

Dealing with guilt and shame

Removing the sense of guilt and shame associated with abuse can be a very important part of empowering the child. Providing information, seeding ideas (e.g. 'The adult is always to blame'), reframing (e.g. 'You're very brave to talk about this'), and normalizing (e.g. 'No wonder you feel like that!') can be very reassuring and help to build confidence and self-esteem.

The way that we phrase our questions and comments plays an important part in helping the child to place guilt and blame where they belong — with the offender. This is clear in such questions as 'What did he make you do?' and 'How did he trick you?'

Respecting the child's pace

Finally, we help children to feel empowered when we respect their tolerance for therapy. It is essential that we do not abuse them further by making them do or say anything unwillingly. If they are unwilling to talk about something we do not try to force them. If one activity is too difficult, we try another. If it is not the right time for them to engage in therapy, we ensure that they are safe and that they know that help is available if needed in the future. This should not be portrayed as a step backwards, but as the right decision at that time.

Throughout therapy we are careful to move at the child's pace, sometimes shifting away from a topic which proves to be too stressful, and allowing time for the child to recover their strength. While we try to find ways to facilitate discussion of difficult topics, we also have to respect that a child may choose not to share certain information. When this happens we may discuss with the child why that particular topic is so hard to talk about, or when they think they might be ready to address it, e.g. later today, next week, 'after the holidays', or 'after your next birthday'.

EXAMINING THE EFFECTS OF ABUSE

Current effects and effects over time

Details of how a child has been affected by the abuse are obtained from the child, from the family, and from observation by the therapist of behaviour in the playroom. Significant information may also be collected from other people involved such as a teacher or referring social worker.

Some of this information is offered spontaneously in discussion, but we need to ask the parents about behaviours such as compliance, regression, aggression, sexualized play, and any signs of fear or insecurity. Significant changes in a child's behaviour at the time of the abuse, nightmares, eating disorders, and bedwetting are common effects of abuse. We need to enquire about each of them specifically, and be ready to deal with them when necessary.

Many of these effects diminish as time, family support, and therapy relieve the effects of trauma, but in the meantime parents may need practical advice on how to deal with them. Ideas for helping parents deal with some of the common behaviour problems associated with abuse are described in Chapter 9.

GOING OVER THE ABUSE IN A THERAPEUTIC WAY

Several stages are involved in going over the abuse scene in a therapeutic way:

1 Describing the abuse

In order to communicate the details of the abuse children may use words (spoken or written), or enlist the aid of drawings, puppets, dolls, or action methods to show the therapist what happened (see also Chapter 7). Whichever method is used, this stage of therapy needs to be conducted very carefully. We respect the child's pace, we often acknowledge how hard it is to talk about it, and how brave they are for sharing the information. We enquire gently about how they felt, what was done, and what was said. We prompt with such general questions as 'What happened next?'

We need to know where the abuse occurred, who was there, and what happened. When more than one incident is involved we try to find out how often the child was abused and in what ways. Care may need to be taken to keep different incidents separate, to avoid confusing either the child or the therapist. We support and encourage the child to tell us about the abuse with such comments as:

'That must have been really hard.'

'No wonder you were scared.'

'He shouldn't have done that, should he?'

It should not be necessary to go over the details of the abuse repeatedly. In many cases once will suffice, although we may choose to check twice to confirm that there is no evidence of remaining trauma.

Particular care is needed with those children who have been traumatized by abuse. It is important that they be put in touch with the feelings that go with the abuse, so that these can be dealt with effectively in therapy.

Consequently, it is essential to obtain information from the child about anything which might trigger a traumatic response. Sometimes the triggers are details which the child may not volunteer unless specifically requested. For example, we ask about the sights, sounds, and smells that the child recalls, whether any objects were used, and whether anyone else was present. It is also wise to check on whether the child was shown any pornographic photographs or videos. This is a situation where leading questions may be asked legitimately, and is quite different therefore from a diagnostic or assessment interview where such questions are clearly not appropriate.

So long as the child remains traumatized, their behaviour is likely to be affected by the abuse and various triggers will continue to elicit symptomatic responses.

2 Catharsis

It is essential that we do not simply recreate the abuse experience, but help the child to experience the abuse scene/s in a different way. Once we have elicited the details of the abuse we immediately move on to a stage of catharsis or expression of feelings. This is a time when the child is helped to express grief, hurt, anger, etc. which they have experienced.

This catharsis can be encouraged in a number of ways, but usually it involves saying or doing something to a symbolic version of the offender.

We might ask, for example, 'What would you like to say to him now?' or 'Tell him what you think about what he did.' Using a drawing, a clay-model, or a doll to represent the offender, the child is encouraged to address 'the offender' directly. Any tentative comments, such as 'I'd like to tell him he's a bastard' can be developed with the therapist's encouragement: 'OK, tell him.' The emphasis is on 'doing' something in the present rather than talking about it.

If the child is inhibited from entering fully into the activity the therapist can help. The therapist might decide to go first, using the child's words to tell the offender, 'You're a bastard.' Alternatively, the therapist might repeat the child's words in a stronger and louder voice. This gives permission for a more powerful response from the child, when they feel shy or uncertain about how far they are allowed to go. The therapist's role is to help the child to express their feelings. It is important to be careful not to encourage any activity for which the child is not ready, or which is not congruent with the child's perception of reality.

We might ask the child 'What would you like to do to him?' or 'What should happen to him now?' The symbolic offender, if represented by a drawing, can be stabbed, ripped apart, jumped on, inked over, or taken outside for burning. When a doll is used to represent the offender he can be beaten with a rolled-up newspaper, kicked across the room, punched, or jumped on. An 'offender' on a whiteboard can have wet clay thrown at him, be attacked with wads of wet paper, or have appropriate words written all over him and then be wiped out of existence. A playdough figure can be painfully dismembered, squashed, or squeezed out of shape. Any activity appropriate for the child which safely allows them to express their feelings is helpful at this stage.

To make catharsis more powerful we encourage the child to put words to their feelings. As they deal with the offender by ripping, beating, burning, etc., we prompt them with such suggestions as 'Tell him what you think of him' or 'Let him know how much he hurt you.' If their response seems a little tentative we may repeat it ourselves in a loud, strong voice, or encourage them to 'Say it again' or 'Shout it out louder.' In this way we validate their feelings and help them to feel more empowered in dealing with the offender.

Before engaging in these activities it is important that the child knows that they can say or do things which usually are not permitted. Shouting, use of 'swear' words, symbolic forms of aggression such as cutting, ripping, or burning paper, and throwing, punching, or stamping on dolls are acceptable as forms of catharsis in the playroom. When we encourage this sort of behaviour during therapy we also need to teach children that aggressive behaviour outside the playroom is not acceptable. We establish clear boundaries around what they can do in the playroom and what is allowed outside.

We also set limits in the playroom which include the rule that they must not hurt themselves or anyone else. We give parents advice about dealing with any aggressive behaviour which may be occurring at home in response to the abuse. This is described in more detail in Chapter 9. By establishing behavioural limits we make a clear distinction between anger, which is a natural reaction, and unacceptable forms of aggression, which can be damaging for the self and for others.

3 The rescue scene

A useful method for going over the abuse in a different way is the creation of some form of rescue scene. This is a technique used more commonly in therapy with adults, and is not necessary or appropriate for all children. For some, however, it can provide an opportunity for expressing feelings, or for developing a different perspective.

The 'rescue scene' can be created using any of the tools of therapy described in the previous chapter. For example, the child might draw a scene similar to that of their own abuse, but include in the drawing a rescuing figure with whom they identify. Older children may write a story, in which they rescue themselves from the abuse scene. As the rescuer, they may be older, stronger, or suitably armed. The use of action methods to create a rescue scene is described in detail in Chapter 7 and can be a very powerful and effective form of therapy.

The essential factor about a rescue scene is that the situation portrayed parallels the abuse actually experienced, and the child takes on the empowering role of rescuer to effect a shift from the powerless role of victim.

4 Checking for remaining trauma

Usually children leave sessions involving catharsis or rescue scenes feeling better about themselves and less traumatized by the abuse. They are often cheerful and even exhilarated by the new experience of taking charge of the abuser or the abuse situation. Because these methods are very powerful, it is often possible at the next session to move on to the final phase of the therapy process.

Before doing this, however, we need to check at the next session how the child is feeling about the abuser and the incident of abuse previously dealt with. It is important to assess whether they remain traumatized in any way.

To check this we often ask the child to describe the details of the abuse once again.

If the child feels that they have not finished with the incident and/or feelings of trauma remain, it is necessary to go over the abuse again, dealing with either the same or separate abusive incidents in the way described above. In such cases it may be just a matter of consolidating the new experience with repetition, or it may be helpful to try using different methods (e.g. action methods instead of drawing) for greater impact. It may be useful also to first spend some time with the child, developing a stronger image of the hero who could help them to deal with the abuse.

PREPARING FOR THE FUTURE

Highlighting changes made

As therapy draws to a close we find many ways to help both child and family put sexual abuse in the past. The messages we give at this stage include:

'You may never forget what happened, but you have come through it.'

'It is in the past now and you can look at it in a different way.'

'It's not going to ruin your life.'

'You have a lot of strengths.'

'You are OK — there is nothing wrong with you as a result of what happened.'

and most important:

'You can lead a normal life.'

It is important to mark the progress of therapy in some way so that all concerned know when this final stage has been reached. Children can be helped to list their achievements, perhaps describing how they were when they first came to therapy and how they are now. Changes to look for might include lack of nightmares, control of aggression, better relationships with family and peers, improved performance at school, and feeling better about themselves. The idea can be reinforced by getting them to draw pictures of themselves as they are today, looking secure, busy, and happy in various settings.

In the child's presence we highlight with the family any progress made at home, at school, and in the playroom. Both child and family are congratulated on the progress and given as much credit as possible for changes made. They need to know that their efforts and persistence have effected these changes, so they know that they have the ability to maintain them. The therapist should take as little credit as possible. Our job is to put child and family in touch with their strengths and to facilitate their progress towards healing. Without their efforts the therapist is powerless.

Sometimes progress is marked with the award of certificates (e.g. 'Award for bravery') or letters of congratulation. Conclusion of therapy is seen as a cause for celebration and the family is encouraged to mark it in some way, perhaps with a special dinner or treat. We convey the message that 'You don't need me any more' or 'You've done me out of a job' in a way that helps survivor and family to feel proud of themselves rather than rejected by the therapist.

Another way of marking progress, especially for children whose therapy has extended over months rather than weeks, is to space therapy sessions further and further apart. This way the child is able to acknowledge progress and to get on with their life, while having the security of ongoing therapy as needed. Gradually increasing the time between sessions also helps to avoid the risk of a child or family feeling rejected or betrayed by the therapist, and allows them the time and opportunity to develop confidence in their own ability to cope.

Safety education

Ensuring that children know how to keep themselves safe in future is an important part of finishing therapy. Safety education may not enable the child to protect themselves totally, but it does improve the likelihood that they will tell someone if any attempt is made to abuse them. Safety education therefore plays a major role in minimizing the extent and effects of any future abuse, and contributes to a child's sense of power and confidence.

Comprehensive details of how we teach children to keep themselves safe are described in Chapter 7.

DEALING WITH THE EFFECTS OF CHILD ABUSE:
Advice for Parents and Guardians

Many of the behaviours which develop as a result of abuse need to be dealt with by parents as soon as possible. It is wise not to wait for the benefits of therapy to take effect. While some of these behaviours will disappear when the child no longer feels traumatized, others can become habits. Some habits remain long after the trauma of abuse has abated, and can instigate vicious cycles which compound the original effects of the abuse.

Some habits, such as aggression, drug and alcohol abuse, and sexualized behaviour, put others at risk. Some, such as withdrawal or loss of concentration, can lead to long-term disadvantage as children get behind in their schooling and become socially isolated. Other habits, such as nightmares, can be distressing to child and parent alike, and can impact on the whole family with disturbed sleep by night and fatigue by day.

Parents need help to cope with these problems while they are happening. Empowering parents with practical suggestions, and giving them support to persist in their efforts, is therefore a vital part of therapy for both child and family.

This chapter discusses some of the more common issues which parents may have to deal with, and includes practical suggestions for assisting parents to make changes in their child's behaviour. Many of the ideas described here are derived from Behaviour Therapy, which advocates that parents give a lot of attention to behaviour they want to encourage, and that they respond to undesirable behaviour either by ignoring it or by imposing immediate consequences. The underlying assumption is that a particular behaviour is likely to occur more frequently if it elicits attention from others

(Corsini 1984). Attention may include praise and encouragement for acceptable behaviours, but also includes shouting, repeating, complaining, arguing, and smacking in response to unacceptable behaviours.

COMPLIANCE

There are a number of reasons why compliance may suffer as a result of abuse. A confused, angry, or unhappy child may act out their feelings by becoming sullen, withdrawn, disrespectful, and unco-operative. A parent may not provide the usual guidelines because they feel guilty, distressed, or sorry for their child. The parent may choose to make allowances for problem behaviours, as they would with a child who was ill. Parents may be uncertain about what their children need and reluctant to upset them further by taking a strong stand against unacceptable behaviour.

We encourage parents to establish firm guidelines for their child's behaviour, and where necessary we teach parents how to set effective limits. Having normal expectations of a child's behaviour avoids feeding into the pathology of abuse. It contributes to a sense of re-establishing everyday life and leaving the abuse in the past. It also provides the child with the security of boundaries and a sense of having parents strong enough to take care of them at a time when they may feel unable to control themselves. In addition, by setting limits on unacceptable behaviour the parent is limiting the effects of abuse. They do this by controlling the unhelpful habits developed by a child as a response to their abusive experience.

In dealing with non-compliance we make the same suggestions that we would for any parent whose child was not doing what they were told. These are described in detail by Seymour (1987). Parents are taught to distinguish between three different categories of behaviour: The behaviours they like and want to encourage, the behaviours that they find irritating but tolerable, and the behaviours that are totally unacceptable. They are encouraged to notice and praise when their child does what they are told, and to reward good behaviour with smiles, cuddles, and special treats or privileges.

Usually it is more effective if the parents focus on specific behaviours which they want to encourage. Then they can be particularly enthusiastic when there is any sign of co-operation or improvement in these areas. They can praise children for the absence of the unacceptable behaviour. They can also be prepared to use immediate and consistent consequences when there is a lack of co-operation.

Consequences commonly recommended include ignoring and Time Out. Behaviour which is irritating but tolerable is best ignored in a very obvious way, while Time Out is used for children who do not do what they are told after two commands.

Time Out consists of sending or taking the child to a safe, boring room and leaving them there with the door closed for up to five minutes. They should never be left for longer than five minutes, because Time Out then loses its impact and becomes unnecessarily punitive. Nor should Time Out be used with children who are sick, tired, or very distressed. For such children a good night's sleep, a cuddle, or firm holding may be more appropriate.

Time Out means that children receive no attention while in the specified room, and parents also get time to calm down and plan their next move. When the period of Time Out is complete the incident is over and parents are encouraged to help direct their child to some positive activity from which they can derive pleasure or praise.

Before Time Out is used the process should be explained clearly to the child. It is helpful if this is done in a positive way, assuming that the child will do what they are told and emphasizing how pleased the parent will be when they comply. The parent might say something like:

> 'I'm going to be really pleased when you do what I tell you without making a fuss. I'll be able to tell everyone what a good girl you've been. But if you don't do what I say I'm only going to tell you once more, and then you'll go to Time Out. That means two minutes in the laundry with the door closed. And when you're in Time Out I'm not going to talk to you or take any notice of you.'

Compliance can be encouraged in other ways. Withdrawal of privileges (e.g. bike, television) can be very effective, as can rewards for specific behaviours. It is often most effective if parents target one or two behaviours which particularly concern them.

With younger children rewards need to be as immediate as possible, rather than something earned on a points system over an extended period. The task required should be sufficiently manageable to ensure success and continuing interest from the child, and rewards should be accompanied by praise and encouragement. Some of the most effective rewards are not material, but involve extra time with the parents, for example, playing games or reading together.

AGGRESSION AND TANTRUMS

Much of what has been said about co-operation (above) also applies to aggression and tantrums.

Aggression is not an uncommon response to sexual abuse, because it is based on natural feelings of anger and frustration. It can be directed towards care-givers who failed to protect the child, towards those they feel most secure with, or towards anyone within striking distance. It can also be directed against property, in outbursts of destructive behaviour.

Children can be taught that their anger is normal in the circumstances, but that expressing it in aggression towards others is not acceptable.

Therapy in the playroom helps children to express their grief and anger, as they do, for example, when they address a doll or drawing that represents the abuser. At home they need to develop other strategies for coping with anger. They might practise making assertive statements, try removing themselves from a difficult situation, or learn to express their anger through some form of physical exercise which is not harmful to themselves or others.

Parents and therapists can act as coaches for children, helping them to develop strategies for controlling their aggressive behaviour. Many children have good ideas about what situations make them most vulnerable to anger and about ways that they have managed to control aggression. When asked about these they may say, for example, that going for a ride on their bike helps. Alternatively, they may prefer to do something active like playing sport, running, or punching a pillow. They may prefer to calm themselves by spending some quiet time in their room, or walking away from someone who is bothering them. Sometimes they develop a phrase they can say to themselves, such as, 'I'm strong and I can control myself', which helps them to avoid aggressive behaviour.

When children can come up with ideas of their own and a list of times when they have managed to control aggressive impulses, these should be highlighted by a therapist and presented to both child and parent as evidence of their strength and ability. We ask questions that assume they can control themselves when they choose to, such as:

'Tell me about a time when you've really felt like hitting someone but you've managed to stop yourself?' and

'What's the best way you've tried to keep yourself calm when you feel a tantrum coming on?'

Parents may see their child in a more positive light if this discussion is held in their presence, or reported back to them after a session with the child. They can be encouraged to notice and praise any improvements in the child's self-control, and to 'coach' them with suggestions for coping with the difficult times.

Coaching by parents is obviously best done at a time of calm when the child is more receptive. It is most effective when child and parent do not see themselves as pitted against each other, but as team-mates pitted together against the problem. This may involve a shift in thinking for both child and parent, and can be facilitated by externalizing the problem to something like a 'hitting habit' or a 'tricky temper' which is separate from the personality of the child. For more details about externalization see Chapter 5.

Our goal always is to help the child to vent their anger in therapy and to control their own aggression. Until children are able to control themselves, however, parents may need help to control them. Once again we may advocate some form of Time Out as a consequence for aggression or a tantrum — usually three to five minutes in a safe, boring room with the door closed. Some children can simply be sent to their rooms, while others need a safe place where there is nothing they can damage or use to hurt themselves.

There are no warnings about aggressive behaviour. If children are to learn that aggression does not work they need an immediate consequence after every incident. A simple statement is made, such as, 'You do not hit — you are going to Time Out' and there is no further discussion. For tantrums they may be given one warning (e.g. 'Stop that screaming!') before Time Out is used.

Children also need parents who themselves are not modelling aggressive behaviour with physical punishments. Parents may need help to coach and model non-violent ways of expressing anger and resolving conflicts.

It is essential that parents demonstrate in their manner and actions that they are not overwhelmed by the anger that their child expresses. Parents who indicate that they are afraid or unable to cope can expect increased anger and aggression as their child gets even more frustrated and seeks the security of firm limits. They also inadvertently give their child the message that aggressive behaviour is acceptable, because it is not dealt with effectively.

Empowering parents to deal with a child's aggressive behaviour may be an important part of the therapist's job. This is done by helping parents to discover where their beliefs about their own powerlessness come from, and putting them in touch with their own strengths. Planning with them practical strategies for dealing with the child's aggressive behaviours is also essential. This may involve Time Out, loss of privileges, or use of support people such as family, neighbours, or parenting groups. In extreme cases it may involve contacting statutory authorities such as child-welfare services or police.

Parents may also need 'time out' for themselves to maintain their ability to cope with an aggressive child. They may need permission to take better care of themselves. Providing the child is not left alone, it is useful for parents to set aside time to do things for themselves and to spend time with other supportive adults. Use of family, friends, or foster-care to get a temporary break from their child may be beneficial for all, particularly if not presented to the child as a punishment. This is most important for single parents, who may have to cope unsupported with the stress of a child's sexual abuse.

SEXUALIZED BEHAVIOUR

As a consequence of sexual abuse some children may confuse sexuality with affection and try to get attention from others in inappropriate sexual ways. They may also act out the abuse in play with other children. Sexualized behaviour makes them vulnerable to further abuse and a danger to others. It can lead to their being socially ostracized and the subject of criticism and blame.

We advise parents that inappropriate sexual behaviour is a normal response to abuse, but while it is helpful to understand why it is happening, it is not helpful for parents to tolerate it. Sexualized behaviour towards others should be treated the same as any other form of aggression. Children are told simply and firmly something like, 'You do not touch other people's bottoms. You are going to Time Out.'

Sexualized behaviour often can be dealt with quickly and effectively, providing children get adequate help in the playroom (see Chapter 7). Parents, teachers, and others also must be encouraged to deal with it firmly and consistently. It is not likely to go away of its own accord once the child is no longer traumatized by the abuse. This is because often it becomes established as a habit. It therefore requires specific attention from both therapist and family to ensure that it does not continue to be a problem (Johnson & Berry 1989).

EXCESSIVE MASTURBATION

Another form of sexualized behaviour which can follow abuse is excessive masturbation. While this is not harmful to others it can lead to social isolation and vulnerability to further abuse if carried out in public. It can also be very irritating or embarrassing for parents.

Some masturbation is normal for most children, and probably is best ignored if it occurs in the privacy of their own bed. It is not uncommon for children who have not been abused to play with their genitals in the bath or to masturbate over their clothes as a form of comfort.

Usually, parents are best advised to avoid making an issue of masturbation unless it becomes excessive, or is done in inappropriate places. Clear rules and a firm stand taken calmly against masturbation in public might include a warning (e.g. 'Please stop playing with your penis') and the use of Time Out if this is not sufficient. Suggestions can also be made about some alternative activity, for example, 'Why don't you put your hands in your pockets?', or 'Try holding the book with both hands.'

LOSS OF SELF-ESTEEM

There are many ways a parent can help a child who is feeling bad about themselves as a result of sexual abuse. The most important are to demonstrate their love and support, and their unambiguous belief that the child is not to blame for what has happened.

Noticing the things they do well, and taking every opportunity to praise and encourage the child's good behaviour and new skills is also important. When a child shows a particular interest or aptitude in a hobby or sport, for example, this could be pursued enthusiastically by enrolling them in extra classes, encouraging them to join a team or club, or perhaps providing relevant equipment, such as art materials, books, or computer games. Success in any positive activity helps to increase the child's skills, their confidence, and their ability to cope in social situations. Even small steps and unsuccessful attempts should be noticed and encouraged if the child is to persevere with making changes.

Sometimes low self-esteem is manifested in withdrawal and social isolation, and at other times it may be demonstrated in an attempt to dominate, control, or even bully others. Children may benefit from coaching on how to make friends. Opportunities to practise their skills in structured extramural activities also can be helpful. They can be encouraged to have friends home to play, one at a time being easiest for those who do not cope well in a larger group.

Parents who set firm limits on their child's behaviour are also helping the child's self-esteem. Children do not feel good about themselves if they are constantly being reprimanded, criticized, or punished. Dealing quickly and effectively with unacceptable behaviour avoids lengthy negative interactions, and allows the child to develop self-control. It also leaves more time for the child to behave in ways that they feel good about and which should earn them praise from others.

Another way of improving a child's self-esteem is to provide extra help in those areas which they find difficult. Sometimes the stress of sexual abuse affects concentration in class, school attendance, and academic performance. Remedial reading provided through their school or privately can help a child to catch up and restore a sense of personal achievement. It can also help them to feel important by providing undivided quality time with an adult. Coaching in subjects where the child has fallen behind can be a valuable investment for parents who can afford it, particularly if it is presented as a help rather than as a punishment or sign of failure.

Regular quality time with parents or with a care-giver is absolutely essential for the development of self-esteem. This does not have to be a long time. Fifteen minutes of relaxed undivided attention each day is better than two hours spent in the same room busily occupied with other priorities. For younger children this might be a time to read a story, have a cuddle, and talk about the day's activities. For older children it is a quiet, relaxed time, perhaps including a brief game, which gives them the opportunity to discuss any issues and review the day's achievements.

At these times it is most helpful if parents provide their children with the opportunity to raise issues, rather than pressuring them for too much information. They can, however, be encouraged to ask open questions (e.g. 'What was the best thing you did today?') rather than closed questions (e.g. 'Was school OK?'), which tend to provide less scope for discussion.

Parents help to raise their children's self-esteem when they show that they value them the way they are and enjoy being with them. Having fun together in shared activities such as going on outings, throwing a ball about, playing games, or reading together can all be beneficial.

When there are difficulties in the parent–child relationship which pre-date the abuse this is likely to get in the way of the parents providing the love and support needed by the abused child. Therapy with the parent needs to acknowledge and address these relationship issues in a non-blaming way.

Usually in such cases it is necessary to go over the history of the parents' own upbringing and marriage, as well as details of the pregnancy, birth, and the child's early years. This helps us to understand the difficulties and to plan appropriate therapy. If we are unable to deal with these problems ourselves, we may choose to refer the parent to another counsellor who specializes in individual or marital therapy. In extreme cases the extra stress created by the abuse and its effects on the child's behaviour may lead to further deterioration in the parent–child relationship. It may warrant at least temporary separation while the issues are resolved.

FACING FEARS

Some children become fearful and withdrawn as a result of sexual abuse. This in turn can contribute to social isolation and low self-esteem, because the children avoid situations which would give them the opportunity to develop skills and friendships. Small children may cling to a parent and be terrified of being left at kindergarten. Older children may spend a lot of time alone in their room or avoid any situation in which they may stand out. Some children consciously underachieve at school for fear of drawing attention to themselves.

The longer that fears are not faced, the worse they are likely to become. Parents are advised to help children face their fears by taking small manageable steps. The parent with the clingy preschooler may stay with their child at the kindergarten for gradually decreasing amounts of time. The parent of an older child may encourage them to bring home one friend at a time to visit, or get them involved in some activity which parent and child may enjoy together (e.g. aerobics, camera club, bushwalking), just to get the child out of the house. Ideally teachers can be involved, supporting the parents by encouraging children to cope with their fears in the school setting.

Children should not be belittled for being fearful, but noticed and encouraged when any progress is made towards overcoming the fears.

NIGHTMARES

One particularly common and distressing effect of sexual abuse is nightmares. Children may even develop a fear of going to sleep and spend wakeful hours at night trying to avoid the bad dreams. As a result they may be overtired by day as well as terrified by night.

Children's nightmares are also distressing for the parents who have to deal with them. Parents may suffer from broken sleep, and from the strain of coping with a child who is tearful or even hysterical.

Nightmares are likely to decrease in frequency and intensity as the trauma of sexual abuse is dealt with in therapy. In the meantime the parent can be involved in various ways to help the child overcome them. They may encourage activities previously described (Chapter 7), such as encouraging the child to draw ___ rip it up, stomp on it, bury it, or hang ___ courage the use of a hero figure or fav ___ *night mares may decrease as trauma of sexual abuse is dealt with in therapy* ___ light to protect them. They can help ___ to the dream, using positive fantasies ___ he nightmare.

For some time pare ___ eep in order to provide the child with ___ ary after a bad dream. These parents n ___ from the therapist. They also need a ___ ies to take care of themselves. Only by taking care of themselves will they have the energy required to care for their children. Strategies they might try could include making regular opportunities to get some relaxed time to themselves.

They could benefit, for example, from some relief from childcare during the day to enable them to catch up on sleep. They could also benefit from the information that this is only a temporary stage in their child's healing from abuse.

Sometimes nightmares are eased by allowing the child to share a bedroom with a sibling, or to sleep in the parents' bed. It may help to have a night-light, or a door left open. These are options parents may consider, particularly when night has been a frightening time for a child who has been abused in their own bed. For parents who are anxious not to encourage the habit of having their child in their bed, it can be seen as a temporary stage in their child's healing. The habit can be unlearned when the trauma has passed.

WETTING AND SOILING

Regression in toilet-training is another common problem which may follow the sexual abuse of young children. It can show up in bedwetting at night, or in wetting and soiling by day.

Children should not be punished for regression in toilet-training. It is likely to be an indication of emotional stress and trauma which is outside their immediate control, rather than a purposeful misbehaviour. It may also be a symptom of infection. If the child has not been medically examined already, parents are advised to check this possibility with a doctor before taking any other action.

As with other behavioural problems, regression in toilet-training is likely to disappear as the child feels less traumatized by their abuse. In the meantime it is important that parent and child do not get into a battle over toilet-training or bedwetting. As with aggressive behaviour, the problem could be 'externalized' (White 1989) as 'Sneaky Wees' or 'Tricky Poos' which catch them out when unprepared. This helps to pit parents and child against the problem instead of being against one another. Together they can devise ways of outwitting the 'Sneaky Wee', such as toileting before bedtime and regular toilet stops in the daily routine.

Children need to be encouraged by their parents for any successes in beating this problem. The use of rewards and/or 'star' charts could be considered. When they are not successful it is best if parents remain calm, and say something non-blaming, such as 'Never mind, better luck next time.' Parents irritated by their children's 'accidents' may need help from the therapist to develop their own strategies for remaining calm, such as 'biting their tongue' or walking out of the room.

It is helpful for both parent and child if the child is given as much responsibility as is age-appropriate for cleaning up the mess. Mopping up their own puddles for younger children, or washing their own pants and bedding for the older ones, takes the pressure off the parents and makes it clear where the responsibility for making change must lie. This is a problem parents cannot solve for their child, but they can support any efforts made by the child to defeat the problem.

Other problems relating to toileting may occur as a response to sexual abuse, including wetting in inappropriate places or smearing faeces. These behaviours may be indicators of a child in distress, but should not be excused on these grounds. While punishment may not be helpful, nor is it helpful for the child to believe that these behaviours are acceptable. The parents can be supported to deal with them calmly and consistently, getting the child to take as much responsibility as possible for cleaning up. At the same time, work with the child to help deal with any unresolved feelings of trauma should be continued.

Behaviour problems sometimes continue after the trauma has been resolved. The family may need to continue dealing with them in ways similar to those described above.

SEXUALLY TRANSMITTED DISEASES

Unfortunately, one of the possible effects of sexual abuse is that children can be infected with sexually transmitted diseases. These can be a problem even when a child appears to be symptom-free. Whenever there is *any* possibility that infection may have occurred, it is important that a proper medical examination is carried out.

A medical examination can also be very important for a child or parent who is concerned that some sort of physical damage may have been caused by the abuse. For some it may be an immense relief to be reassured that they are not damaged and that their bodies are functioning normally.

Medical examinations must be carried out by a doctor who is sensitive and skilled in the specialist area of sexual abuse. Otherwise it can be invasive, frightening, and even abusive in itself. It is important that therapists are well informed about appropriate medical and other professional services in their area, to ensure that they make the best possible referrals.

In New Zealand, the specialist group Doctors for Sexual Abuse Care provides an excellent service in training doctors, and in referring people who have been abused to physicians with the necessary skills and understanding of the issues involved. A similar group in Australia is Doctors for the Protection of Abused Children, but national organizations of doctors such as this are lacking in other countries.

ISSUES FOR PARENTS OF ADOLESCENTS

Some of the suggestions already made in this chapter will be useful for parents of adolescents. Some issues, however, relate specifically to problem behaviours during adolescence.

One of the most obvious differences between parenting adolescents and parenting younger children is that with adolescents there is more room for negotiation. Parents need to be prepared to allow more choices in some areas, but also to be clear about the things that are not negotiable.

It may be more difficult to enforce meaningful consequences with an adolescent. Realistically, adolescents cannot be confined to a room, or within the house for that matter, against their will. Parents need to think clearly about consequences they can impose, and to use these consistently, for example, 'If you swear or abuse me, you cannot use my car for the next month.' Once parents establish a rule, it is important that they do not yield to pressure when the rule has been broken.

Adolescents expect more freedom than younger children, but this needs to be accompanied by an increase in responsibility. We encourage parents to expect more of their adolescents, but also encourage adolescents to understand that increased trust and freedom must be earned by responsible behaviour.

When problem behaviour is extreme, parents need support from others, such as a support group or statutory agency. They also may consider making an official complaint to the police, particularly when physical abuse or destruction of property is involved. They need to know that this is an option for them to consider when circumstances warrant. Alternatively, they may decide to arrange a respite for themselves or their teenager by arranging alternative accommodation in a hostel, in private board, or with other family members.

Parents also need to continue helping adolescents to develop self-esteem. Encouraging them in the things they are good at, and allowing them opportunities to develop appropriate skills, are major roles of the parent at this stage.

When self-esteem is particularly low, when the adolescent is subject to mood swings, or when they feel overwhelmed or hopeless, the risk of suicide cannot be ignored. Parents may need help to recognize danger signs, such as suicidal threats, depression, withdrawal, giving away personal possessions, or having no sense of the future. At such times they may need to seek extra help for themselves and their child. (See also 'Suicide Prevention' in Chapter 11, pp. 231–234.)

Adolescents also may need help with other problems which have developed as a result of sexual abuse. These might include anger management, drug and alcohol abuse, or difficulties in self-assertion and self-defence. It is useful for both therapists and parents to be aware of the relevant resources available in their area. Group work relating to specific problems such as these can be particularly helpful for adolescents.

Details of specific issues involved in therapy for adolescents who have been abused are discussed in Chapter 10.

10

ISSUES FOR THERAPY WITH ADOLESCENTS

Adolescence is a time when feelings about previous sexual abuse may surface, as the abuse takes on a new meaning with the development of sexuality and cognitive maturity.

Adolescence is also a time when young people are experimenting with sexual behaviour and are particularly vulnerable to abuse by acquaintances, as in 'date rape', for example. Gavey (1991) reported that studies of female students in the United States and New Zealand have found that over one quarter had experienced rape or attempted rape. For adolescents, acquaintance rape is the most common and possibly the least acknowledged form of sexual abuse.

There is no evidence that rape by an acquaintance is any less traumatic than rape by a stranger, and it is likely to be much more difficult to report. This applies particularly to adolescents because they tend to be unwilling to admit to being in situations with friends or acquaintances which they are unable to control. The importance of the peer group for adolescents may also act as a restraint on reporting someone from within their social circle. This in turn can make it difficult for them to get the help they need.

When adolescents do seek help, the process of therapy is the same as for children and adults. The therapeutic tools used are also the same as for other age groups, as described in chapters 5, 7, and 11. There are, however, a number of issues specific to work with adolescents. Also, some of the effects of abuse commonly experienced at any age can present particular difficulties at adolescence.

EFFECTS OF ABUSE ON ADOLESCENTS

Adolescents may experience any of the difficulties previously described as a consequence of sexual abuse. Some difficulties, however, surface for the first time at this stage, and there are others to which adolescents appear to be particularly vulnerable. In this section we discuss some of the more common effects which adolescent abuse survivors may experience.

Poor self-esteem

Lowered self-esteem may be a consequence of sexual abuse for survivors of all ages, but adolescents are particularly vulnerable because their sense of their own identity is still developing, and because they tend to place considerable value on peer relationships. Their opinion of themselves is therefore more likely to be influenced by the opinion of others.

Feeling different or inferior leads to difficulties interacting with friends. It can also lead to withdrawal from social situations and ostracism by others. Adolescents who have been sexually abused are therefore more likely to be drawn towards those who are on the fringe of social acceptance by their peers — the underachievers, those lacking in social skills, those with social, emotional, or behavioural problems of their own. Gravitation to this group may compound the problem by setting in motion a vicious cycle. By behaving in ways generally considered to be undesirable, they become even more socially marginalized and develop even lower self-esteem.

Poor sexual self-esteem

Lack of confidence about sexuality and sexual relationships is a major problem for sexually abused adolescents. As part of their normal development they are learning to cope with physical maturation and sexuality, and may be under pressure from their peers to engage in sexual behaviour. Adolescents with a history of sexual abuse have already experienced powerlessness and sexual exploitation, and may find it difficult to say 'No' to unwanted sex. They may have no clear concept of their own needs, nor of their rights to set boundaries on relationships. As a consequence of past abuse they may see themselves through the eyes of the offender as a sexual being whose feelings are irrelevant.

Those who are known to have been abused may also be seen as sexual candidates by their peers, and consequently subjected to increased pressures to engage in sexual activity. They may have learned to use sex as a way of meeting their emotional needs, confusing sex with affection or intimacy.

Those who feel inferior or socially isolated are therefore likely to find it more difficult to resist sexual invitations.

Self-blame

Adolescents are more likely than younger children to blame themselves for abuse, because they have a more developed understanding of the concept of blame. They will be asking more questions about what happened and why they were 'chosen'. Lucy Berliner,* at a 1992 workshop in Auckland, stated that those who are older or more intelligent are likely to have even greater difficulty with this issue of self-blame.

Adolescents tend to have relatively entrenched ideas. They also find it difficult to admit to being vulnerable, and may be particularly resistant to the notion that someone had taken advantage of them. Consequently, it may be easier for some to blame themselves than to acknowledge that they were not responsible for being abused. Like some survivors from all age groups they may recognize that other people are not responsible for being abused, but still consider that their own circumstances are different.

Self-blame can be a particularly difficult issue for those who were sexually aroused by the abuse or who found some aspect of it gratifying. It can also be difficult for those who accepted money or gifts, and for those who were drawn to the abuser despite warnings from others that he was unpleasant or untrustworthy.

In extreme cases self-blame is demonstrated in resistance to any idea that the adolescent was abused or powerless, and an insistence that they were a consenting participant. This in turn feeds into a heightened sense of shame and guilt, and a lowered self-esteem.

Confusion about sexual orientation

Confusion about sexual orientation and homophobic responses are common problems for adolescent boys, particularly when they felt sexually aroused while being abused by a male (Watkins & Bentovim 1992). These concerns occur so frequently that it is wise to enquire about them, rather than risk that they may be causing anxiety which remains unexpressed.

Boys anxious about their sexual orientation may show this in inappropriate attempts to exert their masculinity (as with aggressive or dominating

* Lucy Berliner, Research Director, Harborview Sexual Assault Centre, Harborview Medical Centre, University of Washington, Seattle : Clinical Assistant Professor, School of Social Work, University of Washington, Seattle.

behaviour), in the need to 'prove themselves' within numerous hetero-sexual relationships, or in demonstrating homophobic attitudes.

There is a lack of research which specifically examines possible confusion about sexual identity in adolescent girls who have been abused. However, childhood abuse often involves what Finkelhor (1990) describes as traumatic sexualization, which includes such responses as heightened awareness of sexual issues, confusion and misconceptions about sexual self-concepts, and negative connotations about sex (Tharinger 1990). As adolescence normally is a stage of developing identity and sexuality, and since fears and confusion about sexual identity are already widespread within the general community, sexual abuse may well have the effect of confirming such preoccupations and fears (Watkins & Bentovim 1992). This seems likely regardless of whether the survivor is male or female, heterosexual, gay, or lesbian.

For adolescents who are gay or lesbian, it is important that their experience is validated and that they receive appropriate support and assistance. This can be facilitated by a gay or lesbian counsellor, or by referral to an agency which specializes in the issues with which these young people are dealing. (See also 'Abuse Does Not Create Gays or Lesbians' in Chapter 1, pp. 13–14)

Sexualized behaviour

Adolescent girls who have been sexually abused sometimes behave in ways that indicate a preoccupation with sex. Usually this is manifest in premature involvement in sexual relationships, or in frequent changes of sexual partners. It is reflected in the high correlation between teenage pregnancies and history of sexual abuse. It can be explained in terms of early sexualization, low self-esteem, or difficulty setting limits. For some it reflects a search for acceptance and intimacy.

Some adolescent girls may engage in sexual activity in an attempt to triumph over the abuse experience. A young woman may become involved in sexual relationships as a way of proving to herself that she is able to control what happens. This is particularly evident in the tendency for some adolescent girls who have been abused to choose older boys or men as partners. These girls often consider that abuse has made them more mature than their contemporaries, but in choosing an older partner they also make themselves more vulnerable to further abuse. They want to prove to themselves that they are stronger than they were before, and that they can now participate as equals in a relationship with an older man. Frequently, however, these relationships are in fact quite unequal, and the adolescent experiences domination and revictimization while having the illusion of being in control.

Boys who have been abused sexually may also become involved in frequent sexual relationships, starting at an early age. As with girls this is related to premature sexualization, and to a need to counteract the abuse experience with experiences of feeling powerful in situations relating to sex.

There is a high incidence of sexual abuse amongst prostitutes, both male and female (Search 1988). For some, this too can be explained as an attempt to take control of sexual relationships. For some it involves a recognition learned through abuse, of the power that sex can give them. For others it reflects an avoidance of intimacy, or a loss of self-esteem, either of which can occur as a consequence of sexual abuse.

Sexually exploitative or abusive behaviour

Most adolescents who have been abused will not abuse others. However, there appears to be a higher rate of sexually abusive behaviour in adolescents who have been abused in some way (Watkins & Bentovim 1992). This is not surprising. Children who have been abused experience early sexualization, and a role-model of abusive behaviour. If they choose to experiment with sexual behaviour, they also are likely to experience some gratification, which in turn encourages them to repeat their activity.

In addition, abuse of others can be an expression of the anger adolescents feel about their own abuse. Probably this applies more to males, who seem more likely than females to express their anger in behaviour directed at others (Summit 1983).

Abusive behaviour is neither a necessary consequence of sexual abuse nor excused by it. Higher rates of abuse amongst adolescent offenders, however, compound the effects of one person's abuse by contributing to a cycle of abuse which can continue over generations. Fortunately social, moral, and legal considerations frequently deter adolescents from perpetuating this cycle. (See also 'Fear of Becoming an Abuser', p. 197.)

Substance abuse

Abuse of alcohol or drugs can emerge as a problem in adolescence, and increasingly in even younger age-groups. For those who have been sexually abused use of drugs is a way to forget, to feel good, to be 'their real self', to numb the pain, or to block out feelings completely. Combined with poor self-esteem it also may be a way of finding acceptance within a sub-culture which espouses non-conformity.

Substance abuse may lead to other difficulties, including poor school or job performance, and failure to develop other coping skills. In more serious instances it can lead to addiction, brain damage, and a criminal lifestyle.

Self-injury

Self-injury lies at the end of the spectrum of those self-defeating behaviours which may result from sexual abuse. Most commonly it involves cutting, burning, injecting, inserting foreign materials, picking skin, pulling hair, or breaking bones. It is an addictive behaviour which usually results from early childhood trauma, and most frequently affects females. While it is evident amongst all age groups, because of its progressive nature it can be a major problem by adolescence. It is described in more detail by Blume (1990).

Self-injury has been explained variously by survivors as an expression of self-blame and hatred of the body, as a way of converting deep-seated emotional pain into more manageable physical pain, as a way of exercising control, as an expression of anger, and as a way of blocking out feelings.

Self-injury needs to be treated as a choice rather than a disease. The therapist should explore with the client ways of controlling it, and help them to plan alternative ways of dealing with the feelings which lead to it.

Eating disorders

The whole range of eating disorders may occur as a response to sexual abuse. Anorexia nervosa has been explained by a number of abuse survivors as a way of feeling in control of themselves, and also as a way of displacing anxiety about abuse onto a more manageable form of anxiety about body shape. Bulimia nervosa has been described as a way of purging guilt or expressing self-disgust. Some abuse survivors over-eat, using food as a source of comfort. Others deliberately try to gain weight in the hope that they will become less attractive to others, and thus safer from sexual advances.

While the various eating disorders may have other explanations, there is evidence that they occur more frequently amongst those who have been sexually abused (Browne and Finkelhor 1986). Problems are exacerbated by the pressure on adolescents, particularly girls, to achieve a prescribed body shape. Eating disorders are thus more likely to occur at this stage, or to become more serious at adolescence.

Depression and anxiety

Both males and females who have been abused may experience depression and anxiety, but these responses are more common in females (see Chapter 1, pp. 6–7). As with other effects of abuse listed previously, they occur in younger age groups but may become acute at adolescence. For a few, the possibility of suicide becomes a serious concern. Psychosomatic illnesses and dependence on medication are also possible, and may contribute to other problems, such as time off work/school, difficulty concentrating, or the need for expensive medical investigation.

Running away

Running away from home becomes a realistic option by the stage of adolescence, and may be a way of escaping from ongoing abuse. Unless the adolescent has somewhere safe to go, however, it can leave them vulnerable to revictimization, or to becoming involved in a criminal lifestyle as a way of surviving.

Aggressive and antisocial behaviour

While abused people of all ages commonly respond with aggressive behaviour, adolescent aggression has the potential to create major problems for both males and females. Picking fights, destruction, marked disobedience, and a generally hostile or confrontational attitude can make adolescents a danger to themselves and others. Adolescents may also risk compounding the effects of abuse with the legal and social consequences of their own aggressive behaviour.

Sexual difficulties

Problems with sexual performance or response are consequences of abuse which may first become obvious at adolescence. When this effect of abuse is reflected in anxiety or avoidance of sex it can heighten self-consciousness and lower self-esteem. It need not have major long-term repercussions, however, and can be dealt with effectively with education and counselling. Therapy which focuses on the development of trust and communication within a specific relationship is particularly helpful. Resources for dealing with sexual difficulties are described in more detail in Chapter 11.

Anger with a non-abusing parent

Anger indirectly related to the abuse can be a major issue for adolescents, especially if they feel that they were not adequately protected by others. Sometimes, this anger is greater than the anger with the abuser, and becomes a major focus of therapy. It is important to acknowledge and validate this anger, but it is also important for the client to place responsibility for abuse where it belongs. Clarifying the distinction between abuse and failure to protect is helpful at this stage.

Rarely does a parent want their child to be harmed. It is possible, however, that they may fail to provide adequate protection, either through lack of information or through their own sense of powerlessness. A useful way to help adolescents reach an understanding of their situation of supposed neglect is to ask a series of questions, rather than try to persuade them to accept a particular viewpoint, for example:

'Do you think your parents would have wanted something like this to happen to you?'

'If you were a parent would you want your child to be harmed in any way?'

'What do you think made it difficult for your parents to give you the protection you needed?'

'Do you think anything in your parents' history made it difficult for them to recognize the signs that something was wrong?'

Clients may also need help to express their anger within the therapy room, or in the form of a family meeting or letter to the parent concerned.

Difficulty in relationships

Loss of trust, fear of intimacy, and perhaps even fear of abusing others, are common problems for adolescents who have been sexually abused, and contribute to difficulties in relationships generally. This is reflected in difficulties with both same-sex and opposite-sex friendships, and can lead to withdrawal from friends and avoidance of social situations. In turn it impinges on their self-esteem and their ability to enjoy satisfying and healthy sexual relationships.

ISSUES IN THERAPY

Just as sexual abuse may have specific implications for adolescents, work with adolescents has specific implications for therapists. This section describes some of the more obvious issues for sexual abuse therapy with adolescents.

Reluctance to talk

In our clinical experience one of the significant differences between working with adolescents and working with younger children is that adolescents make it clear whether or not they are willing to co-operate. This is a problem for boys particularly, who appear to be more difficult to engage in therapy at adolescence. Wherever possible we need to identify the restraints that prevent clients from engaging in therapy.

Such issues as shame, embarrassment, or lack of trust, may make it difficult for them to confide. They may not like a particular therapist or style of work. They may be ambivalent towards the offender, or even have a sense of loyalty to him which makes it difficult to describe what happened, or to expose him in any way. They may simply not have reached a stage where they feel willing or ready to engage in therapy.

Nobody can or should be forced into therapy. When an adolescent does not wish to engage in therapy their decision must be respected. The adolescent and their family may be given information about other resources, and advised about help available should they seek assistance in the future.

When the adolescent is prepared to continue with therapy but finds it difficult to talk, we need to address the restraints that get in their way. For example, we can model talking about abuse by being open and direct, and discussing it without embarrassment. We can also help them to direct any shame or guilt experienced onto the offender. We can normalize loss of trust, and facilitate an understanding of how other relationships, including their relationship with the therapist, might be affected by abuse. We must also be prepared to take time over developing the therapeutic relationship, and to proceed at the client's pace.

The therapeutic relationship

The nature of the relationship between the therapist and the adolescent client is an important factor in developing the necessary co-operation for work together. The therapist must walk a very narrow path in developing a special relationship with the adolescent whilst remaining in the therapist role. This includes refusing invitations to take sides in parent–adolescent conflicts. Comments made in support of the adolescent may be used by them at home as ammunition in a dispute with parents, and the therapist runs the very serious risk of losing the parents' confidence and co-operation.

The adolescent may be very critical of their parents, but it is almost invariably a mistake for the therapist to align themselves with the adolescent against a parent. Not only does this risk losing the parents' support, but it may invoke the adolescent's natural tendency to defend their family against comments from outsiders. This can leave the therapist isolated when volatile family relationships and changing alliances shift between sessions.

Adolescents are likely to be less trusting than younger children and more sensitive to any sign that the therapist lacks commitment, interest, integrity, or the necessary therapeutic skills. As in sexual-abuse counselling generally, it is essential that the therapist is seen to be honest and reliable, and that particular care is taken to avoid the things that have gone wrong in the previous abusive relationship. This includes taking care to be reliable and predictable about appointments, and negotiating ahead about times when we will, and will not, be available.

Confidentiality

Establishing clear rules of confidentiality at the beginning of therapy is one way in which we nurture our client's trust. In doing this we need to be quite explicit about what is not confidential. This may include defining what information will be given to parents and what will be included in reports to other agencies.

Adolescents are very sensitive about confidentiality and may not want anything to be shared with their family. Usually there is room for the adolescent to have considerable choice about confidentiality, and the issue needs to be discussed in detail. We might ask, for example, 'What do you want me to say if your Mum or Dad asks how things are going?' or 'How much can I tell your social worker when he joins us at our meeting tomorrow?'

We also need to be clear about any limits to confidentiality imposed by legal or ethical considerations. We do not guarantee confidentiality if there is a danger that a client may harm themselves or others, nor if we believe that others may be at risk from the same offender.

Contracts

Establishing a clear contract for therapy is another essential factor in avoiding confusion and distrust. Adolescents need to know why they are coming to therapy and what is likely to happen. They need to know that they are the client, and they need to be clear about the role of their family in the therapy process. (See also 'Joining' in Chapter 4, pp. 45–46)

Maintaining the focus of therapy

Maintaining a focus on sexual abuse can be very difficult in therapy with adolescents. They are likely to bring many other, often more immediate, issues to therapy. While we may need to respond to these issues, it is important that we do not lose sight of the primary goal of dealing with the abuse experience.

Should current events in the adolescent's life make it too difficult to focus on therapy for abuse, this needs to be discussed. The adolescent may be asked whether it is the right time for sexual-abuse counselling to proceed, and a new contract might be negotiated to clarify the purpose of therapy. It may also be necessary to discuss this with the family.

Self-disclosure

Issues about self-disclosure by the therapist are more likely to arise in therapy with adolescents than with younger children. Clients may want to know, for example, if we have been abused ourselves, or how old we were when we had our first sexual experience. We must be careful to be honest with adolescents as they are very sensitive to evasion and lies. This does not mean, however, that we cannot refuse to answer some questions, preferably providing a good reason. We also need to be wary of answering in such detail that it shifts the focus of therapy away from the client.

Reference to our lives outside therapy, mention of our families, and photographs on the wall, all represent a form of self-disclosure which has meaning for both therapist and client. It is important that we are aware of our intention when we self-disclose, and that we are sensitive to the meaning it may have for our clients. For example, a family photograph or reference to some event in our own family can serve as a painful reminder to an adolescent who is lacking in family support. It can also serve to distract from the purpose of therapy by taking the focus away from the client's needs.

Support systems

Ensuring that adequate support systems are in place becomes an issue for therapy with those adolescents who are socially or emotionally isolated from their families. Many in this age group lack the resources to function safely independently, though they may not be prepared to acknowledge this. They may also be too old to enlist the same degree of support from social service agencies as would younger children in need of care.

It is important to develop a list of places where adolescents can go if in crisis, and to ensure that they have someone they can contact for help 24 hours per day. A telephone contact for the therapist might be provided, or a system of letter-writing initiated to provide a link between adolescent and therapist between sessions.

Flexibility about location of interview

Providing a comfortable place to talk is essential for any therapy, and for some adolescents this includes escaping from the confines of an office. Going for a walk or sitting in an appropriate place outside may help to facilitate discussion, and is particularly helpful for those nicotine addicts who are used to lighting up a cigarette at times of stress.

As in therapy for children, strict guidelines need to be adhered to when an adolescent is taken away from the usual meeting place. This is important for the safety of both client and therapist, and is dealt with in more detail in Chapter 7, pp. 121–122.

The role of friends in therapy

Bringing friends to therapy may be an adolescent's way of enlisting support for themselves or getting help for others. It can raise some difficult issues for therapists, especially when it happens unexpectedly and we are not clear about the role that our client expects their friends to play in therapy.

It is important not to be diverted from the focus of therapy, and friends brought as support usually are best made welcome in the waiting room, but not included in the therapy session. Friends in need of help for themselves can be given the information they need about resources available. In most cases they are best referred to another therapist to avoid issues of confidentiality and possible competition for one therapist's attention.

The therapist's response to the adolescent

The feelings evoked in the therapist by an adolescent client need particular attention. Normal aspects of adolescence such as emotional volatility, swinging attitudes, and experimenting with new behaviours often are exacerbated by sexual abuse and the process of therapy. The adolescent's response to the therapist may alternate between hostility and co-operation. Their behaviour may evoke feelings such as sympathy, anxiety, frustration, or anger in the therapist.

In all cases we need to be clear about how we are responding, and how our feelings might be affecting our therapy. If we are aware of any strong feelings we need to stop and think, and, where necessary, seek supervision. If we are doing anything different from the usual we need to be particularly clear in acknowledging what is happening and why. Outside supervision provides a valuable check in such situations.

Denial of vulnerability

Adolescents find it particularly threatening to admit to vulnerability, whether it be in the past, present, or future. This can present a major stumbling block for therapy.

Adolescents may blame themselves for abuse rather than admit to past vulnerability, and may not recognize their vulnerability to revictimization in a current unequal relationship. They are also not likely to respond positively to a direct statement of opinion about these matters from the therapist.

It is preferable, therefore, to take an indirect approach to this problem. Adolescents can be helped to think about it for themselves with a series of careful non-blaming questions designed to help them make their own discoveries. Questions which help an adolescent discard self-blame by acknowledging relative powerlessness in the past might focus on differences in the relative age and size of adolescent and abuser, on the child's habit of obedience to elders, or on the fears that get in the way of assertion and disclosure. (See also 'Self-blame' p. 186 and 'Placing Responsibility Where it Belongs', pp. 37–38.)

In therapy with all adolescents it may be helpful to draw out the issues of self-blame, anticipating the client's concerns by asking such questions as:

'Why do you think he chose you?'

'Do you ever worry that you could have done something earlier to stop him?'

'Often I see girls and boys who blame themselves for what happened: Is this something you ever do?'

An adolescent who is being dominated or even revictimized in a current relationship can be helped to understand how the abuse has affected them. They can be asked questions which help them to identify a non-exploitative relationship that would meet their needs. They are then in a position to examine current relationships in a more objective way.

Examples of the sort of question that may be helpful include :

'How big were you when you were abused?'

'How big was your stepfather?'

'Are kids usually taught to do what adults tell them?'

'What happened in your family if you didn't do what you were told?'

'Did you get the idea that you had done something wrong?'

'Did you think your Mum might be really upset or angry if she knew?'

'What effect do you think the fear had on you?'

'What were you afraid might happen if you told anyone about it?'

'When do you think it's OK for two people to have sex?'

'Do you think anyone should force another person to have sex?'

'Do you think men and women should have equal power in a relationship?'

'What sort of things make a relationship equal?'

'Are there times when you agree to do something your boyfriend wants just to keep him happy?'

'What would happen if you said "No"?'

'Do you think you got a message from your past abuse that your feelings didn't count?'

'How do you think that has affected you?'

'A lot of people who have been abused find it difficult to stand up for themselves. Is that a problem for you?'

Fear of becoming an abuser

Some adolescent survivors of abuse fear that they may become abusers themselves. Therapists need to convey clearly to adolescents that they are responsible for their behaviour and that a history of abuse is not an excuse for abusing others. Like survivors of all ages, adolescents need information that abusive behaviour does not necessarily follow abuse, and is in fact a choice made by the perpetrator. They also need reassurance that they are less likely to have any problems in future because they are getting the help they need now.

It is helpful to bring fear of abusing out into the open. For example, we might ask clients questions about whether they have ever wondered what it would be like to abuse others, and about strategies they could develop to ensure that this never happens. Similarly, questions which focus on the pain which abuse has brought them can help to highlight their determination not to hurt others in the same way.

It is also helpful to reframe thoughts of abusing as a way of trying to make sense of their own abuse experience. It is quite normal for them to wonder what the perpetrator felt, as they try to make sense of his abusive actions. Clearly there is a vast difference between normalizing the thought and condoning the action.

Shame and anxiety relating to sexual arousal

Sexual arousal at the time of abuse can be the source of extreme anxiety or shame for an adolescent client. Sometimes it is helpful to normalize it as a sign that their body was functioning as it should. The ability to respond sexually can be described as a normal reaction to stimulation. It can also be reframed as a way their body coped with the abuse experience, a way of blocking out the fear, confusion, and pain.

Another useful way of dealing with this problem is to ask the adolescent whether they would have chosen to have the arousal experience in those circumstances. Once they acknowledge that they would not have wanted it we can then make it clear that it is not a matter of choice, and therefore not a matter for shame. It was a matter of the body responding to circumstances over which it had no control.

Ambivalence regarding the offender

Conflicting feelings about the offender can be issues for people of all ages who have been abused. While we should not assume that all survivors will feel ambivalent towards the abuser, such feelings need to be acknowledged by the therapist when they do occur. It is not sufficient to only acknowledge feelings of anger and disgust when there are also feelings of love and loyalty.

In more extreme examples the relationship with the offender may have met needs which were not met in other relationships. The client may have enjoyed feeling that they were 'special' to someone. They even may have thought that they were 'in love' with the abuser. Disclosure may only occur when they discover that someone else is being abused by the same person, when they recognize the full impact of what has happened, or when someone else discovers the abuse.

The therapist who fails to acknowledge a client's conflicting feelings about an abuser does not understand the full impact of the abuse, and may feed into feelings of confusion and guilt. The progress of therapy will be blocked until these issues are dealt with.

Conversely, we must not imply in any way that survivors *should* experience feelings of ambivalence. It is a mistake also to question a client extensively about mixed feelings, when they are clearly conveying a reaction of pure hatred or anger towards the abuser.

Safety education

Education about sexual safety is particularly important for adolescent survivors. As we have previously noted, adolescence is a developmental stage where young people are usually experimenting with sexual behaviour and are vulnerable to peer pressure. They may become sexually attractive to others before they develop the self-confidence and social skills to deal with unwanted advances. Sexual harassment, rape, and attempted rape by acquaintances are common (see also p. 184).

For a number of reasons the adolescent who previously has been sexually abused can be particularly vulnerable to sexual harassment or victimization. They may be thought of as a 'sex-object' by others or even by themselves. They are more likely to be sexually active and to have difficulty setting limits. (See also 'Poor Sexual Self-esteem', p. 185.)

One of the basic concepts that the adolescent may need help with is the right to say 'No' to any unwanted sexual advances, at any time, and at any stage of sexual activity. We help them to get in touch with their own feelings about what they want and do not want, and to set their own boundaries.

We teach adolescents to say 'No' clearly and forcefully, and to accompany it with congruent body language. Planning ahead is one way of doing this. For example, they can prepare such excuses as 'My mother won't let me' to avoid a particular situation, without having to admit that they do not want do be part of it. We also tell them that they have a right to be angry if their limits are not respected, and encourage them to get help when necessary.

We also encourage adolescents to trust their own intuition: If a situation feels uncomfortable or risky, it is wise to get out of it. There may be indications from another person's body language that their safety is threatened, although nothing explicit has been said to indicate this. Watching what other people do and not just what they say is a useful skill to encourage. For example, noticing when another person stands too close, touches too much, or tries to get them alone.

While we encourage adolescents to take care of themselves by avoiding situations in which they may be vulnerable, we also stress that they are not to blame if their own clear limits are violated at any stage. It is important to stress that the abuser is always responsible. Adolescents can be subject to criticism and self-blame if they get into abusive situations because they lack the protection of wisdom and experience. Even carelessness does not make them responsible for another person's abusive behaviour.

PART 5

THERAPY WITH ADULTS

11

TOOLS FOR THERAPY
WITH ADULTS

As we noted in Chapter 7, it is important for therapists to have a working knowledge of a variety of tools for therapy. There are several major reasons for this:

- Some tools are more appropriate for a particular age group. Those described in this chapter are most suitable for adults and for some adolescents. They apply to adults abused as children and to those individuals abused more recently in their adult life.
- Different clients respond more to some methods than to others, and feel more comfortable with some methods than with others. Providing a variety of options allows clients to choose methods they feel comfortable with, and to reject others. This is an important part of empowerment for people who have experienced the powerlessness of abuse.
- Different therapists prefer different methods, finding that some fit better with their personal style, their belief systems, and their areas of competence and confidence.
- Some of the tools we describe in this chapter are more useful at a particular stage or stages in the therapy process. A variety of techniques is therefore needed to assist the client at different stages of therapy.
- The variety of ways that our clients are affected by sexual abuse calls for a variety of responses. We need tools that address specifically beliefs, emotional responses, physical symptoms, and behaviour.
- A review of the research suggests that a combination of therapy that activates memories of the abuse with therapy that addresses unhelpful beliefs about it, is likely to be more effective than either type of therapy

alone (Resick & Schnicke 1990). This is why in our work we combine different ideas for taking the client back over the abuse experience with ideas that deal at a more cognitive level with the client's perceptions of the abuse and its effects.

For clients who have been traumatized by abuse, an important part of therapy is for them to feel empowered to face the abuse experience and to express the feelings that this engenders. Huge steps towards healing can be taken when the client 'revisits' the abuse scene and rescues herself or himself in some way from the sense of powerlessness associated with the abuse (Parks 1990). Retraumatization may occur, however, if memories of the abuse increase the sense of powerlessness previously experienced.

In this chapter we have included a number of methods designed to help the client face the abuse experience in a way that is both safe and effective. The therapist can choose the technique that seems most appropriate for a particular client, or may use a variety of techniques at different times with the same person. These techniques are all used to create a different experience of the abuse.

The different methods that we use most commonly in sexual abuse therapy with adults are described here in detail under the following headings:
- Building a Powerful Part of Self
- Identifying a Powerful Person
- The Rescue Scene — Drawing and Action Methods
- Fantasy
- Solution Talk
- Writing Exercises
- Thought Stopping
- Suicide Prevention
- Dealing with Sexual Difficulties
- Stress Management
- Relaxation Exercises
- Anchoring a Resource
- Visual Kinaesthetic Dissociation
- Trance/Hypnosis.

BUILDING A POWERFUL PART OF SELF

The technique that we call 'Building a Powerful Part of Self' is particularly useful because it acts quickly to put clients in touch with their own strengths and wisdom. It enables them to experience a new sense of their own power at an emotional level. This sense of power, therefore, becomes more completely integrated as part of themselves, than it would if it were restricted to an intellectual understanding.

The technique combines a simple trance-like experience with the development of a new and more powerful role within the client. The use of trance is described in more detail later in the chapter (pp. 245–246), and is based on the work of Milton Erickson, Richard Bandler, and John Grinder. In this exercise it involves careful choice of words, slowing the pace of speech, speaking relatively softly, matching the rhythm of the client's breathing, and regulating the tone of voice. This facilitates the client's ability to hear and respond to new information while retaining the ability to reject ideas that do not suit them.

The aim of the exercise is to develop a new role within the client that embodies power, wisdom, and self-nurturing. Ideas about the development of new roles are based on the work of Jacob Moreno (1975). According to Moreno's Role Theory, each person develops a variety of roles, and consequently behaves differently in different situations. These roles are being changed continually on the basis of information from the environment and from social interactions.

Using Moreno's model we can see that many survivors of sexual abuse have developed roles (made up of beliefs, behaviours, and emotional and physical responses) that are unhelpful and self-defeating. These roles do not reflect their potential as human beings. The goal of the therapist, therefore, is to help the client to develop new roles that enable them to live their life more fully.

One of the roles that we help our clients to develop is the powerful part of themselves. The aim of this is to build within the client a resource or support 'person' before entering the abuse scene. Development of this role also provides them with an ongoing resource for facing difficulties and solving problems.

This exercise could be used any time after the therapist has established some rapport with the client and has gathered basic information about the client's concerns. It requires that the room is set up with four chairs, two to be used at different times by the client, and two by the therapist.

The basic steps towards building a powerful part of self

1 Explain the process and establish a contract to proceed. This includes obtaining the client's informed consent.
2 Facilitate a trance-like experience with careful choice of language, slow pace, repetition, and quiet, regular tone of voice. Usually the therapist sits just outside the client's line of vision to avoid distracting them — a place close to the client, a little to the side, and behind.
3 Set the context, drawing from the knowledge of the client, for example:

'There are many things going on for you at the moment. Before we talk about the things that concern you, you need to feel ready to face them. We will spend some time today getting to know a part of you that may be able to help.'

'What I mean, is that each of us has different parts. There is the part that is funny, the part that is sad, the part that is adventurous. Sometimes a part of you may doubt yourself, while at other times you are aware of a strong part of yourself, a part that helps you to do things you didn't think were possible. Today we are going to get to know a part of you that is supportive, caring, wise, and knows how to help you through a difficult time. This is a strong part of you. We are going to spend some time today creating an image of what that strong part of you looks like.'

4   Ask the client to picture, seated in the chair opposite them, a strong, caring person capable of providing support and solutions for their problems, for example:

'I want you to look at that chair, and as you look, think carefully about what you see, about what image begins to form. It may be an imaginary person, or a person you know from your past ... someone who represents strength, wisdom, and caring. It may be someone you have yet to meet, or something else, like a mountain, river or tree. This image may form slowly or quickly. Give yourself time, and as you look at the chair notice what starts to take shape. Let me know when you have your picture of this strong, caring image.'

5   Ask for details of the person or image. If it's a person, ask about their gender, physical features, the clothes they wear, their facial expression, their personality, and their name. As the process continues, make opportunities to imbed suggestions relating to their strength and wisdom, for example:

'As she sits there staring back at you, you are aware of the expression on her face. This strong, caring, and wise person ... You know this person really well, you know that she could support you and give you good advice about anything that was bothering you.'

6   Ask the client to think about a problem they have, and to formulate a question for the powerful person — a specific request for advice about the problem. The client is then requested to ask the question, either silently or out loud, as they prefer.

7   Ask the client to reverse roles with the powerful person:
'I want you to come over here and be Betty.'
This requires that the client shifts to the opposite seat, where the powerful person was pictured previously. The therapist also shifts, remaining just outside the client's immediate line of vision as before.

8 Help the client to develop their new role, repeating the words used previously by the client to describe the powerful person, for example:
   'You are now Betty. You are about forty, with a quiet manner, and a
   kind smile. ... Take your time to settle into being Betty. ... How do you
   sit, Betty? ... How are you holding your head? ... Where are your feet?'
9 The client, in the role of powerful person, is asked to picture herself or
   himself in the other chair, for example:
   'Betty, can you see Jan over there? ... What is she wearing? ... What is
   she feeling as she sits there? ... How do you feel about Jan as you see
   her sitting there?'
10 As the powerful person, the client is asked if they heard the question that
   was directed to them, for example:
   'Betty, Jan has asked you a question. Do you know what it is?'
   The client is then given a pen and paper and asked to write a letter
   answering the question. The first sentence of the letter is to begin with
   the words 'I love you because ... ', for example:
   'Betty, you have the strength that Jan needs at the moment. I want you
   to write her a letter answering her question, and giving her the advice
   she needs. Take as long as you need to do this. I would like you to start
   with the words "Dear Jan, I love you because ... ". Let me know when
   you have finished.'
11 When the letter is completed, the client is asked to place it on the empty
   chair opposite, where they sat originally.
12 The client is then asked to reverse roles and return to their chair, collecting
   the letter before sitting down. The therapist also returns to their original position. The client is asked to read the letter, silently if they prefer,
   for example:
   'Now I want you to come back here and be Jan ... You are now Jan,
   and Betty is over there. Jan, you asked Betty a question which she has
   answered. I want you to read the answer to yourself, silently or out loud,
   whichever you prefer. As you read it you may find her answer really
   helpful, and something you can keep with you. Or it may only answer
   your question partly, or not at all. Take from it what you find helpful.'
13 The client is given as much time as they need to study the letter. They
   are then advised that the powerful person is a part of them, and asked
   to integrate that part in some way. The therapist suggests, for example,
   that they may like to go over to the second chair and physically 'pick up'
   the powerful person, holding him or her close. Alternatively, they may
   remain still, silently absorbing a sense of this powerful self.
     This technique of building a powerful part of self is illustrated fully in the
case example at the end of the chapter (pp. 249–252). It can be a very pow-

erful emotional experience for clients, and can also surprise them with the wisdom of their own advice expressed in the letters they write.

IDENTIFYING A POWERFUL PERSON

Although usually we work to help our clients to construct a sense of power within themselves, some people prefer to focus on a source of strength which is more separate. This would be represented by people or identities whom the client respects, admires, and acknowledges as a positive influence. By imagining the presence of a separate powerful person or identity beside them, they identify a resource that can always be available to them.

This identification can be done variously, just as there are different ways in which we help our clients to create a sense of power within themselves. One client may choose to have an empty chair beside her to represent God's presence in the room. Another may picture her grandmother seated next to her. In both of these examples the client is able to feel supported through some of the difficult stages of therapy, and to check regularly with this source of strength and caring for affirmation and advice.

Similarly, people from real life, from novels and films, as well as fantasy heroes and heroines can be enlisted by our clients to accompany them on their therapeutic journey. The therapist may assist by getting them to visualize these support people in detail, or even by getting clients to draw pictures of their mentors. We can prompt our clients to ask these people for advice and encouragement. We might ask, for example:

'Can you feel the presence of your grandmother taking care of you here today? … What advice does she have for you? … What does she think of the courage you have shown?'

Maori colleagues have advised us about a cultural variation of the 'Building a Powerful Part of Self' exercise, in which the image of the powerful person seated opposite is elicited as before, but no role-reversal occurs. This is because the powerful person may be an ancestor or god, and it would be inappropriate for a human to take on their role. Nevertheless the ancestor or god would be considered by clients to be part of themselves, and a significant ongoing source of strength, wisdom, and caring.

THE RESCUE SCENE: DRAWING AND ACTION METHODS

In this exercise of taking the client over the abuse experience we combine drawing with action. The details of how we do this are illustrated in the case study at the end of the chapter. Briefly, the process is as follows:

1 Establish a contract, explaining what the process involves, and obtaining the client's agreement to proceed.

2 Empower the client to talk about the details of the abuse by putting them in touch with their strengths in some way. This might involve, for example, making contact with their 'powerful part of self' if this exercise has been used previously (see pp. 203–207). Alternatively, they can be reminded of who they are now and of the strengths that they have been able to acknowledge earlier in therapy. Check with this strong part of them that it is safe to proceed.

   Continue to take the client back to this sense of their own strength whenever the process becomes difficult. If they become anxious or upset, remind them of their strengths and of the support available to them, before checking whether it is safe to proceed. If the exercise for 'Building a Powerful Part of Self' has been used, they can reverse roles with the powerful person for advice and/or reassurance.

   If the client feels unable to proceed, stop at this stage. Further work may be needed before the client feels sufficiently empowered to resume this exercise at another session, or before another way of going over the abuse scene is attempted.

3 'Warm-up' to the abuse scene by eliciting background information, for example:
   'How old were you?' ... 'What sort of a child were you then?' ... 'Where did you live?'

4 Begin to get background information about the abuse, such as where it occurred, how they came to be there, who else was there. Start with the less threatening details, and keep the pace slow. Make use of opportunities to reframe, seed ideas and normalize, for example:
   'That must have been awful.' ... 'So that's how he tricked you.' ... 'He was much older than you — he had no right to do that, did he?' ... 'How did he manage to get alongside you?'

5 Ask about the offender, who he was, his name, what he looked like. Ask the client to draw him. Provide a large sheet of paper and a selection of felt-tip pens. The drawing may be of his face only, or of his whole body. It can be a very rough sketch or a precise impression, depending on the client's preference and artistic skills.

6 Ask the client to place the drawing of the offender somewhere in the room, for example:

'If you were to put him anywhere in this room, where would you like to put him?'

7 Ask the client to draw an occasion when they were abused by this person. As they draw, elicit the details: What was happening? ... What were they thinking? ... What were they feeling? ... What was said? ... What memories remain the strongest?

8 Ask the client to stand over the drawing, absorbing its impact. Then ask them to place the scene aside somewhere in the room.

9 Go back to the drawing of the offender. Ask the client to stand over him and address him. If necessary, warm them up to the idea, by using their own words. For example:

'There he is, with that sly grin of his. He was 43 and you were only 12. He's ruined 10 years of your life. What do you think of him now?'

The therapist may also prompt the client to express their feelings, for example:

'Tell him how frightened you were.' ... 'Tell him what you think of him.' ... 'Tell him how it affected you.'

Encourage the client to speak assertively, perhaps by joining in or by acting as a role model, repeating their words in louder, more powerful tones. Ensure that they speak directly to the offender, not just talk about him. If they find this too difficult, it may be helpful to ask them to reverse roles with their 'powerful self' to elicit advice about what needs to happen next. Some way of stepping out of the scene to get more in touch with a sense of their own strengths may be required before the client is able to proceed.

10 Find out what the client would like to do to the offender. Allow them to express their anger physically, by stomping on the drawing, ripping, cutting, screwing it up, and/or burning it. Get them to dispose of the remnants as they choose.

11 Go back to the drawing of the abuse scene. Ask the client to carefully cut herself/himself out of the scene, and to put this part of the drawing in a safe place. For example, some may choose a pocket, brief case, or handbag. They may first like to address the child representing themself in the drawing, offering comfort and reassurance. The client is then encouraged to dispose of the rest of the scene as they see fit.

12 If the exercise for 'Building a Powerful Part of Self' has been used, ask the client to check with the powerful 'person' that it is all right to leave the process at this stage. They do this by asking the powerful person if it is all right to finish, and then reversing roles with them for the answer.

They can also seek affirmation for what they have done, before reintegrating the powerful person back into themselves.

If the exercise for 'Building a Powerful Part of Self' has not been used, help the client to get back in touch with the strong person that they are now, check that they feel all right about finishing here, and ask them to affirm themselves. The therapist also offers affirmation for the difficulties they have faced and for the powerful steps they have taken in dealing with their abuse.

13 Make a final check that the client feels OK. Discuss what they might do to celebrate and/or take care of themselves after the session. Ensure that they will have any support they may need between sessions.

The case study at the end of this chapter illustrates this way of using Drawing and Action Methods in more detail.

FANTASY

Fantasy is useful in therapy with both adults and children. Sometimes it involves relatively simple ideas, but at other times it requires advanced verbal skills and an understanding of difficult concepts. Most commonly we use fantasy in work with adults to:

- Create a 'safe place' from which the client can think about the abuse.
- Dialogue with the child who was abused.
- Vent anger.
- 'Rescue' the client from the role of victim.
- Deal with nightmares.
- Plan for the future.

Providing a safe place from which to view the abuse and/or the abuser

Describing the details of the abuse may be very difficult and painful for the client, so it can be helpful for therapist and client to first create an image of a safe place from which to view the abuse. This safe place can also serve as a retreat if the client needs to escape from memories or feelings that are too painful.

We begin by asking the client to describe a place where they feel warm, comfortable, and safe. As they start to describe this place we help them to 'be' there in fantasy by shifting to the present tense. We put them in touch with the sensory experience of being in this place with such questions as:

'Are you sitting or standing?' ... 'What can you see?' ...'What are the sounds that you hear?' ... 'What are you feeling as you sink into the armchair?'

Once established in this safe place the client can begin to view the abuse scene. If it becomes too difficult we remind them that they are safe. When necessary we help them to experience being in the fantasy place again, recreating the image with the details described previously by the client, for example:

'Remember that sunny courtyard you told me about?' ... 'Can you see the high walls, with the ivy growing across them?' ... 'Remember how safe you feel there. Can you feel the warmth of the sun?' ... 'Can you see the flowers in the garden?' ... 'What does it feel like to be back there, with the fresh air, and the birds calling, and that lovely peaceful sound of the bees droning?'

Some people like to distance themselves from the abuse scene by picturing it on an imaginary television or cinema screen. Similarly, they can imagine themselves to be invisible, or as a bird hovering overhead, or as standing behind a one-way screen. In this way they are able to see the abuser while he is unable to see them.

These methods of viewing traumatic experiences with a minimum of discomfort represent simple forms of visual kinaesthetic dissociation, a method which is described in detail later in this chapter.

Dialogue with the child

Another way in which we use fantasy is to help adults who have been abused as children. Through fantasy we facilitate a dialogue between the adult client and the child who was abused. The adult is asked to picture themselves as a child sitting in the therapy room, and is prompted to ask the child questions about the abuse. They are also helped to make explicit statements to the child which provide information, comfort, and affirmation. This method has the advantage of enabling the client to recall the details of what happened, express their feelings relating to the abuse, and to deal with unhelpful beliefs and emotional responses.

An important part of this process is ensuring that the client is ready to face the memories of the abuse. This can be done by explaining the exercise, obtaining a clear contract to proceed, helping the client to get in touch with their strengths, and ensuring that they have people available to support them as needed. They also need reassurance that they do not have to proceed any further than is comfortable, and that they can stop the process at any time they wish. We might say, for example:

'The person you are now, with all your strengths and resources, has come through a lot and survived. That person now feels that it is safe to talk about some of the frightening things that have happened. If the feelings get too frightening or upsetting, remember that you are no longer a child, but an adult who has learned how to be strong and wise, and who knows how to take care of herself. If you decide that this is not the right time to proceed, we can stop the process at any time you choose.'

We then help the client to get a clear sense of their adult self in their present circumstances. This is important to give them a sense of strength, safety, and distance from the powerlessness and vulnerability of the child who was abused. One of the most effective ways to do this is through questioning:

'You sit here as an adult. How old are you?' ... 'How tall are you?' ... 'Are you safe in this room?' ... 'What are some of your achievements?'

The next step is to help the adult to picture the child sitting in the room. At different times this child can be pictured at different ages, but for this exercise it is helpful at some stage to picture the child at the age when the abuse occurred. Concrete details are elicited about how she looks, what she wears, how she sits, what name she is known by. To aid in the fantasy, once again questions are asked in the present tense. We start with simple questions to elicit an image of the child's physical appearance, for example:

'How old is she?' ... 'How does she wear her hair?' ... 'What does she wear?'

These are followed by more sensitive questions about the child's emotional state, for example:

'Is she a happy child or a sad child?' ... 'How is she feeling about being in this room today?'

In this last exchange an increased sense of safety is achieved by referring to the child as 'she' and to the adult as 'you'. This helps the client to feel separate from the vulnerable child, and to maintain a sense of themselves as an adult with strengths and resources which they previously lacked. If they become upset by memories of the abuse they can be reminded that they are now an adult, that they are in a safe place, and that they now have many skills for coping.

When ready, the adult is encouraged to engage in a dialogue with the child, which is prompted by the therapist, for example:

'Margaret, ask Margie if she feels ready to talk.'

With appropriate prompting from the therapist, the adult then can ask the child questions about the abuse, and report the answers back to the therapist. When opportunities arise, the therapist prompts the adult to praise the child for her bravery, or to comfort her distress. Opportunities are also taken to help the adult reassure the child with information, and to normalize, reframe, and seed ideas. The adult client thus develops their own resources to help the child.

The therapist also helps the client to maintain a sense of their own power by providing ongoing support and affirmation, and by ensuring that the client is able to control the direction in which the exercise proceeds. This can be offered directly through such statements as, 'You are doing well', or by offering choices, for example, 'What else would you like to ask her?' or 'What do you think she needs now?' It can also be offered in a more indirect way, by prompting the client to affirm herself or himself, for example:

'Margaret, tell Margie that you have learned a lot since then. Tell her that you have a lot of resources now and that you know what she needs.'

From time to time the therapist may also suggest that the adult checks with the child whether they wish to continue. The 'child' should be allowed to avoid, distract, or 'go out and play' if the questions are too difficult or if they are not ready to answer.

If the adult becomes too distressed they should be gently brought back to the present and reminded of how old they are now, that they are in a safe place, and that they have lots of maturity, wisdom, and strength which has helped them to survive. They should be affirmed for the progress they have made, and allowed to stop at any time they choose.

Successful variations of this exercise can be used by asking the client to alternate the roles of adult and child, changing chairs as they change roles. The dialogue continues as before, with the client being brought back to their adult role any time the 'child' becomes distressed or needs attention or information.

Alternatively, concrete descriptions of both adult and child can be elicited, but both are described in the third person as 'she'. The therapist obtains a description of the adult by phrasing questions slightly differently from those previously quoted, for example:

'The adult sits here now. How old is she?' ... 'How does she sit?' ... 'What is she wearing?'

The exercise continues as previously described, but now allows the client to be an observer of the dialogue between adult and child and so to look at the abuse without the same level of emotional involvement. The distance inherent in this 'observer' position creates a sense of safety and allows for the development of a new understanding. Whenever the client becomes overwhelmed by feelings about the abuse they can be brought back to the present with reminders that they are observing events from a safe distance.

Venting anger

Fantasy can be a very powerful way for survivors to express their anger about the abuse and how it has affected them. It is particularly useful for people who do not feel comfortable using action methods.

As we have noted previously (Chapter 4), it is important not to stay in the abuse scene once the client has described the details of what happened. If we are to provide a different experience of the abuse we must move on immediately. One of the ways in which this can be done is to help the client to develop fantasies about what they would like to happen to the offender. We begin this process by asking such questions as:

'What would you like to do to him now?' or

'Have you thought about what you would like to happen to this guy?'

Many people have already developed some favourite fantasies of revenge which they are only too delighted to share. Having their anger validated, their fantasies normalized, and the opportunity to vent feelings in a safe place, is an empowering experience and a vital part of therapy. Sometimes the client gets enormous pleasure from sharing their fantasies with an understanding therapist, and the fun engendered can be therapeutic in itself.

The therapist helps to develop the fantasy by drawing out the details. The client could choose to be themselves, or take on the role of a hero figure with whom they can identify. They could, for example, choose to be a powerful figure from current affairs, history, film, or legend. Or they may choose to be themselves, appropriately armed and protected with weapons that help them to feel powerful. They might use long spears, for example, which help to keep them at a safe distance, or strong hands which twist and strangle. Long-handled weapons tend to be more 'suitable' for women, who may not feel so strong imagining themselves punching, kicking, or getting too close. For the same reason women also sometimes enjoy picturing the offender tied up and unable to retaliate. How the offender came to be in that position is not important.

Through fantasy a powerful experience is created by shifting to the present tense and drawing out concrete details:

'How are you moving?' … 'What are your weapons?' … 'What do you say?' … 'What are you thinking?' … 'What do you do next?'

This powerful experience of being in control does not replace the abuse experience, but it can be placed alongside it in the client's mind to provide another perspective, and another more positive memory.

When the abuser has been dealt with to the satisfaction of the client we need to ensure that he is suitably disposed of. Just because he is 'dead' or 'mortally wounded' does not mean that the client has finished with him. Such questions as 'What are you going to do with him now?' can help to conclude the fantasy with details of burial, burning, dismemberment, etc.

In another very effective way of helping the client to express anger, fantasy can be combined with action methods. The abuser is pictured sitting on a chair in the room, while the client addresses him and tells him how they feel about the abuse and the ways that it has affected them. The imagined offender can be pummelled with real cushions or beaten with various 'weapons', such as a tightly rolled-up and taped newspaper or a length of plastic or rubber hose.

When fantasy is used without action methods, the client may feel the need for some form of physical activity after the session. Digging a garden, scrubbing the floor, smashing a squash ball around a court, or just getting out for a walk are various ways which allow for the release of pent-up emotions.

Once anger has been expressed, it may not be necessary to repeat this sort of exercise. At the next session the therapist checks the client's energy levels for signs of unresolved anger, for example:

'Remember what we did last time to Uncle Bob — how do you feel about him now?' or

'Do you think we've finished with this guy?'

If the client shows little interest in the offender, and seems relatively calm when talking about him, it is probably time to move on to the next stage of therapy. If there are signs of continuing anger and distress, more work on the abuse scene and more venting of feelings are indicated. The therapist may then choose to continue using fantasy in the next session, or try changing to a different technique which offers variety and helps to maintain the client's interest. A change of style also allows for the possibility of finding a way which is more effective for this particular client.

The rescue scene

Fantasizing about a rescue from abuse can be a powerful way to follow a detailed description of the actual incident. Fantasy used in this way can combine the expression of anger towards the abuser with an opportunity for the adult to comfort and reassure the abused child. By using fantasy to provide the child with what they needed at the time of the abuse, the adult creates a different experience which is both empowering and healing. The fantasy will not erode memories of the abuse, but it will create a more positive memory of power and success which helps to desensitize the client to memories of powerlessness and victimization.

To develop this fantasy the client is invited to view the abuse scene from the position of strength inherent in their present adult status. They might be reminded of their age, their size, their relative wisdom, and maturity, for example:

'Now you're no longer a young child — you're a grown-up woman with a lot of strength and resources that you didn't have then. I want you to picture yourself as you are now, 35 years old, 160 cm tall, with all the wisdom you have gained about sexual abuse. You walk into the bedroom where that little nine-year-old who was you is about to be touched by her grandfather. What do you do? ... What do you want to say to that guy? ... What does that little girl need now? ... Where do you take her? ... What do you do for her? ... What do you want to say to that little girl about how she survived and coped?'

As with the expression of anger, the rescue scene shifts from mere fantasy to an emotional experience. We achieve this by using the present tense, by eliciting concrete details, and by the use of slow, carefully chosen and spaced words that are almost hypnotic in their effect.

'Happy endings' to nightmares

Another effective use of fantasy is in devising 'happy endings' to nightmares, which for some survivors of sexual abuse can be a frequent cause of terror and distress. Nightmares are a product of the imagination, and it is therefore good to use the imagination to develop the dream into a more positive experience.

Some people are able to consciously control their dreams while not fully awake, so they can choose what happens next. The majority, however, first have to wake themselves to stop the nightmare, and then use fantasy to devise a suitable ending. They should be encouraged to choose endings that put them in powerful roles, and that deal effectively with the people or things which frighten them.

Sometimes planning 'happy endings' for recurrent nightmares can be an enjoyable task for client and therapist to engage in together. It can have the effect of removing some of the fear associated with anticipation of the dreams.

Fantasy can ease the distress of nightmares and give the client a way of coping with them, but it is not likely to stop the nightmares until further therapy has dealt with the trauma of the abuse.

Future fantasies

One of the most useful issues to discuss with clients is how they view the future once their problems have been solved (Furman & Ahola 1992). This helps them to be more optimistic, and to view their present difficulties as a transitory phase rather than a permanent predicament. For sexual-abuse survivors who feel overwhelmed by the effects of their abuse, a vision of the future without these feelings and problems can be inspiring and energizing.

In creating a positive future fantasy the language used is important. We talk about 'when' the problems are solved, for example, rather than 'if'. The underlying assumption that the problem *will* be solved is part of what makes future fantasies so powerful.

We also elicit concrete details, perhaps going through various modalities:

'How will you be walking?' … 'Will things smell differently' … 'What will you notice about colours that you might be missing at the moment?'

Examples of questions which elicit future fantasies and which encourage imagination and optimism include:

'What are your dreams for the future when you've finished with this?'

'Imagine we meet in two years' time when you are through this bad time in your life. How will your life be different?'

'What will you be doing?'

'What will your relationship with your mother/partner/son/daughter be like?'

'What will I notice about the way you look?'

'What might other people be saying about you?'

'What would you like to be doing in 10 years' time?'

SOLUTION TALK

The use of fantasies is extended by Ben Furman and Tapani Ahola (1992) into a style of therapy they call 'solution talk'. Furman and Ahola base their ideas on the work of Milton Erickson and share his focus in being much more interested in knowing the details of the solution, than the details of the problem. Although work with sexual-abuse survivors requires an understanding of the problem, 'solution talk' can be a powerful and positive part of therapy. It is a way of getting people in touch with their strengths and giving them hope for the future. It is most useful during the stages of therapy when we are empowering our clients, and when we are planning for the future.

As outlined by Furman and Ahola, the process of 'solution talk' involves four major steps:

1 A vision of the future when the problem has been solved.
2 Noticing the steps already taken towards the future vision.
3 Giving credit to oneself and others for solving the problem.
4 'Problems as Friends' — acknowledging anything positive which has come from the experience.

1 The future vision

We have described already the creation of future fantasies in the preceding section. The 'Miracle Question' is another method for eliciting future visions, and is used frequently by such solution-oriented therapists as de Shazer (1985) and Furman and Ahola (1992). The 'Miracle Question' is in fact a sequence of questions exploring the consequences of an imagined critical change. It may be asked in many different versions, such as:

'Let us imagine that a miracle takes place and you wake up one day to find that all your problems are over.'

'What will you notice first?'

'How will things be different?'

'How will you feel?'

'What will other people notice about you?'

'What positive things will begin to happen now the problem is no longer there?'

Usually in this context the problem being dealt with is not the fact that abuse has occurred, but the many ways in which the survivor has been affected by the abuse. The problem being addressed might be depression, poor self-esteem, anxiety about sexual performance — or, more likely, a combination of many concerns.

It is also possible to use the 'Miracle Question' format to ask useful questions about the problem of sexual abuse. By eliciting a picture of a person who has healed from abuse, we can help the client to develop a different vision of their future. We might ask a sequence of questions such as:

'Imagine that a miracle has happened, and you wake up one day to find that a process of healing has occurred.'

'How will you be different?'

'What is the first difference you will notice?'

'How will you walk?'

'What is the expression on your face?'

'What differences will other people notice?'

Clearly the client must be ready to imagine the possibility of healing for these questions to be useful. Such questions would not be appropriate for a client who was feeling hopeless or overwhelmed by feelings of grief and anger.

2 Noticing the steps already taken

Once a positive vision of the future has been described, we help the client to acknowledge the progress they have already made towards their goal. We might ask directly:

'Have any of these changes begun to take place?'

Alternatively, we might stay with the future fantasy, looking 'back to the present' to discover how the goal was achieved:

'How did you do it?' or

'What did you have to do to make such progress?'

Once the necessary steps towards the goal have been elicited we then enquire about which of these steps has been taken already.

Furman and Ahola also use questions that ask the client to rate their achievements or their problems on a scale. This provides a context for discussing the steps required to make changes, for example:

'Let's suppose your problem at its worst rated a ten. What number is it now?' ... 'How do you explain this change?' ... 'What would you have to do to move up to the next point on the scale?'

They also ask such questions as:

'Which of your solutions so far has proven most effective?' ... 'What else have you thought you might try?'

Another way of highlighting progress made towards the goal is to ask about the times when the problem does not occur. These are the 'unique outcomes' or 'exceptions' described in Chapter 5 (pp. 58–59).

There will always be times, places, or situations in which the client has success and shows signs of strength. Helping them to notice the times when they are not totally overwhelmed by the problem is a way of putting them in touch with their strengths. A mother who lacks confidence in dealing with authority figures as a result of her abuse may, for example, take an assertive stand with the teacher when her child is being treated unfairly at school. A man who feels depressed may enjoy taking his dog for a walk. Noticing such times when the problem is not controlling their lives helps clients to acknowledge their power and to plan ways of extending their control over the problem.

3 Giving credit for progress made

Often survivors of sexual abuse feel so overwhelmed by its effects that they have lost touch with their strengths. They may make a number of helpful discoveries, however, if we make such statements as:

'Other people would not have made it through what's happened to you without going crazy'.

and asking such questions as:

'How did you survive so well?'

'Where did you find the strength?'

Other questions used by Furman and Ahola which might help sexual-abuse survivors to give credit to themselves and to mobilize their strengths include:

'What is your best quality? ... How have you used that quality so far in handling this problem?' ... 'What else can you do to make use of that quality in solving the problem?'

They also ask questions which help survivors to appreciate and apply to their own lives the things they have learned as a result of their experience. Sometimes asking them to help someone else frees them from the feelings that restrain them from solving their own problems, for example:

'Let's suppose that someone you really care about has something similar happen to them, and they come to you for advice. What would you tell them?' or

'Imagine you receive an invitation to give a lecture to a group of professionals about the kind of problem you have had to deal with. You tap into the wisdom you have gained from your experience to tell them what they need to know. What do you say?'

Often our clients stun us with the brilliance of their answers to such questions. It can be really helpful to record their answers word-for-word, and have them typed up and sent out in letter form after the session. This provides clients with a permanent record to remind them of their own wisdom and strengths. In this way it can help to empower them in dealing with the abuse and its effects. The example below is based on a letter sent to a client, and uses her own words of advice. Like others who have received these letters she was surprised by her own wisdom and carried it with her for some time afterwards. It is reprinted with permission:

'Dear ——

You already know that you are a survivor. At times you are also beginning to appreciate just how much strength and wisdom you have gained along the way, and this gives you confidence and hope for the future.

I thought it might be useful to record some of your discoveries for those times when your energy level runs low and tricks you into losing confidence. Here is some good advice from the best expert you could consult:

- Don't ever stop fighting for the things you believe in.
- Maintain a sense of balance in your life.
- Realize when you need to step back and get a rest from it all.
- Be genuine and open and real, and then you'll attract the same sort of people.
- Trust your instincts.
- Don't give up — even when others tell you it's hopeless.
- You can learn something from everyone and everything.
- Children and old people have a lot of wisdom.
- Hardships make you stronger.

I look forward to hearing more of your discoveries when we next meet.'

In addition to acknowledging their own strengths which have helped them to survive, it can also be useful for clients to acknowledge others who have helped them along the road to healing. When trust has been destroyed by abuse, it can be therapeutic to appreciate the love and support provided by others, perhaps family, partner, or friends. This does not change the abuse experience, but does put it in a context which allows for hope in the future and for the rebuilding of trust within non-abusive relationships.

4 'Problems as friends'

While we would not wish sexual abuse on anyone, clients at the end of therapy sometimes acknowledge something valuable that they have gained through their experience. This is what Furman and Ahola (1992) mean by 'problems as friends' — the learning, the strengths of character, and the sensitivity gained through surviving and healing.

Acknowledging something positive does not negate or minimize the distress experienced, but it does help our clients to leave it in the past. We need to be careful, however, not to imply in any way that something positive should come from the experience of sexual abuse. Rather, when it is useful, we allow our clients to make their own discoveries about any gains they have made. Questions that could be asked at this stage would include:

'If this problem has taught you something important about life, about yourself, or about other people, what would it be?'

'Many people believe that problems and suffering are not in vain. What do you think?'

'What can you do now, because of your experiences, that you would not have been able to do before?'

'What do you know now, because of what you have been through, that would not have been available to you otherwise?'

'What can you be now that you would not have been able to achieve if you had not had all these experiences?'

WRITING EXERCISES

Writing is one of the most widely used tools for work with adult survivors of sexual abuse. It can be used at any stage of the therapy process, but is probably most effective for writing about what happened, for looking at the effects of the abuse, for going over the abuse in a different way, and for planning the future.

Any client who can put words on paper can be encouraged to write. These are exercises where self-expression is important, not spelling or grammar. Some clients may choose to write in logical ordered sequence, while others will have a jumble of ideas and incomplete sentences. They may revert to the baby-talk of early childhood, or use of a different language associated with their upbringing. There are no rules about what is right or wrong. We simply suggest that they use whatever words they find to express their thoughts and feelings. Consequently stream-of-consciousness writing is one of the styles most often suggested. This involves recording thoughts as they occur and without stopping, including perhaps such thoughts as 'I can't think of anything else to say', or 'I'm finding this exercise really difficult'.

Other useful writing includes making lists, keeping a journal, writing poetry, writing letters, or writing a metaphorical story that relates to their own experience. Many of the ideas for children's writing in Chapter 7 are equally suitable for adults.

When we suggest that our clients try any of the writing exercises, we ensure that they choose a suitable time and place. They need to be free of worry about interruption and they need to allow time afterwards to recover from any feelings triggered by their memories. For some exercises ten minutes may be sufficient. Others may be done slowly over an evening, over a week, or in bursts as inspiration and opportunity allow.

The advantages of writing exercises are that they can be done by just about anyone, without any special equipment, and at a pace that suits them. By expressing their thoughts and feelings clients can validate their own experience. This is an important step for those who have been told to think and feel something quite different from what they really experienced, such as 'Doesn't that feel nice,' or 'You made it all up,' or 'It's all your fault'.

Sometimes clients find it easier to put on paper words that they are unable to express face-to-face. The distancing effect may help them to cope with the their sense of shame or embarrassment in describing what happened. It can also help them to express the strong feelings of anger and distress engendered by the abuse, or to confront an abuser they are too anxious or too angry to face safely in person.

If, however, a writing exercise is likely to arouse strong feelings, it is important that clients are not asked to write at home unsupported. They may be left to write alone for part of the therapy session, with the therapist checking regularly to ensure that they are coping. Before the end of the session, therapist and client would discuss the exercise and ensure that the client is able to leave the session feeling emotionally intact. Some form of catharsis may be required before they leave, particularly if they have been writing about abuse.

Useful resources for those who want to read more about writing exercises are *The Courage to Heal*, by Ellen Bass and Laura Davis (1988), *Rescuing the Inner Child*, by Penny Parks (1990), and *Broken Boys, Mending Men*, by Stephen Grubman-Black (1990).

Writing about the effects of abuse — past and present

Writing about any of the effects of abuse is a useful way of acknowledging the distress experienced at the time, and the difficulties faced afterwards. The client may like to write about feelings of fear, confusion, anger, or powerlessness, about effects on family relationships, parenting, friendships, and self-esteem, or about the things they have lost and need to grieve for, such as innocence, trust, or childhood.

Similarly, writing about how they have coped can be useful. Some coping strategies might have created further problems which need to be addressed, such as drug and alcohol abuse or emotional withdrawal. Other ways of coping will have led to the development of strengths, such as persistence, wisdom, sensitivity, and heightened awareness of danger signs. Writing about coping can be a validating experience, and a valuable part of becoming empowered.

Some clients feel able to write about the effects of abuse while at home, providing that they have the necessary support. For others it is preferable to do this exercise during a session with the therapist. Sometimes the therapist might do the writing, asking about the effects of abuse, and highlighting them by writing a list on a whiteboard, or on a sheet of paper for the client to take away. This might be done, for example, to help the client develop awareness of their underlying anger, as well as to help them acknowledge the strengths that enabled them to survive in spite of difficulties. When a whiteboard or large sheet of newsprint is used to list a client's positive attributes, the therapist can copy these out later and send the list to the client.

Writing about the effects of abuse is an exercise that can be done once or several times, depending on the client's energy for writing and the benefits gained. Often it is useful to break it down into separate sections, such as 'Effects at the time of abuse', 'Current effects', 'How I coped', 'What I learned'.

Writing about the abuse

When the survivor feels empowered to face the abuse, writing is one way of going over their experience. Where appropriate, it can be shared with others.

However, when writing exercises are the only way used to help the client describe the abuse, it is important for them to include the same sort of detail that we elicit using other methods. These are not necessarily details of what the abuser did, but may include background noises, a characteristic gesture or facial expression, sensory details such as the feel of rough skin or hard ground, the smell of the abuser's breath. Anything that reminds the client of the abuse can trigger the feelings of panic, anxiety, nausea, or emotional withdrawal that often accompany the abuse experience. Systematic desensitization (p. 51), catharsis (pp. 166–167), searching for unique outcomes (pp. 58–59), and thought stopping (pp. 227–230) are various methods described in this book which could be used in conjunction with writing exercises to deal with these feelings.

We should encourage our clients to write only about the things that they feel ready to cope with. They may like to start with a less difficult incident, or provide limited details at first. They may need to do this exercise several times, or to use the written exercise as a basis for discussion in therapy.

When the details are not present in the written record, they can be drawn out by the therapist who simultaneously ensures that the client is ready to face them. *Clients should never be encouraged to fill any gaps in their memory by imagining details they do not recall.*

Providing a different experience of the abuse

As stated previously, it is important to move on quickly once the client has described the details of the abuse experience. We are trying to alter the emotional impact of the abuse experience, not repeat it. This can be done in a number of ways using writing exercises. The most common of these are:

- Catharsis
- Rescue-scene stories
- Writing to the child who was abused.

Catharsis

Writing can be a useful way of expressing the anger, pain, and grief associated with sexual abuse. This is perhaps most usefully done in the form of letters to the offender, or to other people held partly responsible, such as an adult who failed to believe or protect.

These letters need not be sent, though it is important for some clients to convey their feelings directly to those concerned. It is not even necessary that the person addressed is still alive, or that they will ever be available to read the letters. The essential part of catharsis is that the client finds a way of unburdening themselves of destructive feelings. This exercise, too, can be repeated as often as necessary. Letters do not have to be polite or reasonable. They only have to express feelings.

If the letters are to be sent, it is important to discuss with the client what they hope to achieve. They might write a very different letter, for example, if they want understanding or reconciliation, than they would write if they want to express anger and wish for no further association. We may need to question them about how realistic their goals are if they are hoping for an apology, and to discuss strategies for coping if they do not achieve what they want from a confrontational letter.

Rescue-scene stories

Writing rescue-scene stories is a variation on the use of fantasy to create a different experience of the abuse. The client who was abused as a child writes about themselves as an adult or hero/ine figure arriving on the scene of their previous abuse. They include details of what they did and what they said, how they dealt with the abuser, and how they provided what was needed for the child. Again, they should be encouraged to express themselves in the present tense and to provide concrete details which help to make this experience more real, for example:

'I burst into the room, throwing open the door to find little Joe lying on the bed with Uncle Grant leaning over his bare body. "Don't you dare touch that child," I say coldly and calmly. "Just get out of this house right now." He can tell by the intensity of my tone and my barely controlled fury that I am deadly serious, and stumbles out of the room to be met by the waiting detective. I take Joe in my arms, comforting him as I gently help him back into his clothes. "It's all right now," I tell him as he sobs with relief, "I'm here to take care of you. Uncle Grant is in serious trouble and I'll see that he can't ever hurt you again."'

Writing to the child

The concept of 'the child within' or 'the inner child' is one widely used with adult clients who were abused as children. It describes that part of our client which represents the child who is still suffering from the abuse experience. From this perspective the primary purpose of therapy is helping the adult client to provide that inner child with the help that they need for their healing.

Dialogue between the adult and the child can be facilitated in a number of ways. One way was illustrated in the previous section on fantasy, when the adult engaged the 'child' in a 'dialogue' about the abuse. Another form of dialogue is the adult writing letters to the child which convey information and comfort, including such messages as 'It was not your fault', 'No wonder you feel so bad', 'You are a normal healthy girl' and 'You are safe now and I'm going to look after you.' In this way the adult gets in touch with their own resources to become therapist to the child, offering information, reassurance, and comfort. Such messages employ seeding, reframing, and normalizing as opportunities arise, just as a therapist would do in response to a survivor's story. Writing down this information, repeatedly if necessary, helps the client to integrate different beliefs, which in turn form a foundation for different emotional responses.

The adult client can also write letters to the 'child', asking for details about the abuse. They then write letters in which 'the child' replies, thereby helping themselves to go over the abuse experience. The next step is for the adult to write back to 'the child', providing information and comfort. This 'correspondence' method is described in detail by Parks (1990), who encourages her adult clients to engage in it for as long as seems helpful. Parks also suggests they write letters to people who have hurt them, expressing their feelings. These are not letters for posting but letters for catharsis. As a separate exercise, clients then write a description of a rescue scenario.

Letters are used to go over the details of the abuse and its effects, to express emotions, to affirm the 'child', to address unhelpful beliefs, and to create a different experience of the abuse. Parks' work is a good example of how writing exercises can be used throughout the various stages of therapy.

Other writing exercises

Often it is helpful for the therapist to suggest that clients focus on a particular area, such as difficulties or achievements. For example, they can be asked to listen to their 'inner voice' and list all the negative messages they give themselves during the day. On a more positive note they can be asked to write down one thing they have achieved each day which they feel good about. Clients can also be asked to write to the therapist between sessions, or to write letters to other people, real or imaginary. The purpose of such letters depends on the client's needs.

Other writing exercises suggested by Bass and Davis (1988) include writing about progress in therapy, about achievements made, and goals for the future. They also suggest writing about the family. Clients can, for example, describe the things they like and dislike about their family, or they can write a family history which helps them to understand the abuse in its context.

THOUGHT STOPPING

Thought stopping is a useful technique for those who have recurring thoughts that make them feel anxious, distressed, or disempowered. It incorporates ideas derived from behaviour therapy, Neurolinguistic Programming, and Ericksonian hypnotherapy. It is a relatively simple technique which can be taught to a client within several minutes, and which they can then practise at home and use as required. The sequence of stages in thought stopping is described below.

1 Explanation and contract

The first step is to explain the purpose of thought stopping, to provide brief details of what it entails, and to obtain the client's informed consent to proceed. We might say something like this:

'There is a way that you can control those thoughts that keep bothering you. It is a technique that I can teach you here in a few minutes. You can use it any time the thoughts bother you, wherever you are. It involves your dwelling briefly on the thoughts, which I then interrupt by shouting "Stop". I then ask you to imagine being somewhere that is really positive, pleasant, and relaxing, so the thoughts lose their impact. Would you like to try it?'

2 Identify a negative thought

Having established that a client is troubled by a thought that they want to stop, it is necessary to define the precise words of the thought. It might be, for example, 'I am no good' or 'I cannot cope with this'.

3 Identify a positive scene

The client is then asked to picture a scene where they feel really positive, relaxed, and comfortable. A concrete description of the scene is elicited, including visual, kinaesthetic, and auditory details. This helps to focus the client on the experience of being in this place, while providing essential details for use later in the exercise. We obtain this information with such questions as:

'What can you see there?'

'What are the sounds you hear?'

'What does it smell like?'

'How do you feel when you are there?'

4 Move to position

To remove distractions and so facilitate the process, the therapist shifts to a position to the side of the client, and sufficiently behind so they are out of sight. Alternatively, the client might be asked to turn their chair around so they cannot see the therapist.

5 Explain the process

The therapist explains to the client in more detail what they are going to do. This involves the client thinking the negative thought until the therapist shouts 'Stop!' They will then be asked to picture a 'Stop' sign. During the final stage the client is helped to imagine being at the positive place which they have previously described.

6 The client describes the negative thought

The client is then asked to have the negative thought, and to say out loud the words that go with it. Details of what it means to the client and how it makes them feel are elicited. At this stage we are not afraid of causing our clients anxiety, as the more real the impact of the thoughts, the more effective is the thought-stopping intervention, for example:

THERAPIST   Now I want you to tell me about those thoughts that keep bothering you.

CLIENT   Well, whenever I'm in even a slightly difficult situation I tell myself that I can't do it, that I'm no good.

THERAPIST   And how does that message affect you?

CLIENT   Well, I feel really hopeless, really bad about myself, and I tend to give up easily.

THERAPIST   What are the words that go through your mind?

CLIENT   'You're no good.' 'You can't do it.' 'Give up.' 'You're a failure.'

7 The therapist shouts 'stop'

When the client has been describing the thoughts for about 20 to 30 seconds, particularly when a note of anxiety is recognized in their voice, the therapist interrupts, shouting 'Stop!' Shouting helps to magnify the impact of the intervention, and to anchor it as a response to the thoughts.

8 Picture a 'stop' sign

The client is then asked to picture a 'Stop' sign. They may be assisted with brief details:

'Now I want you to picture a 'Stop' sign. It is red with big white letters. Can you see it?'

9 Visualize the positive scene

Having checked that the client has been able to picture a 'Stop' sign, the therapist then requests that they visualize that positive place where they feel relaxed and comfortable. The therapist helps to develop a fantasy of being in that place by repeating details previously described by the client:

'Now I want you to think of that beach that you were telling me about. … Can you see the blueness of the sea? … Smell the salt in the air? …

Where are you standing? ... What do you see? ... What sort of feeling do you have there?'

At this stage the therapist should be speaking quietly, slowly, and evenly, contributing to the development of the fantasy by adopting a hypnotic tone of voice. The therapist's speech should match the rhythm of the client's breathing.

10 Repeat the process

Once the client has successfully placed themselves within the positive scene and described the relaxed feelings that go with it, they are taken through the whole process once again. The therapist might begin with such words as:

'Now I want you to go back to those thoughts you had about how hopeless you feel. ... Do you have them in your mind? ... Tell me about that again.'

The client begins to describe the troublesome thoughts once again. As they begin to feel anxious or distressed the therapist again shouts, 'Stop', gets them to picture the 'Stop' sign, and then returns to the positive place:

'And there's that place where you feel really good. ... Tell me about it.'

This routine is repeated as many times as necessary until the procedure is clear to the client. Usually this repetition is required only once or twice.

11 The client completes the process alone

The client is then asked to go through the process alone, either speaking out loud or just thinking through each stage in their mind. The therapist gives instructions, for example:

'Now I want you to stop those thoughts by yourself. First go back to the thoughts, letting them go through your mind until you start to feel bad. Then shout "Stop!" in your mind. Picture the Stop sign and then move on. Make sure that you see the blueness of the sea ... feel the sun on your face ... '

Once the client has succeeded in going through the process silently by themselves, they have acquired a tool which they can use anywhere and anytime the troublesome thoughts recur. They have taken a step towards regaining control over their lives. We suggest that they continue to practise this technique at home, as well as using it when the negative thoughts arise.

A variation on this exercise is described by Davis, Eshelman, and McKay (1982).

Suicide prevention

Occasionally in work with sexual-abuse survivors, a client makes suicidal threats or feels so unhappy and hopeless that they present a serious risk to themselves. We need to be alert to any danger of suicide and prepared to take action.

Confidentiality

When a client is at risk the usual constraints of confidentiality do not apply. We need to do whatever we can to ensure their safety, and often this means enlisting the help of others. It may mean notifying appropriate crisis or emergency services, informing family or friends of our concerns, or preferably helping the client to tell others how they feel.

This is a situation where the therapist may need to take charge. While we continually try to find ways of co-operating with our clients and empowering them to take care of themselves, this may be insufficient to prevent a risk of suicide. We then need to become quite directive. The message we give is that 'I care about you and I'm not going to let you hurt yourself.'

Involving support people

We assist our clients to identify potential support people, and ensure that they are helpful and accessible. We might ask, for example, 'Who can you ring if you feel desperate?'

This needs to be followed up with plans to notify the support people of the seriousness of the situation before it becomes a crisis. We might suggest that the client telephones them before they get desperate, or even get the client to telephone their nominated support people while they are still in our presence. We can suggest that the client invites their support people to a meeting with us, or we can contact the support people directly when necessary.

It may be difficult for the client to identify appropriate support people, and we attend to the various restraints that get in their way. These may include beliefs about their own worth which need to be addressed, such as 'I'm useless', 'Nobody cares about me', or 'I can't ask for help.' Other restraints might relate to a lack of trust in others, or an unwillingness to hand over control. If the client is socially isolated and has no close friends or family contacts, a support group needs to be created, which might involve referral to an appropriate therapy group, making contact with neighbours or community resources, or enlisting the help of other professionals and voluntary agencies.

Crisis services

The therapist should keep well informed about emergency services, such as 24-hour telephone counselling services and community psychiatric services which visit homes at short notice. Both our client and their support people need to know that such crisis help is always available.

Decreasing risk factors

We should help our clients and their support people to make it as difficult as possible for any impulsive suicidal behaviour to occur. Clients should have access only to their immediate medication requirements, for example, and other people in the household should be told to keep their medication in a secure place.

Any excess pills should be stored safely or disposed of, preferably in front of a witness. When no witnesses are available we can instruct our clients to dispose of the pills and telephone us as soon as they have done so. They should be told that failure to telephone would be regarded as a signal that further action was required (e.g. notify family, contact emergency services, make a home visit).

Addressing the issues

When a client is threatening suicide we do not always have time to deal effectively with the feelings that underlie these threats, such as despair, anger, or low self-esteem. Before therapy can address these feelings we need to deal with the risk of suicide. We discuss with the client their beliefs about suicide, and try to provide them with a different perspective. Somehow we need to convey our belief that their feelings will pass with time, and that they are considering a permanent solution to a temporary problem. Suicide can be presented as a way of saying 'No' to hope and denying the possibility of change. We can talk, for example, about how they are in a place where it is hard to see any other possibilities, but they will not always be in this place.

Contracts to prevent suicide

A useful tool for work with a suicidal client is a formal written contract between client and therapist. This should cover deliberate acts, and acts carried out through impulse or carelessness. The wording might read something like:

I, Mary Alice Jones, contract that I will not in any way knowingly or unknowingly harm myself.

Signed:

Witnessed:

Date:

It may help to ask the client to read the contract out loud once it has been signed, and both client and therapist should retain a copy of it. It may also be necessary to have some discussion about the contract in order to reinforce its effect in various situations. We might ask, for example, such questions as:

'Are there any particular times when this contract will be more difficult to honour?'

'How's the contract going to feel at night?'

'What will be the signs that you are strong enough to honour this contract?'

We could even predict that the client may feel angry with us, and resent our making them sign the contract at times when they are feeling most desperate.

Contracts for preventing suicide do not provide total security, but are more likely to succeed when the client takes them seriously and struggles with the decision to sign.

Suicidal gestures and attempts

Suicidal 'gestures' and suicide attempts should always be taken seriously. Even when the client does not intend to kill themselves, they may misjudge and do so mistakenly. Attempted suicide is a signal of distress and is sometimes followed by a completed suicide. It is important that the causes of the distress are isolated and addressed, and that all possible steps are taken to prevent further attempts.

Suicide threats

Threats of suicide are very powerful, and for a few clients become the best way they know to be heard. When we suspect that a client may be using the threat of suicide in this way, it is advisable to consult a supervisor. A second opinion is often helpful in such cases, as is support in devising the most effective way of dealing with the situation. We may choose, for example, to discuss with the client our belief that they do not really want to die, and that there are more positive ways for them to solve their problems. We may help them to find other ways to communicate their distress or to achieve their goals. Sometimes they need help to accept and grieve for the things they cannot change.

While we take all possible practical steps to prevent suicide, the threat of suicide does not mean that we try to meet every demand of a client, or that we encourage the family to do so. We need to resist the power of the threat to manipulate us into doing something which is unreasonable or unhelpful. We may need, for example, to make a statement which acknowledges the client's ultimate responsibility for any choice they make about suicide. This is an extremely difficult position for any therapist, but we have to acknowledge that we represent only a part of our client's life and do not have absolute power over decisions they make, nor can we be totally responsible for their actions.

When the client does not seem able to act in a way that is safe, we may need to ask psychiatric services to provide for their immediate safety.

DEALING WITH SEXUAL DIFFICULTIES

It is not uncommon for adults who have been abused to experience difficulties in sexual relationships. This is not surprising as they have often experienced sexual contact in ways that are frightening, confusing, and which have not allowed for their own needs and rights. Sex therefore can trigger responses of fear, anxiety, or emotional dissociation. This situation may be compounded by lack of trust, fear of intimacy, and difficulties in communicating the individual's own desires and limits, all of which are common reactions to sexual abuse.

Difficulties can be further compounded by the response of the sexual partner(s). If a partner does not understand the effects of abuse, sexual difficulties may be regarded as individual issues, rather than as an inevitable response to the circumstances. Feelings of inadequacy, and criticism or blame of self or partner can occur.

Problems may also be exacerbated by any of the issues that can create difficulties in any sexual relationship, such as poor communication, inequality of power or status, competitiveness, and issues relating to intimacy, personal boundaries, and drug or alcohol abuse. Society's definitions of 'normal' sex, and differences between the partners' expectations of each other can present further difficulties.

It is important for any therapist working with sexual problems to take into account the historical, political, social, and interactional context of the problems. This enables the therapist to normalize the client's difficulties as a natural response to their circumstances. It also helps to avoid pathologizing feelings and behaviours which can cause considerable distress and anxiety within relationships. Clearly it is not sufficient to deal only with the client's concerns about specific emotional or behavioural responses. Therapists need to be familiar with all the issues that may contribute to sexual difficulties. When the client is in a relationship, it is important to include the partner in any discussion of these issues whenever possible. It is also important to ensure that the client is ready and willing to make changes for their own benefit, and not just because they are being pressured by a partner. It is not helpful for survivors to try to make themselves have sex, or to do anything sexually, just to please someone else.

Sexual problems which have not become deeply entrenched within a relationship often respond to normalizing, and to the provision of information or suggestions (Annon 1974). This includes education about physiology, and a lot of the behavioural interventions first developed by Masters and Johnson (1970). Some problems require medical investigation and treatment, while others require more intensive counselling. Therapists who lack skills and confidence in working with sexual difficulties may prefer to refer their clients to someone who specializes in this work.

The following list of references provides a starting-point for those interested in learning more about working with sexual problems.

For a useful framework for dealing with long-standing sexual problems, we recommend Roughan and Jenkins (1990). Crowe (1982) describes behavioural techniques based on the work of Masters and Johnson, as do Kilman and Mills (1983). Heiman, LoPiccolo, and LoPiccolo (1984) combine information about normal physiology, behavioural techniques for dealing with problems, and a good appreciation of context in an excellent guide for heterosexual women. Loulan (1984) provides similar assistance in a valuable book for lesbian women.

For gay and lesbian clients, books edited by Coleman (1988) and Gonsiorek (1985) both have useful sections on dealing with sexual difficulties. Davis (1990) has a section appropriate for most survivors outlining guidelines for healing sexually, and includes written exercises. Bass and Davis (1988) and Davis (1991) both have useful sections for partners as well as survivors.

A book specifically written for female survivors of sexual abuse by Maltz (1991) is recommended for both client and therapist.

STRESS MANAGEMENT

Anxiety and stress can be major problems for abuse survivors. Over time, chronic stress resulting from emotional trauma can cause physical symptoms such as the breakdown in the body's immune system and consequent vulnerability to a wide range of health problems, including high blood pressure, hardening of the arteries, peptic ulcers, migraines, and rheumatoid arthritis. Therefore it is important for therapists to be aware of the many ways in which clients can be helped to reduce unnecessary or excessive stress, and to cope with the normal stresses of everyday life.

There are a number of useful skills for managing stress, some of which we have already described. These include the various ways of examining unhelpful beliefs and values, and reframing ideas to develop more useful perspectives (see Chapter 5).

Going over a traumatic event such as an abuse experience can also help to reduce stress when it is done in a way that is different from the original experience. The ways of going over the abuse scene which we described earlier in this chapter help to reduce stress and anxiety by providing a different experience of the abuse, and by dealing with the memories and emotions which trigger anxiety (e.g. the rescue scene, fantasy, writing exercises). Thought-stopping is another technique described earlier in this chapter for dealing with ideas that increase anxiety and stress.

Stress can also be alleviated by helping an abuse survivor to communicate more effectively either within individual therapy or preferably in sessions involving partner, family members, or friends. Where appropriate they can be referred to courses or books on communication, assertion, and conflict resolution. Learning how to ask for what they want more effectively, and how to say 'No' to unreasonable or excessive demands, can play a vital role in helping most people to reduce the level of stress in their life.

Encouraging better self-care is another way of helping clients to deal with stress. This includes attention to nutrition and exercise, getting proper medical attention as needed, and building appropriate support systems. It may involve attending to unhelpful beliefs which prevent the client from giving priority to their own needs. Such beliefs would include, for example, the belief that they were not deserving of the time and attention required to take care of themselves, or the belief that the needs of others should always come first.

Improving organizational skills helps to deal with stress by focusing attention on priorities and time management. Sometimes it becomes clear that a client is feeling unduly stressed because they are trying to achieve too much in too short a period of time. When we can normalize stress as an inevitable response to their circumstances, we help to remove some of the sense of self-blame, weakness, and failure which can accompany it.

Relaxation exercises also can play a major part in stress management, and various forms are described in the next section.

RELAXATION EXERCISES

It is important that we all enjoy times of relaxation in our lives. This helps to prevent the accumulation of stress and can be particularly relevant for a client who is dealing with difficult and painful issues in therapy. It is always useful, therefore, to discuss relaxation and leisure with our clients, and to ensure that they practise some form of relaxation which suits them. For example, they might enjoy reading, listening to music, gardening, arts, crafts, sports, time alone, or time with friends.

The type of relaxation that makes a difference in dealing with chronic anxiety, however, is the daily practice of some form of deep relaxation (Bourne 1990). The resulting physiological benefits of decreases in heart rate, respiration, blood pressure, and muscle tension help to counteract the physiological changes created by chronic and excessive stress. Other benefits which have been documented include increased energy levels, improvements to concentration and memory, increased self confidence, and reduction in insomnia, fatigue, and various psychosomatic symptoms (Bourne 1990).

The most common methods used to achieve deep relaxation include deep breathing, progressive muscle relaxation, mental relaxation, visualizing a peaceful scene, meditation, and autogenic training. Clients and therapists who are interested in learning more about any of these methods are referred to the invaluable self-help manuals prepared by Bourne (1990) and Davis, Eshelman, and McKay (1982). These books not only provide practical information on the various ways of achieving deep relaxation, but also include a resource list of useful books, and audio- and videotapes.

When we teach relaxation exercises it is important that we think of this as providing the client with a resource that they can use when they choose, and not as a form of treatment provided by the therapist.

Summarized here are some of the more popular and practical relaxation options. One of the tasks of the therapist is to assess which method would best suit a particular client.

Deep breathing

Deep breathing can be practised in a variety of positions, but is usually learned while lying face up on a rug on the floor. Legs and back should be straight, and the feet slightly apart. One hand is placed on the abdomen, the other on the chest. Long deep breaths are taken in through the nose and into the abdomen. The abdomen should rise as much as is comfortable, while the chest moves only a little. The breath is then gently blown out through the mouth. As more breaths are taken, the focus is on the feel and the sound of the breathing, and the growing sense of relaxation that accompanies it. This exercise should continue for five to ten minutes at a time, once or twice a day. When the client develops more ease, it can be practised at any time during the day, sitting or standing.

Progressive relaxation

Progressive relaxation is a physical relaxation technique developed by Edmund Jacobson (1938). Variations are also described by Atkinson and Raeburn (1987), Bernstein and Borkovec (1973), Bourne (1990), and Davis, Eshelman, and McKay (1982).

The technique involves tensing and releasing various muscle groups throughout the body. Usually it is practised in a comfortable chair, with the eyes closed, for a period of 10–20 minutes, and is enhanced by a quiet environment. The first step is to focus on the breathing. The various muscle groups of the body are then alternately tensed and relaxed over several seconds each in a specific order, usually beginning with the hands and arms, and then proceeding downwards from head to toes.

Audiotapes can be used for instructions on the way each muscle group is to be tensed and relaxed, and for the order in which this is done. Commercial tapes are available or the therapist can record tapes for a particular client. Some people prefer to memorize the sequence and exercise without tapes.

Meditation

Exercises for mental relaxation can be used either in conjunction with physical relaxation or separately. As with progressive relaxation exercises, they require a quiet environment, the setting aside of a period of up to 20 minutes, and a comfortable position.

One form of mental relaxation is a simple form of meditation described by Atkinson and Raeburn (1987), Benson (1975), and Bourne (1990). It involves repeating a sound or word with each breath. Atkinson and Raeburn, and Benson, for example, suggest that the word 'one' is silently repeated with every exhalation. The Mental Health Foundation of New Zealand has produced an excellent tape with written instructions for this meditation technique, which also includes instructions for learning progressive relaxation. Similar resources are available in other countries.

Davis, Eshelman, and McKay (1982) provide a useful chapter on meditation, along with detailed instructions for a variety of meditation exercises.

Visualization

Another form of mental relaxation involves visualizing a pleasant, relaxing scene. This can be facilitated by a therapist in person, or by the use of an audiotape. As with progressive relaxation, tapes are available commercially or can be recorded by the therapist.

In some visualization exercises the scene described is determined by the therapist, or by the speaker on the audiotape. A calm, relaxing scene is described, perhaps a forest or a beach. Often the description is artfully vague, to allow the client to fill in details which have meaning for them. For example, the speaker might include such statements as, 'Notice what you see ... see the colours'. In this way a picture rich in sensory detail is created, with references to the sights, sounds, smells, and textures of the scene. Usually this is accompanied by such suggestions as 'Your cares and worries are far away ... Let feelings of peace and calm flow over you ... Your body and mind are at peace ... You feel calm and relaxed.'

Alternatively, the client can be invited to recall a place where they have felt really relaxed, and to imagine being in that scene. The fantasy can be guided by prompts to recall the sensory details experienced.

The client can learn to use visualization exercises at home, either with or without the help of an audiotape. They can use tapes recorded by others or can record tapes for their own use. Sometimes these act as a form of self-hypnosis.

During these exercises the speaker uses a soothing almost monotonous tone, with trance-like qualities. Hypnosis is not necessary however, for visualization exercises to be effective, and some deliberately avoid it.

A variation on the use of visualization is described in the case study that follows this chapter (pp. 258–260).

Autogenics

Autogenic training is a systematic programme for teaching the body and mind to respond quickly to verbal commands to relax. It is one of the most effective ways to reduce chronic stress, and is described more fully by Davis, Eshelman, and McKay (1982), and Luthe (1969).

Essentially, autogenics involves sitting or lying in a relaxed undisturbed position, concentrating on statements that suggest warmth and heaviness in the limbs. Simple statements such as 'My right arm is heavy ... My arms and legs are heavy ... My right arm is warm' are repeated over a period of several minutes, several times a day. The exact wording changes each week, shifting the focus onto the heart, the breathing, the stomach, and the forehead.

Autogenic training has been found to be effective in the treatment of various bodily disorders, and in reducing anxiety, irritability, and fatigue. It has the benefits of enabling the client to create a trance-like state without dependence on a therapist.

Use of relaxation exercises in sexual-abuse therapy

Relaxation exercises are useful for anyone who is experiencing stress from emotional trauma following sexual abuse. A review of the literature by Bernstein and Borkovec (1973) suggests a number of other ways in which relaxation techniques could be relevant for therapy.

One of the most basic and important ways that relaxation training can be employed is in helping clients to discuss emotionally charged subjects. In this way relaxation techniques taught early in therapy can help to reduce tension and make it easier for the client to communicate their concerns. The techniques constitute a positive and non-threatening intervention which aids the development of the therapeutic relationship by providing immediate assistance. They also help the client to develop confidence in the therapy process, because they represent an added resource to cope with the potentially difficult times ahead.

Relaxation exercises can be practised before and after taking a client over the details of the abuse. Both progressive relaxation and hypnosis have been demonstrated to significantly lower the physiological responses (e.g. heart and respiration rates) to a stressful image (Bernstein & Borkovec 1973). Because of this they can be used to help the client to describe the details of the abuse.

Similarly, relaxation exercises can be used at the end of a stressful interview, or in conjunction with thought-stopping to deal with troublesome ideas or memories. Because they help to alleviate tension, the exercises are also useful for those experiencing insomnia, or for psychosomatic symptoms such as headaches and stomach pains.

Finally, relaxation exercises can be practised by therapists to help relieve the stress often associated with our work. When we practise relaxation exercises regularly ourselves, we are well prepared to teach them to our clients.

ANCHORING A RESOURCE

'Anchoring' is another empowering skill that we can teach our clients. It is a technique used in Neurolinguistic Programming (NLP), another school of therapy which has been greatly influenced by the work of Milton Erickson, and is described in detail by Bandler and Grinder (1979).

Anchoring involves creating an association between a simple physical response and a positive emotional state. Usually, the physical response is something which can be done easily and unobtrusively in any situation, such as silently saying a certain word, looking at a certain place, or doing something like clenching the fist, sniffing, blinking, or touching the elbow. The positive emotional state might be feeling calm, strong, or in control.

When this technique is used the positive emotional state is connected or 'anchored' to the physical activity in such a way that the desired emotional state can be induced by performing a simple physical act. Once 'anchored', this positive feeling can be used as a resource by the client when needed, to induce a sense of strength or well-being, or to contain distressing feelings by triggering a more desirable response.

Anchoring is a resource that clients can use to develop self-control over thoughts or feelings that bother them, and as a way of empowering them-selves to deal with a variety of difficult situations. They may also use this tech-nique during therapy to help themselves cope with distressing feelings or painful memories.

The basic steps of anchoring are as follows:

1   The client identifies the resource they want, e.g. 'feeling confident'.
2   The client identifies the physical act or 'self-anchor' they will use, e.g. pressing the left thumb into the index finger.
3   The therapist elicits details of a time in the past when the client has experienced the desired feeling. This is done by asking such questions as: 'Has there been a time in your life when you have felt more confident?' ... 'What did it feel like?' ... 'How did you stand?' ... 'How did you speak?' ... 'What did you do?'
4   The therapist listens carefully to the words used by the client, as the experience of the positive emotional state is described. In particular, the therapist observes any signs indicating that the client is beginning to experience the feelings they describe. This would be indicated, for exam-ple, by changes in facial expression or posture.
5   As the client describes this time in the past, they begin to experience the positive feeling that went with it. The therapist can comment on what is happening, for example:
    'I have a hunch that you may be feeling some of that confidence now.'
6   When the client is able to experience the specified feeling, they are asked to anchor it by using the self-anchor they had selected, for example:
    'I'd like you to talk about that feeling of confidence. ... When you begin to feel it you can press your thumb into your index finger to anchor it in place. ... Notice that confident feeling as your thumb presses into your finger', or:

'Go back to that time when you were feeling really confident. ... Press your thumb and finger together. ... Hold your breath and stand tall as you feel the confidence sweeping over you.'

7 At this stage the feeling may not be well anchored and it is useful to deal with any potential problems, for example:
'If that confidence starts to fade away, separate your thumb and finger.'
'If it stays and you get tired of pressing your thumb and finger together, you can separate them and keep feeling confident.'

8 The client practises several times, recalling the feeling and anchoring it each time with the physical response. The therapist facilitates this by repeating the words previously used by the client when describing their positive experience. The therapist reminds the client to anchor the physical response as they re-experience the feeling.

9 The client is then asked to use their anchor first and to then feel the feeling. The therapist checks whether the anchor is working, for example:
'Now I want you to press your thumb and index finger together, and you may be surprised to feel that sense of confidence returning. ... Can you feel that confident feeling?' or
'When you are ready, I'd like you to press your thumb and finger together and notice what you experience. Stop when you wish. What did you experience?'

10 If the anchor has not elicited the desired emotional state the client is asked to stop the physical response and continue practising, for example:
'If that confident feeling hasn't returned, separate your thumb and finger again. ... Good, the feeling is in the tips of your fingers. ... Practise once more.'

11 Once the connection between the physical response and the emotional state has been established, the client is asked to imagine a specific situation in the future where they will want to use the resource they have chosen. As they picture this potentially difficult situation they are asked to anchor in the desired resource with their anchor or physical response. Initially the therapist may remind them to do this, but they should practise to the stage where they can self-anchor without assistance.

12 The client is able to use their anchor as needed. They can elicit the resource in difficult situations during therapy, or in their life outside the therapy room.

VISUAL KINAESTHETIC DISSOCIATION

Another useful therapeutic technique derived from NLP is Visual Kinaesthetic Dissociation. It is often used in conjunction with anchoring and is described in more detail by Lankton (1980).

Literally, visual kinaesthetic dissociation means that visual perceptions or memories are separated from the emotions that are usually associated with them. Specifically, it is a technique for reviewing in the mind the sights and/or sounds of a traumatic experience, while feeling secure and comfortable. It is used to enable clients to recall and understand an experience such as sexual abuse without having to re-experience the feelings associated with it.

The client is asked to imagine the scene and to watch it unfold from an emotional distance. Usually this is facilitated by asking them to imagine that they are watching the scene on television, in a crystal ball, or in a movie theatre. A sense of comfort is created by helping them to picture themselves watching from a safe and pleasant place. They might be seated in a cosy room in an armchair, for example, or in a familiar movie theatre. Before proceeding, anchor(s) for comfort, security, and well-being are developed and tested, as described in the previous section.

It is important when using this technique that the client first practises by imagining only a mildly unpleasant scene, unlikely to include sexual abuse. The therapist should help them to go over the exercise several times, testing their ability to dissociate and with each session gradually moving to scenes that are more unpleasant. It might take several sessions before any attempt is made to view a really traumatic event.

When the client is ready to go over an abuse scene, additional resources can be enlisted. For example, they can be asked to imagine an invisible shield around them, a strong supportive person seated beside them, or a remote control switch that allows them to stop the film or change the channel any time they choose.

The basic stages in the process of visual kinaesthetic dissociation are as follows:

1 Develop an anchor for comfort and safety as described in 'Anchoring a Resource', pp. 240–242. Check that it is working.
2 Ask the client to imagine being in a movie theatre (or watching a play, or television) while feeling a sense of comfort, security, and well-being. Check that they are able to do this and elicit details of the comfortable situation in which they have placed themselves. Remind them that they can use their self-anchor any time they need to reinforce the sense of well-being, and/or suggest that they get in touch with their own sense of strength before proceeding, for example:

'I'd like you to imagine being somewhere like a movie theatre or at home watching TV ... somewhere there can be a screen or a stage. Where would you like to be? ... Where are you sitting? ... Now you may close your eyes and imagine feeling really comfortable and secure. What are you experiencing? ... I'd like you also to bring in your self-anchor, or you might like to get in touch with that sense of strength you have. Make sure you have that with you so you know you can use it anytime you want to.'

3 Ask the client to imagine a mildly unpleasant scene on the movie screen while feeling comfortable. It is important that this is drawn from the client's own experience or imagination, and not suggested by the therapist. Ask them to let you know when they have completed the scene. Check that they are able to do this, for example:
'How was that?'

4 Ask the client to imagine a mildly unpleasant scene from their own life, while feeling comfortable. Remind them that they can bring in their self-anchor or their sense of strength if needed. Check for their response:
'What happened?' or 'How was that?'

5 Ask the client to imagine being in the projection booth of the theatre, looking down on themselves feeling comfortable as they watch the mildly uncomfortable scene, for example:
'Now I'd like you to imagine being in the movie theatre, sitting up high in the projection booth. You are looking down on yourself in Row K. You can see yourself watching comfortably the unpleasant scene, feeling your sense of strength. If necessary use your anchor to maintain that comfortable feeling. Watch yourself watching, don't watch the scene. How do you look? ... How was that?'

Visual kinaesthetic dissociation is another resource our clients can use any time they want to uncover memories or to process an experience. To ensure that an abuse survivor is not overwhelmed by a flooding of memories, it is important to develop this skill gradually over time, and to continually re-check how it has affected them. This should be done at the end of each session, and again at the beginning of the next session. The therapist also checks that appropriate support people are available between sessions, and where possible meets with them to explain the client's needs and the ways that they can be most helpful.

This method is not used for catharsis, because it is designed to separate the client from their feelings about the abuse. It therefore needs to be used in conjunction with other techniques for helping the client to express their feelings.

Trance/hypnosis

One of the tools we use in therapy which can be traced most directly to Milton Erickson is the use of trance or hypnotic suggestion. Erickson used trance to help his clients utilize abilities and potential that already existed, but which remained unused or underdeveloped. This may occur through lack of training or understanding, or because 'learned limitations' or unhelpful beliefs prevent clients from noticing and fully using their own abilities (Erickson & Rossi 1979).

The benefit of trance is that our usual assumptions and beliefs are temporarily interrupted, so the mind is more receptive to new solutions and attitudes. When we help clients to suspend habitual beliefs we also help them to suspend the limitations imposed by these beliefs. Then they can learn more about themselves and express themselves more adequately. Clients are not changed by the trance, but put in touch with resources that they had not recognized previously.

Trance is another way of using indirect suggestion, which can be used when more direct methods such as giving advice and information are not successful or appropriate. It is not fundamentally different from any other form of effective communication. Grinder and Bandler (1981) describe it as acting somewhat like an amplifier, amplifying information that is already present but beyond consciousness. Trance also amplifies behaviour by eliciting more intense responses. It involves an altered state of consciousness, similar to that observed anytime in therapy when a client is particularly attentive, receptive, or involved.

Although we may not consciously intend to use hypnotic techniques, therapists are always making choices about the language, rhythm, and pace of their communications. Establishing a trance involves a combination of slow even speech and careful choice of words, and generally the therapist's pace of speech matches the client's breathing or blinking. Each client has their own way of going into a trance, and it is part of the therapist's skill to find an approach that works for a specific client.

Before trance is used, it is essential to obtain the client's informed consent, to join with them, and gather relevant information about their life, their personal resources, and their current concerns. Erickson and Rossi (1979) describe five stages in 'the dynamics of trance induction':

1 Helping the client to relax and to focus their attention. Often this involves reference to conscious beliefs and current behaviour because it is easier to focus on something which is immediately verifiable.
2 Interrupting habitual belief systems using distraction or surprise.

3 Accessing the unconscious with questions, puns, metaphor, and other forms of indirect suggestion.

4 Initiating an unconscious search for a new experience or solution to a problem.

5 Assisting in the development of a new response by the client as they access abilities, beliefs, and behaviours not previously explored or utilized. Therapeutic change appears to occur almost spontaneously.

Erickson took pains to answer claims that trance involves mysticism or a misuse of therapeutic power, as did other therapists whose work includes use of trance (e.g. Gilligan 1987; Grinder & Bandler 1981). Erickson described trance as a 'common everyday' event, experienced, for example, when we become absorbed or preoccupied and momentarily lose track of our outer environment (Erickson & Rossi 1979). Trance can occur spontaneously in many other forms (e.g. amnesia, age-regression, hallucination, time distortion), and can also be induced by suggestion and used for therapeutic purposes.

Erickson explained that the therapist only stimulates the client into activity, and that the client's task is to learn through their own efforts to understand their experience in a different way. The way in which they do this will be in terms of their own life experience. It will be guided by their own memories, attitudes, and ideas, and not by those of the therapist (Erickson & Rossi 1979).

Grinder and Bandler (1981) further explain that hypnosis is not a process of taking control of people, but a process of giving them control of themselves by providing information that they would not normally have. They believed that people are more discerning in a trance, and less vulnerable to being tricked than they are in a waking state. They claim that it is more difficult to get someone in a trance to behave in ways that do not lead to something meaningful and positive.

We acknowledge the power of trance, as we acknowledge the power of other forms of therapy, but with regard to the ethics and quality of our work, it must be subject to the same expectations as other therapeutic tools that we use. This includes ensuring that control remains with the client. We do this by using language that makes it explicit, for example, 'You are in control, I am just on the sidelines … You can choose to participate only so far as you feel comfortable.'

Here we provide only a brief introduction for those interested in trance. Its use is described in greater detail elsewhere, and those interested are referred to the writers mentioned above. Examples of two different ways of using trance are provided in the following case study.

CASE EXAMPLE
Building a Powerful Part of Self, The Rescue Scene, and Visualization Exercise

The following example is a composite case based on several young men seen at the Leslie Centre. It illustrates such techniques as normalizing, reframing, seeding ideas, and questioning to elicit new perspectives. It also illustrates three specific techniques commonly used in counselling adults who were sexually abused during their childhood or adolescence. We call these Building a Powerful Part of Self, The Rescue Scene, and Visualization. Each exercise is outlined in Chapter 11, and it may be useful to check the case example against the processes previously described.

In our example we describe 'Mike', a 19-year-old man, who was referred to the Centre because he had been sexually abused between the ages of 12 and 14. He experienced neglect and physical abuse from parents who each had a history of alcohol abuse. Consequently, Mike turned to a male neighbour for the affection and support he lacked at home.

The neighbour 'groomed' Mike under the guise of giving him the care and attention he craved. This person proceeded to sexually abuse Mike over a period of two years, committing the acts of masturbation and fellatio, and getting Mike to reciprocate.

Following this abuse, Mike was immensely troubled by thoughts that he must be homosexual. He worried about having engaged in sexual acts with a man, although he did not experience any sexual feelings towards men. Consequently he felt anxious and confused about his sexual orientation.

Mike also blamed himself for getting involved with the abuser, and experienced an enormous amount of guilt relating to the things he had done.

Continually thinking about this caused Mike to feel very anxious. This led to his use of alcohol and drugs as a coping mechanism, to the extent that he developed a serious problem with substance abuse from the age of 15.

SESSION ONE

During the first session an outline of Mike's story was obtained, and his response to the abuse was normalized:

'No wonder you responded to sexual abuse by using drugs and alcohol. All through your upbringing you learned that this is the way to handle stress and tension. This was part of the modelling you received from your parents.'

Mike's confusion about his sexual orientation was further normalized with an explanation from the therapist. Mike was told:

'Children naturally have a huge need for love and attention. When they are not receiving it at home they respond very easily to attention from an abuser. They are particularly vulnerable if the abuse is disguised in a package of care and support, as it was for you.

'It is also really normal for men who have been abused to be confused about their sexual orientation, especially when they feel too embarrassed or guilty to talk about it. Getting abused by a man does not make you homosexual, but unless you share your worries, you don't get a chance to sort out this confusion. You don't even get a chance to find out that you were not responsible for what happened.'

Mike's coming to a therapist for help was then reframed from a weakness to a strength.

'You have had a long history of neglect. Your parents were drinking instead of taking care of you, and then the person you turned to for love sexually abused you. Yet here you are taking steps to stop drinking and to deal with these issues of sexual abuse. This makes me wonder where you have got this enormous amount of strength from. Can you tell me, Mike, where this strength comes from?'

Mike was left to consider this question at the end of the first session. A contract was negotiated for several more sessions to deal with the issues Mike had raised.

SESSION TWO

The beginning of the second session was devoted to the re-establishment of rapport with Mike. He was also questioned about any changes that might have occurred since the previous session. Mike explained that he felt less anxious after talking about the things that had happened to him, but continued to place some blame on himself for having allowed the abuse to occur.

Mike was then told about a technique for helping people to feel more powerful. (See 'Building a Powerful Part of Self', pp. 203–207.) He was advised that we often use this exercise to help people who want to deal with issues relating to sexual abuse. The steps involved were explained, as was the unusual nature of the technique. Mike was advised that he did not have to participate if he felt unable or unwilling.

This opportunity to reject any technique we offer is very important for clients who have experienced sexual abuse. Providing choices, and allowing them to proceed at their own pace, gives our clients the control they need to develop trust and to overcome the sense of powerlessness they have previously experienced.

Mike agreed to continue, and the following dialogue occurred. Note the therapist's careful choice of words, and the even, rhythmic pattern which matches the client's breathing. This is typical of simple trance induction (Grinder & Bandler 1981).

THERAPIST   I will put this chair on the other side of the room in front of you, and I will move here to the side so I won't distract you. I would like you to look at the chair ... and as you look I would like you to imagine a powerful person. This may be a part of yourself ... a powerful person within yourself. Or it might be someone you know ... someone who has influenced you ... or someone you imagine. Someone who is strong and wise. Imagine what sort of person would be in that chair. Someone who could support you, someone in that chair. What do they look like? ... Is it a man or is it a woman?

MIKE   It's a man.

THERAPIST   As you look at that man in the chair ... and as you begin to notice different things about him ... you may notice his age. How old do you think he is?

MIKE   Thirtyish.

THERAPIST   As you look at him ... you may notice his hair ... the way it's combed ... how it's parted ... it may not even be parted.

What colour hair does he have? ... What form does it have?

MIKE   It's brown, and kind of wavy.

THERAPIST   Look really closely at his face ... his eyebrows ... the lines ... notice his eyes ... notice all those things. What sort of eyes does he have?

MIKE   They're blue. They crinkle up a bit at the sides when he smiles.

THERAPIST   So he's thirtyish, with brown wavy hair, and blue eyes, and his eyes crinkle when he smiles. Now look at his clothes ... and notice what he is wearing. ... Notice how he sits ... and notice how big he is. What do you see?

MIKE   He's medium build. He looks relaxed but he doesn't slouch.

THERAPIST   What does he wear?

MIKE   He's casually dressed, but neat. He wears jeans and a blue jersey.

THERAPIST   Does he remind you of anybody ... someone you've known before ... someone you may know now?

MIKE   Parts of him, yes, he reminds me of someone.

THERAPIST   As you continue to look at him ... just staring at the chair ... I would like you to think how this person would be able to help you. Would a person like this have the strength ... would he have the knowledge? As you look and notice I want you to wonder if this person is someone who could help you?

MIKE   Uhuh. Yep.

THERAPIST   What would his name be?

MIKE   John.

THERAPIST   As you look at John ...I would like you to think of some problem ... some difficulty that you may have ... relating to the things we have been discussing. And as you look at John, I would like you to think of a question that you could ask him. This would be a question about your problem ... a question that you would like some help with. You may need to think for a moment, about the question you would like to ask ... or you may have a question, one that immediately comes to mind. And as you think of that question, it may be interesting to note how a person like this could help you. All sorts of things may be going through your mind as you look. This may even seem a little strange, very strange. In your mind I would like you to ask John the question. ... Have you done that?

MIKE   Yes.

THERAPIST   Now I want you to come over here and be John.

The therapist asks Mike to sit in the chair opposite, and sits next to him out of Mike's visual field. Soon he will be asking Mike to write a letter, so he takes care to sit in a position where he would not be able to see what Mike is writing.

Note the care now necessary to help Mike take on the role of John, using the description previously elicited:

THERAPIST   You have now become John. You are thirtyish, with brown wavy hair, and blue eyes that crinkle when you smile. You sit straight ... but relaxed ... in your chair ... and you feel strong and wise. ... John, over there you can see Mike. Notice how he sits. Notice what he's wearing. How does he look?

JOHN (MIKE)   He looks pretty anxious.

THERAPIST   As you look at Mike you will want to support him and help him. You will want to provide whatever help he needs, because you know that you have the resources to do that. Your abilities and strength will enable you to help this young man. As you look at Mike, knowing that he looks pretty anxious, think about the things that are troubling him. Can you recall the question he asked you?

JOHN (MIKE)   Yes, I can.

The therapist hands Mike a pen and paper, and continues as follows:

THERAPIST   I would like you to write a letter, to Mike. And when you start that letter I would like you to start with the words 'Dear Mike, I love you because ... .' Tell Mike all the things you love about him, all the things you admire and respect. Following that I would like you to answer the question, to answer the question that he asks. Maybe that's giving him some ideas, or maybe it's giving him some choices, but however you choose to answer it, just make sure that it's helping him to find some solutions.

In the role of John, Mike proceeds to write the letter. The process takes about five minutes and about two pages are used.

THERAPIST   I would like you to fold the letter, and place it on the chair opposite.

Mike places the letter on the other chair.

THERAPIST   Now I want you to come back here and be Mike. ... Pick up the letter, and sit down in the chair. And, Mike, I would like you to recall the question that you asked this man over there, the question that you asked John. Do you remember the question that you asked John, Mike?

MIKE   Yeah.

THERAPIST   I would like you to read the letter, and think about the question that you asked.

≥ therapist allows Mike to spend as much time as he needs to read and digest the letter.

THERAPIST   Is that useful?

MIKE   Yes.

THERAPIST   I would like you to keep that letter and read it whenever you need to. It might be of some use in the future.

Mike puts the letter in his pocket.

THERAPIST   I would like you to look over there, Mike, and I would like you to look at John ... and somehow I would like you to think of a way of making him a part of yourself ... because John is a part of you, and he's a part of you that is able to support you, and to heal you, and to take care of you through difficult times. So I would like you to think of a way that you can make that other part fully part of yourself, so it can look after you and become one with you. Some people pick it up and imagine that they are rubbing it into themselves, some people just sit here visualizing that it becomes part of themselves. People do different things. I would like you to allow John to become part of yourself, in whatever way that is right for you.

Mike walks across to the other chair, and visualizes himself picking up John and holding him close. The therapist then checks with Mike that he feels all right, and that he is ready to continue with his day. They make another appointment and the therapist ensures that Mike has people to support him between sessions. Mike is advised on how to make contact if he has any concerns before the next appointment.

Mike is also given some homework. He is asked to practise the process of building a powerful part of himself between sessions. He is to choose a special time of day that suits him, and to go through this exercise on two separate occasions. This homework is designed to help him to develop a way of consulting with himself. Through such dialogue he can begin generating solutions for himself, and begin allaying some of the fears and anxieties he has experienced as a result of sexual abuse. It may also help him to deal with some of the issues that are being brought up in therapy.

SESSION THREE

At the beginning of the third session Mike stated that he was feeling less guilty about the abuse, saying, 'The neighbour took advantage of me because I was vulnerable and needed love.' However, he was still experiencing some anxiety about being sexually aroused by a man. When he stated, 'I got sexually excited when he did those things to me', the therapist responded by looking at Mike directly, and said, 'Thank God you're normal.' The therapist then explained:

> 'Boys who get erections, or in fact anybody who gets sexually aroused when they are being fondled, is just responding normally, because that's how our bodies are built. Bodies are made to respond to being touched.'

Mike is told about another client who was made to take off his clothes at knife point. In this case the perpetrator then committed the act of fellatio until the young man ejaculated. The story provides Mike with a different perspective, because it very clearly separates choice and pleasure from sexual response. It helps to normalize Mike's responses, seeding information through the use of metaphor. The story of the other client parallels Mike's story in only one crucial aspect, but allows different conclusions to be drawn. The following dialogue then took place:

THERAPIST   Do you think it was the young man's fault?

MIKE   No.

THERAPIST   Why?

MIKE   Because the guy had a knife and he had no choice.

THERAPIST   No, he didn't have a choice but his body responded anyway.

MIKE   Umm.

THERAPIST   There is something I don't understand, Mike. You worry about being gay but you think only about women in a sexual way. If you were gay, would you think about men sexually or would you think about women sexually? Think about it and we will discuss it in the next session.

By asking Mike to consider this question, the therapist has given him the opportunity to develop a different perception of the issue. Once again, the therapist has not dwelt on the subject, but seeded an idea, leaving Mike to make his own discoveries. Following this question the session continued. The following dialogue highlights the techniques used in the rescue scene.

THERAPIST   Today, Mike, I would like to explore in a more in-depth way, how this man sexually abused you. How do feel about that?

MIKE   OK.

THERAPIST   The way I would like you to do that is by getting you to draw pictures of the offender and some of things he did to you. This will give you an opportunity to express your feelings in a more powerful way than you have been able to do before. ... I understand that it might be really difficult for you, so I just want to check out again if that is OK.

MIKE   I feel nervous, but I will try.

THERAPIST   Before we do this, I would like you to put John on a chair over
              here just like we did in the last session.

The therapist assists Mike to develop a clear image of John, using the
description elicited in the last session:

THERAPIST   You recall that John is that powerful part of yourself. He's about
              thirty, with brown, wavy hair, and he has blue eyes that crin-
              kle when he smiles. Can you see him there, in his neat, casual
              clothes, sitting straight but relaxed?

MIKE   Yes.

THERAPIST   Remember that he is strong and wise, he is someone who
              would support you when you need him. Now I want you to
              reverse roles and be John.

Mike shifts to the opposite chair, and the therapist moves also to be with him.

THERAPIST   John, Mike is going to go back to a time in his life when he
              was abused. Is it OK for him to do that today?

JOHN (MIKE)   Yes.

THERAPIST   If Mike needs any help to do this, I'll get him to come back
              and be you. Is that OK?

JOHN (MIKE)   Yes.

If Mike becomes too distressed while going over the details of the abuse,
it is now possible to get him to take on the role of John. In this way he
can have a sense of his own strength, and can be reminded that he is no
longer the 12-year-old boy who was being abused. At such a time a temporary role-reversal with the 'powerful part of self' usually is sufficient to
allow the client to continue going over the abuse scene. At the very least
it provides a way of stopping the process while leaving the client emotionally intact, and with a sense of control over their therapy.

THERAPIST   Now I want you to come back and be Mike.

They return to their original positions.

THERAPIST   If it gets too difficult we will ask John to help. Where would you
              like to place him in the room while we talk about the things that
              happened to you?

Mike places the chair on which he had sat as John in a corner of the
room, not far from his own chair.

THERAPIST   What sort of person were you when you were 12?

MIKE   Lonely.

THERAPIST   So you were a lonely person. What else was it like being 12?

MIKE   I was scared, scared to go home, in case the old man was drunk.

THERAPIST   So you were a lonely and scared kid. Are lonely and scared kids easy target for child molesters?

Mike looks at the therapist. The point is not laboured, but the question helps Mike to develop a different view of the abuse and its context.

THERAPIST   How did this guy get you to be his friend?

MIKE   He used to give me things, take me out and feed me.

THERAPIST   So this is how he tricked you into being his friend?

This response by the therapist is a simple reframe which is very useful in sexual-abuse counselling. It is developed further in the following dialogue:

THERAPIST   How long was he like this before he tried to do things to you?

MIKE   A while, I don't know.

THERAPIST   Did he try something straight away? Or did he pretend to be your friend for a while?

MIKE   It was a while. I thought he really cared for me.

THERAPIST   He was a good pretender.

MIKE   Ummm.

THERAPIST   Can you draw him for me?

MIKE   Not very well.

THERAPIST   That's OK, it only matters that you draw him.

MIKE   OK.

The therapist gives Mike some felt-tip pens and a large sheet of paper. As Mike begins to draw, the therapist asks him questions to clarify the details, for example, 'What can you remember about his eyes?' … 'He must have been much bigger than you?'

THERAPIST   What was his name?

MIKE   Malcolm.

THERAPIST   Now that you have finished, where would you like to put his picture in this room for the moment?

Mike places his picture of the offender in the far corner of the room.

THERAPIST   Could you draw another picture please, Mike? I would like you to draw a picture of a scene that comes to your mind, a time when you were being abused by Malcolm.

Mike takes the new sheet of paper and begins to draw the abuse scene. As he draws, the dialogue between therapist and client continues. The therapist creates opportunities to seed ideas, shifting responsibility away from Mike and onto the perpetrator. The present tense is used to revisit the scene in the most effective way:

THERAPIST How old is Malcolm at this time?

MIKE 40.

THERAPIST How old are you?

MIKE 12.

THERAPIST Do 12-year-olds generally do what 40-year-olds want them to do?

MIKE Mmm.

THERAPIST Are 40-year-old people responsible for what happens between them and a child, or is the child responsible?

MIKE The adult's responsible.

THERAPIST Where is this happening, whereabouts are you in the drawing?

MIKE Malcolm's house. In the bedroom.

THERAPIST You are here in the bedroom. What do you remember about that room?

MIKE There wasn't much light, because he'd pull the curtains across. I remember how I got to dread it every time he'd close those curtains.

THERAPIST Can you remember anything else?

MIKE Just the bed. It had an old blue cover on it and it creaked when you sat on it. I still feel sick when I think of that creak.

THERAPIST What's Malcolm doing?

MIKE He's sucking me off.

THERAPIST What else does he do?

MIKE He takes my hand and puts it on his penis.

THERAPIST Does he do anything else?

MIKE No, he just gets me to hold my hand there, and he keeps saying how nice it is.

THERAPIST And how do you feel?

MIKE I feel yucky, really sick inside.

THERAPIST When you look at the picture, and you look at Malcolm, and you look at that young part of yourself, who's in charge? Who is making it happen?

MIKE	He's making it happen, he is saying to me that I really like it. But I don't like it. I'm not sure.
THERAPIST	That's a young part of you in that picture. That's the 12-year-old part of you. Now you are bigger and older. Would he be able to do that to you now?
MIKE	No, I'd kill him! I would damn well kill him!
THERAPIST	Where do you want to put this picture?

Mike places the picture in the opposite corner to where he had previously placed 'John', his 'powerful part of self'.

THERAPIST	Stand up, Mike. Come and stand over here.

Mike moves over to the picture of Malcolm in the other corner. Together, therapist and client look down on the abuser.

THERAPIST	When you think about Malcolm abusing you over there in the scene you've just drawn, how do you feel?
MIKE	Really angry, really angry!
THERAPIST	Would you like to say anything to him? Would you like to do anything to him?

Mike rips the picture of Malcolm into tiny pieces.

THERAPIST	Where do you want to put him?

Mike begins throwing the bits of paper out the window.

THERAPIST	That's good. Get rid of him. That's really good.

When Mike has finished the therapist directs him to the picture of the abuse scene. The therapist hands Mike a pair of scissors, asking him to cut himself carefully out of the abuse scene. He is told to be very careful not to damage himself, but not to worry about the remainder of the picture. Mike very gently cuts himself out, very slowly and carefully.

THERAPIST	Put that young part of yourself somewhere else, somewhere you can look after it. What do you want to do with the rest of the drawing?

Mike places the drawing of his younger self carefully into his pocket. He then begins to stamp on the drawing. Then the therapist hands him a long tube of rolled-up newspaper. Mike beats the drawing rapidly, angrily, continuing for about 10 minutes until the paper has torn apart into a number of pieces. He is encouraged to tell Malcolm what he thinks of him as he beats the drawing. The blows are accompanied by strong statements such as 'You bastard!' … 'It's all your fault!' …'You took advantage of a lonely kid!' … 'How dare you try to stuff up my life like that!'. When he is finished, the therapist continues:

THERAPIST   What shall we do with the bits, Mike?

Mike picks up the bits of paper, throwing each bit out of the window.

THERAPIST   That's great, Mike. Now I want you to sit over here and just begin to picture John in that chair. Ask him if it's OK to finish now, or is there something else you need to do before we bring this session to a close.

MIKE   It's OK, I know it's OK.

The therapist then gets Mike to reintegrate John into himself, just as he did in the previous session. The dialogue continues.

THERAPIST   I would like you to bring out that young part of yourself that you rescued and take a good look at it. I'm wondering what you think.

MIKE   It's OK, I'm OK.

THERAPIST   Look after that young part of yourself that survived. You rescued it. How are you different now?

MIKE   I'm bigger.

THERAPIST   Are you stronger?

MIKE   Much stronger. That wouldn't happen to me now. I wouldn't let it.

Mike is directed to think of some ways of looking after that young part of himself, that child within himself, and is given telephone numbers of 24-hour counselling services in case he needs any support before the next session. The therapist reiterates that Mike is welcome to telephone if he needs any help before they next meet.

SESSION FOUR

Mike begins the session enthusiastically, acknowledging that the abuse was not his fault, and says he is no longer plagued by concerns about his sexual orientation. The therapist highlights the changes made by Mike, asking such questions as: 'How come you have stopped doubting yourself?' …'What has made you realize that it was his fault and not yours?' … 'What is it like to put guilt where it belongs?'

Mike is then asked if he minds taking part in a visualization exercise about his future (see p. 239) and the process is outlined for him. Mike readily agrees and the following exercise is facilitated by the therapist. The exercise is conducted using trance (see pp. 245–246).

The specific technique used for this trance is described by Grinder and Bandler (1981) as the '5-4-3-2-1 Exercise'. It begins by focusing Mike's attention on verifiable, sensory-based observations of his current behaviour, for example, 'You sit there listening to my voice'. ... 'You can notice the temperature of your hands.' Five such verifiable statements are followed by one statement that is internally oriented and non-verifiable: 'You're finding yourself feeling more comfortable inside.' Gradually the number of sensory-based, verifiable statements are decreased, the number of non-verifiable statements are increased, and a trance develops.

Each statement is connected by the use of such transition words as 'and' and 'as', and follows an even rhythm which does not differentiate between sentences. The trance combines familiar experiences with the strange and unexpected, and so allows Mike to suspend his usual ways of thinking. He is then free to consider other possibilities, for example, 'Notice yourself feeling certain and strong' ... 'feel all the feelings that go with being healed.'

In the following transcript the pace and rhythm of speech matches the pace and rhythm of Mike's breathing. Pauses between breaths are indicated by a series of dots.

'As you sit there ... listening ... to my voice ... and you can notice ... the temperature ... of your hands ... as they are clasped ... together ... and with your feet ... being supported ... and the noises ... you can hear ... you're finding yourself ... feeling ... more comfortable ... inside. ... And as you continue ... to sit ... with your elbows ... resting ... on the chair ... and your eyes ... closed ... and your head ... fully supported ... you will find yourself ... beginning to drift ... into a more ... and more ... relaxed state ... and while you ... continue to listen ... to the sound of my voice ... and the noise ... of the people ... far away ... more and more ... you are finding yourself ... slipping ... deeper ... and deeper ... into a state ... of relaxation. ... As you lie there ... with your jaw ... beginning to fall ... you know ... in some way ... how different you feel ... and this difference ... is allowing you ... to drift ... a little like ... lying ... in the warm sea. ... As you move up ... and you move down ... with the waves ... as they go in ... and go out ... and as you find yourself ... drifting ... backwards ... and forwards ... you may allow yourself ... to go ... on a little journey ... in your mind. ... And this journey ... will take you ... to places ... where you have perhaps ... not been. ... A safe journey ... a journey ... you can just drift ... into. ... You might like ... to allow yourself ... to think ... of walking ... along the beach ... far away ... from the other people ... and as you walk ... along the beach ... you can see ... in the distance ... a whole lot of trees ... and you become ... very curious. ... As you head ... towards them ... you can notice ... along the side ... of the path ... that you are treading ... all the colours ... as the beach ... begins to change ... to some green vegetation. ... And as you get closer ... and closer ... to the trees ... you can see ... all sorts of birds ... and plants ... that you've not noticed before. ... You find yourself moving deeper ... and deeper ... into the forest ... and listening to the sounds ... all around. ... And you find yourself ... quite safe ... in this forest ... and become interested ... in all the things ... along the way. ... And as you keep going ... moving forward ... further forward ... you see a clearing ... up ahead ... and in that clearing ... you come across ... a pool. ... And that pool ... is fed by a stream. ... And you notice ... all the things around ... the outside of the pool. ... As you watch ... and listen ... and feel ... and as you look ... into the pool ... you can see ... a reflection ... a reflection ... of yourself. ... Look very carefully ... at yourself ... and notice ... how different ... you look. ... Notice yourself ... feeling certain ... and strong. ... See ... how your face ... is different. ... And as you look at yourself ... you may begin to notice ... and to feel ... other differences ... that go along ... with being healed. ... Although being healed ... is not forgetting ... it's remembering ... with a strength ... it's knowing yourself ... it's moving forward. ... And as you look ... very carefully ... at this healed self ... I want you to step inside the picture ... and feel all of the feelings ... that go with being healed ... just like stepping into a canvas. ... Allow those feelings ... to go through your body. ... You may even notice ... some different thoughts about yourself. ... And as you ... step away from the pool ... in a different way ... notice how different ... you are. ... As you walk back ... along the path ... going back ... the way you came ... notice the difference ... as you walk ... back ... towards the beach. ... And as you get closer ... and closer ... you may begin to think ... about all the changes ... that you've made ... or are going to make. ... And as you reach the sand ... and walk along ... further back ... back to where you started ... back to the sea ... back to the comfort ... of people ... rather than the comfort ... of the forest. ... And as you sit there ... feeling comfortable ... and as you breathe ... in ... and out ... taking all the time ... you need ... to come back ... to this room ... knowing that something ... has changed ... or knowing ... that something ... can be different.'

The positive vision enjoyed by Mike while in a trance creates an expectancy of change. The next step is to make the vision more concrete by helping Mike to make specific plans. Before the session ends Mike is asked to write down the steps he needs to take in order to move into the future in a positive way.

Session five

Mike brings to the session a plan he has developed to help himself remain free of drugs. This includes expressing his feelings more openly, mixing with others who are maintaining a drug-free lifestyle, and enrolling in a training course at the local technical institute. He already has in place a good support system to help him put his plans into practice.

Previous thoughts of self-blame relating to the abuse, and anxiety about his sexual orientation are no longer issues for Mike. The therapist explains that people who have been abused sometimes begin to doubt themselves again, and that self-doubt is quite normal at certain times. Mike is advised not to worry unduly about these times, as he has already developed some useful ways of overcoming self-doubt. If necessary he could also get help in the future by talking with friends or going to see an appropriate counsellor.

At this stage Mike stated his belief that he did not need further counselling. The therapist agreed, and congratulated Mike on his courage, his perseverance, and his progress. The therapist thanked Mike for sharing a difficult and important part of his life, and concluded the session early.

The early conclusion was explained in the following way: 'You have done really well. I would just be wasting your time if we continued this session. There is no need for me to help a normal person who has sorted out his difficulties.'

PART 6

THERAPY WITH OFFENDERS

12

SEX OFFENDERS:
Causes and Treatments

The focus of this book is on therapy for sexual-abuse survivors and their families. It is useful in our work with survivors, however, to have some understanding of offenders. This helps us to answer questions that our survivor clients often ask, such as 'Why did he do it?' It provides us with relevant information to seed ideas about 'grooming' techniques used by offenders to gain the trust of their victims and the opportunity to abuse. It helps us to explain that offenders frequently plan the abuse. It also prepares us to deal with concerns the survivor may raise, such as how to respond appropriately to an abuser within the family.

This chapter briefly describes common issues relating to offenders. For those seeking a more detailed understanding we recommend *Treating Child Sex Offenders and Victims: A Practical Guide* (Salter 1988). Other useful references are cited throughout the chapter.

Usually we do not use the word 'victim' in our work with clients who have been abused as we do not find it respectful or helpful for survivors to think of themselves in this way. However, 'victim' is used frequently in this chapter because we find it is useful for offenders to understand the effects of their behaviour in such terms.

The issues addressed in this chapter are:
- Possible Causes of Abuse
- Why Men Abuse more than Women
- The Cycle of Offending
- The Scope of Assessment
- Tools and Procedures for Assessment
- Treatment
- Conclusion.

Possible causes of abuse

Paedophilia is defined as an adult's conscious sexual interest in pre-pubertal children (Araji & Finkelhor 1986). It is demonstrated either by sexual contact with a child or by masturbating while fantasizing sexually about children. Sexual abuse of young children therefore involves both abnormal sexuality, and an abuse of power. Consequently, treatment of sexually abusive behaviour must address issues of power and control (physical and emotional), as well as an element of abnormal sexuality.

Various theories have been proposed to explain paedophilia, originating primarily from fields as diverse as psychoanalytic theory, social learning theory, and feminism. But as no single theory explains the full range of paedophiliac behaviour, a combination of factors must be considered.

Araji and Finkelhor have described four major factors which predispose someone to sexual abuse. A combination of any of these factors may be present in any particular offender. Araji and Finkelhor's model is able to explain the wide range of personality profiles found amongst offenders, because it takes into account a variety of different sources of abusive behaviour. They consider sociological, physiological, behavioural, cognitive, and emotional aspects which can contribute to the development and maintenance of paedophilia.

The four factors described by Araji and Finkelhor are summarized as follows:

1 The adult's emotional needs are met by children

Sexual abuse sometimes involves an adult who finds it emotionally satisfying to relate to a child. This can be explained in a number of ways.

One explanation can be found in psychoanalytic theories where the paedophile is considered to be emotionally immature. He has probably experienced difficulties within his own childhood which remain unresolved. His emotional development becomes stalled at a child's level, so he continues to relate to children.

This idea has been extended by some theorists, cited by Araji and Finkelhor, who believe that abusers are not just emotionally immature, but also often lacking in social skills. Abusers frequently have low self-esteem, and experience a sense of power and control only in relationships with people who are younger and more vulnerable. Sexual fantasies about children are seen to be one way of overcoming the sense of powerlessness they have experienced since their own childhood.

Another explanation for an adult's use of children to fill emotional needs can be found in social-learning theory. This applies particularly to people with a history of childhood sexual abuse who later become abusers themselves. They have experienced role models of abusive behaviour from someone who is more powerful, and may even consider this to be normal. One way in which they try to overcome the trauma of childhood abuse is through identification with the aggressor.

Feminists have extended social-learning theory with the notion that males are socialized to be dominant, and to initiate sexual relationships. They learn to value partners who are younger and subservient, and sexual abuse is regarded by some as an extension of these values.

2 Being sexually aroused by children

A number of reasons have been cited to explain paedophilia in terms of sexual arousal.

One theory suggests that adult abusers have learned to find children sexually arousing from early childhood experiences. Some have been sexually aroused by other children, and continue to find children sexually attractive. A similar theory is that they experienced a traumatic sexual experience as a child. The memories of this experience have become part of their sexual fantasies, and masturbating to these fantasies increases their impact and increases the potential for the adult to act out their fantasies of sex with a child.

Another possible explanation for paedophilia in those who were abused as children is that the role model they have experienced is of an adult being aroused to a child. This theory suggests another way in which socialization may reduce normal inhibitions and so make abuse more likely.

Pornography also contributes to sexual arousal. By objectifying women and sometimes presenting children as sex objects, it fosters attitudes that condone the use of women and children for sexual gratification without any consideration of their rights.

Exposure to adult pornography can be sexually arousing for children as well. This in turn makes adults more likely to be aroused by them. Many paedophiles use pornography quite consciously to try to arouse children sexually, or to sustain their own fantasies about sex with children.

Finally, biological factors such as hormonal abnormalities have been cited as possible causes of paedophilia. According to these theories, sexual arousal to children could be related to a genetic or medical condition. Although such theories have often been taken seriously, generally they fail to explain why children in particular become arousing to paedophiles.

3 Difficulties meeting emotional and sexual needs in an adult relationship

Adult sex offenders frequently possess definable characteristics that make it difficult for them to fulfil their emotional and social needs in adult relationships. These include low self-esteem, feelings of social inadequacy and sexual inferiority, and lack of skills in developing age-appropriate relationships.

Psychoanalytic theories that include oedipal conflict and castration anxiety have been used to explain how these difficulties may occur. Difficulties relating to women are explained in terms of childhood experiences, which hinder the development of adult heterosexual relationships.

Other theories have focused more on crises in the adult's life, such as initial traumatic experiences of sex as an adult (e.g. impotence, rejection) or breakdown in a marital relationship. When such experiences are combined with beliefs which inhibit masturbation or which do not allow for the development of adult sexual relationships outside marriage, some adults will turn to children as a sexual outlet.

As therapists we find it more useful to think of abusers as having inadequate social skills, which provides us with some indications of how the problem might be solved.

4 Lack of conventional inhibitions against having sex with children

A number of explanations have been described which help to account for the abuser's failure to control his abusive behaviour. These include physiological explanations such as psychosis, senility, and alcohol abuse. Psychological explanations which focus on poor impulse control have also been advanced. For some paedophiles, a crisis in their own lives can lead to abusive behaviour. Stress caused by unemployment, separation, or grief can also lower the usual inhibitions.

From feminist theory we have an understanding of the ways in which abuse is facilitated by inequalities in the distribution of power, specifically by the power accorded to fathers within families.

Some people provide excuses for abusers and minimize the impact of their actions with such statements as 'She led him on' and 'He didn't do that much'. The extent to which abuse occurs is also often denied. These issues contribute to difficulties in dealing with abusers and thus act to reduce inhibitions which might deter them from committing offences.

Summary

It is evident that there is a wide variation in the factors that lead someone to abuse a child, and in the reasons why it is difficult for them to stop. Although profiles of the 'typical offender' have been described, relying on these can serve to focus attention on some groups more than others. Paedophilia is a problem that transcends cultural and socio-economic boundaries, so profiles that do not take this into account are of limited value.

Araji and Finkelhor provide a valuable summary of theories about the causes of sexually abusive behaviour. In our work with offenders we have found some of these more useful than others. Some of the issues that we believe need most attention during treatment are attitudes that promote male dominance over women and children, difficulties in meeting emotional needs in age-appropriate relationships, deviancy in sexual arousal patterns, and the use of pornography.

WHY MEN ABUSE MORE THAN WOMEN

By far the majority of all sex offenders are male. It has been estimated that women represent only about 3 to 4 percent of all sex offenders (Farrelly & Sebastian 1984; Russell 1983). When women do offend sexually they often act in collaboration with a man who has instigated the abuse (Faller 1987).

Feminists have described the different socialization processes which help to account for this gender difference (e.g. Gilligan 1982). Finkelhor (1984) has also attempted to explain it; some of the more likely reasons he describes are listed below:

- Women learn earlier and more fully to differentiate between sexual and non-sexual forms of attention.
- Men are socialized more towards expressing their sexuality through separate acts. Women tend to be more influenced by the context of the relationship in which the sex act occurs. They are more likely to be sensitive to their partner's emotional responses and less likely to impose their own sexual desires on an unwilling participant.
- Heterosexual men are socialized to believe that their sexual partners should be younger and smaller than themselves. Heterosexual women are socialized to believe that appropriate sexual partners are likely to be older and larger.
- Men are socialized to believe that heterosexual success is important for their gender identity. Finkelhor believes that this helps men to define who they are and how successful they are, far more than it influences women.

Men are socialized to be dominant in sexual relationships, while women's sexualization teaches them to be subservient.

- Men who have been abused themselves are more likely to externalize their feelings, expressing their anger in abuse of others. Women are more likely to internalize their experience, for example, by becoming depressed or anxious. This, too, is a result of gender differences in socialization which make the overt expression of anger more difficult for women than for men.

The cycle of offending

The factors that typically contribute to sexually abusive behaviour can be illustrated as a cycle of offending (see diagram below). Although this represents a simplified summary of events we have found it useful as an explanation of abusive behaviour because most offenders can easily relate to it.

It may take several days or several years for a particular offender to complete this cycle. Typically the time taken decreases with repeated offending.

As the pattern becomes established the offender may move directly from rationalization to fantasy. This is more likely to occur when the conventional social and emotional barriers that prevent abuse are lacking.

Each offender develops his own pattern of behaviour, thoughts, and emotions which can be incorporated into the cycle. It is useful to illustrate this to provide the offender and others with a better understanding of the factors which lead to abuse. Once the individual pattern has been identified

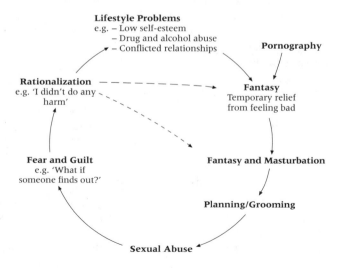

it is also easier to plan ways of breaking the cycle. This is discussed more fully in 'Patterns of offending', p. 277.

Treatment can focus on any stage of the cycle as a way of interrupting its progress, and usually employs interventions at each stage of the cycle. It involves dealing with the behaviours, beliefs, emotions, and life-style problems which contribute to abuse. Identifying the unique characteristics of each individual's cycle of offending is therefore a necessary part of assessment and treatment.

THE SCOPE OF ASSESSMENT

In order to treat an offender effectively it is important to undertake a thorough assessment. This may take place over three or four sessions, as rapport and trust are established.

As in our work with survivors, assessment is an ongoing therapeutic process. It begins with the first information we receive, and finishes with our last contact with the offender. It must be done in a way that facilitates achievement of the treatment goals.

The extent of the initial assessment depends on the resources available, the skill of the therapist, and on whether the therapist is planning to treat the offender or to refer him to specialist services in another agency. For example, a social worker in a child and family agency may only determine that abuse has occurred, while a therapist who works with sex offenders seeks to determine causes and to develop a treatment plan. A thorough assessment requires money, time, and specialized training.

The assessment of sex offenders must cover three main areas:
- Attitudes and beliefs
- Their own sexuality
- Social skills.

As part of our assessment it is also important to check that offenders have undergone a medical screening for sexually transmitted diseases. If positive results are obtained from such a screening, the necessary treatment can take place and we can ensure that their victims are also checked.

Attitudes and beliefs

The abuser's attitude to his offending is an important factor to be considered. Initially most offenders deny the abuse, while many minimize the extent of the abuse and the seriousness of its effects. Some deny having sexual fantasies about children, and many deny planning the offences. Denial and minimization are typical of the offender's response to a disclosure, and are likely to continue into treatment. These responses are largely motivated by fear of possible consequences, which might include imprisonment or rejection by the family. Shame and guilt may also influence their responses. It is important, however, to distinguish that prior to treatment the shame and guilt usually relate to self-pity from the consequences of having been found out, rather than shame and guilt for the hurt they have caused their victims.

Other attitudes to be assessed include the offender's ideas about gender roles in society, the level of their understanding of the effects of abuse on the victim, and the amount of responsibility they take for their behaviour.

Sexuality

It is important to obtain as much information as possible about the offender's sexual experiences and preferences. The therapist enquires about the history and quality of their sexual experiences. What was their first sexual experience? How old were they? How much experience of sex have they had? What was the relative age of their partners/victims? What was the gender of their partners/victims? Have they had sex within an equal, consenting relationship? What was this like for them? Have they had any experiences of being physically or sexually abused themselves? How do they identify their sexual orientation?

The offender's knowledge of sex and their attitudes to it are also assessed. This helps to determine how much treatment needs to focus on education.

Accurate information about the sexual fantasies that an offender has when masturbating is essential for effective treatment. This provides an indication of any deviant arousal patterns, particularly sexual arousal to fantasies about children. Similarly, fantasies which involve the use of force can be reinforced by masturbation until violence becomes part of sexual behaviour. Fantasies therefore play a major role in the development of deviant sexual practice, because they combine with masturbation to lower resistance to ideas about relating sexually to children.

Information about sexual fantasies is likely to be obtained only gradually, however, and only after a level of trust, rapport, and respect has been established.

Social skills and emotional awareness

From the way the offender presents himself in the therapy situation some tentative assessment can be made of his social skills. Ideally, any conclusions should be checked with other people, such as family members, who see him in different contexts.

Questioning can elicit further information about the number, nature, and quality of the offender's relationships. This helps to develop a picture of his personal resources, and of any difficulties he may experience in relating as an equal in adult relationships.

An awareness of any prevailing moods is an important part of assessment of the offender. The therapist notes, for example, if the offender appears to be depressed, anxious, withdrawn, assertive, or aggressive.

It is also useful to assess the offender's ability to identify and understand his emotions. His ability to make changes if his emotions place him or others at risk should also be considered.

TOOLS AND PROCEDURES FOR ASSESSMENT

Assessment of offenders relies mostly on four main sources of information:
• Interviews
• Clinical records
• Plethysmograph
• Questionnaires.

Each of these methods of assessment is summarized below. Those seeking further information are referred to Groth (1979) and Salter (1988).

Interviews

During the interview we establish rapport as in any counselling session. In order to do this it is necessary to demonstrate interest in the offender and respect for him as a person, while being very clear that we do not in any way condone his abusive behaviour. We affirm any signs that he is being honest and taking responsibility, while not minimizing the seriousness of the abuse.

It is important to get information about the abuser's personal history. This may provide clues to understanding the abuse, as well as putting it in a context which can include positive achievements.

As in work with survivors, assessment also involves collecting information about personal resources, family relationships, support people, and their beliefs about the abuse. Details of the offences and information about the offender's current situation and mood level are important as well.

The therapist interviewing an offender should not expect their client to be honest. This applies particularly to the first interview, before trust and rapport have been established. Abusers entering treatment are typically ashamed, embarrassed, and fearful. The consequences of fully disclosing the extent of their abuse or of facing the effects it has had on others could be devastating. This may be the first time they have had to face the reality of what they have done. As Salter (1988, p. 186) writes, 'For many, sexual deviancy does not occur when they commit the act, it occurs when they admit it.'

With many sex offenders, therefore, the story they tell may represent only the 'tip of the iceberg'. The therapist would be wise to assume that they have committed more abuse and engaged in other inappropriate sexual activities which they have not disclosed. It is useful to make this assumption with every offender, and to make a clear statement to this effect. We try to avoid an argument at this stage by normalizing the difficulties in being honest and the tendency to minimize the extent of offending. While confrontation about abusive behaviour is usually necessary, we must also demonstrate respect for the offender in other areas of his life. This is important if we are to help him to get in touch with the strength he will need to break the cycle of offending.

Clinical records

Whenever possible it is useful to check the accuracy of the offender's disclosure with details provided by the victim. Often these details can be obtained from the survivor's therapist (with their client's permission) or from the records of statutory agencies, such as police or child welfare. Any discrepancies between the offender's story and the information provided by the survivor can then be addressed in therapy.

Police and child welfare records are useful as they may document details of past sexual offences. Information about the nature and frequency of past offences can influence the type of treatment required. If no record of other sexual offences exists, it should never be assumed that they have not occurred. Many sex offenders do not come to the attention of authorities, but when they do the frequency of recorded offences often is much lower than the actual number committed.

Plethysmograph

The penile plethysmograph is a machine which provides objective information about the offender's sexual preference. A small device on the machine measures the circumference of the penis, which indicates the degree of arousal. For such an assessment the offender sits in a room alone, with the device placed on his penis. He is shown slides which typically include naked children and adults, while the plethysmograph measures his arousal in response to each of the slides.

The plethysmograph can provide a valuable objective measure for both initial assessment and assessment of the effectiveness of treatment. It should be noted, however, that it provides only a measure of sexual arousal, and an indication of sexual preferences. It does not provide any information about the likelihood of past or future offending. Its usefulness is in providing objective information about the range of potential sexual behaviour, which can help to determine the focus of treatment. It cannot, however, be relied upon in isolation from other assessment procedures, as offenders can learn to suppress their responses to the slides.

Questionnaires

Many questionnaires have been developed specifically for the assessment of sex offenders. As with the clinical interview, their accuracy and usefulness depends partly on the concerns that the therapist wishes to investigate, on the self-respect and honesty of the offender, and on the level of trust developed between therapist and abuser. Salter (1988) provides examples of questionnaires, and a more detailed explanation of their use. She includes questionnaires that assess attitudes to sex, attitudes to women, empathy, alcohol abuse, sexual fantasies, and ability to accept responsibility for behaviour.

TREATMENT

The ideal treatment programme for sexual offenders involves a comprehensive approach that includes individual, family, and group therapy. Such a broad approach is necessary largely because the offender has many needs that cannot be adequately addressed by one method.

Individual therapy is used to address deviant arousal patterns, and personal issues such as self-esteem and depression. Group therapy is especially relevant for dealing with cognitive distortions such as 'She liked it', 'It wasn't serious', or 'I couldn't do it again'. A group also provides a place for ongoing support and motivation. Family therapy can address issues such as the reintegration of the abuser back into the home, the safety of all concerned, the offender's behaviour at home and support for other family members. Family therapy also may be used to address problems that are not directly related to abuse.

Treatment needs to address a number of specific issues which are summarized below under the following headings:

- Cognitive distortions
- Victim empathy
- Patterns of offending
- Sexual fantasies
- Sex education
- Social skills training and anger management
- Reintegration
- Relapse prevention.

For a more detailed account of treatment procedures relating to these issues, we recommend Retraining *Adult Sex Offenders* (Knopp 1984), *Handbook of Sexual Assault: Issues, Theories, and Treatment of the Offender* (Marshall, Laws, & Barbaree 1990), *Treating Child Sex Offenders and Victims: A Practical Guide* (Salter 1988), and *The Juvenile Sex Offender* (Barbaree, Marshall, & Hudson 1993).

Cognitive distortions

The treatment of sexual offending is quite different from other types of therapy. Abusers often deny their offences, and those disclosures they do make frequently represent only a fraction of the number of offences committed. Minimization of the extent of abuse is common, as is minimization of responsibility for what happened. All these factors must be taken into consideration when interviewing offenders, especially in the early stages of treatment.

Unlike other clients, sex offenders often have low motivation to seek treatment and change. Therapists working with offenders therefore may need to adopt a different therapeutic style from that used in their other work. Specifically, this involves challenging and working with denial, as we endeavour to obtain an accurate picture of the details of their offences.

For effective treatment to occur, it is important that the therapist obtains details of the offences which are as accurate as possible. We need to know what types of offences have been committed, the gender and age/s of the children involved, the number of children abused, and the duration of offending.

It may take several interviews to obtain this information. The therapist first must gain the offender's trust, and must maintain a good therapeutic relationship throughout treatment. The therapist must also explain the advantages for the offender of making a full disclosure. These include being able to confront and deal with things which make them feel bad about themselves.

At the same time the therapist must be clear about the limits of confidentiality. The offender needs to know that we will notify statutory authorities if we consider that he or anyone else is at risk of being harmed. If necessary, we seek advice about the most effective way of reporting our concerns that is consistent with the legal rights of the offender.

It is important to remember that the offender may abuse others if left unsupervised with children, and to set clear limits to prevent this from happening. Preferably these limits are established both with the offender and with family members who can ensure that they are observed.

One technique which can be used to engage the offender in therapy is motivational interviewing. This has been employed most often in therapy for people with alcohol problems, but recently has been adopted for work with sex offenders (Garland & Dougher 1990). It is used to motivate offenders to undertake treatment and to continue making changes.

As with other approaches that aim to get an accurate record of offending, motivational interviewing highlights the positive aspects of the offender's being honest and engaging in treatment. Affirmation of the honesty and courage it takes to make an accurate disclosure is an essential part of therapy. Without continuing encouragement the offender is less likely to fully disclose, and less likely to address distorted belief systems relating to the abuse.

Victim empathy

Victim empathy is an essential part of treatment. It involves the offender's experiencing at an emotional level some of the feelings that a victim may experience. It can be achieved through methods such as those described below. Often a combination of methods that address both intellectual and emotional understanding is most effective.

It is useful to begin with discussion about the effects of sexual abuse on victims and their families. Similarly, setting tasks that have offenders reading victims' stories or watching video recordings of victims describing the effects of abuse, can create a shift at an intellectual and emotional level.

Another useful technique is to ask offenders to recall a frightening experience in their own life. By getting in touch with emotions they have experienced, they are helped to understand their victim's experience.

Gestalt 'two-chair' work (Hatcher & Himelstein 1976) can be used to facilitate victim empathy, as can psychodramatic techniques. The use of psychodrama techniques for this purpose is described by Lambie *et al.* (in press), and in Simmonds and Houlahan (1991).

Patterns of offending

Regardless of the nature of the abuse, all sex offenders have planned their offences. It is important for the abuser, as well as the therapist, to understand the pattern of behaviour that led to the abusive acts. This includes details of what the offender did, what they thought, and how they felt, before, during, and after the offences.

Once they have identified their own particular pattern of offending, abusers are able to address any lifestyle problems that may have contributed. These might include lack of peer relationships, social isolation, poor self-esteem, abuse of drugs or alcohol, or use of pornography.

Identifying their own pattern of offending is the first step for abusers in developing strategies to remove themselves from the cycle that leads to abuse. It is important, for example, for them to learn to resolve conflict within their relationships more effectively, to practise masturbating to appropriate fantasies, and to destroy any pornography they possess.

Sexual fantasies

Many adult sex offenders will have been masturbating while experiencing deviant sexual fantasies, though they may not admit to this. These fantasies may or may not have been about the children they have abused. The sexual arousal and pleasure they gain from masturbating to these fantasies strengthens their sexual desire towards children and reduces any internal inhibitions they may have. As a result, the likelihood of further offending is increased.

One method of changing deviant fantasy patterns is the use of 'Boredom Tapes'. Briefly, this involves masturbating to an appropriate fantasy until orgasm, and then masturbating to the deviant fantasy. The appropriate fantasy is first created with the abuser, and involves a sexual experience within a relationship that is equal, consenting, caring, age-appropriate, and non-violent.

The offender is required to record a description of the appropriate fantasy while masturbating using oil as a lubricant. The use of oil reduces the possibility of fabrication, because it makes the activity of masturbation more audible on the tape. Masturbating to the inappropriate fantasy then continues for approximately 45 minutes after orgasm. The purpose of this tedious exercise is to create boredom, and so to make it more difficult for the offender to link pleasure with images of children. This exercise is recorded on tape two to three times each week, for approximately two months. The tapes must be checked regularly by the therapist to ensure that the exercise is being performed as required.

The use of Boredom Tapes is more fully described in such treatment guides as Salter (1988). Another behavioural technique described by Salter is known as covert sensitization. This involves the offender describing on tape a chain of events which preceded their abuse of a child. Before the abuse occurs in their account they describe a painful or frightening event from their own life. The intention is to make a connection between the behaviour that typically precedes abuse, and a powerful negative thought or feeling. Ultimately the negative thought or feeling should arise automatically whenever the offender initiates behaviour that may lead to abuse.

A variation on this exercise is for the offender to describe on tape a situation that normally would lead to his abusing a child, but to interrupt it with a conscious decision not to abuse. He then describes a realistic alternative behaviour which ends with him feeling good and achieving something positive. This recording is played regularly over a set period of time as a homework task.

Thought stopping is another useful technique for interrupting ideas that might lead to abuse. It is sometimes used in conjunction with Boredom Tapes, and is described in detail in Chapter 11 (pp. 227–230).

Sex education

An important part of treating sex offenders is ensuring that they have adequate information about non-abusive sexual relationships. This includes information about physiology, positive ways of enhancing sexual pleasure, methods of contraception, and education about sexually transmitted diseases. It should also include information that normalizes masturbation. The use of books, slides, and films is often helpful in communicating this sort of information.

Sex education of offenders also must challenge traditional patriarchal beliefs and stereotypical opinions about the roles of men and women. It is important to develop an awareness of the power inequalities inherent in abuse, and of any socialization practices which have contributed to behaviour that is controlling and abusive. Beliefs about gender orientation are important and may need to be addressed as well.

Social skills training and anger management

As we have noted previously, many sex offenders are not good at relating appropriately to people of their own age. As a result they are attracted to children, with whom they feel more comfortable and more able to make an emotional connection. They may lack skills in initiating and maintaining adult relationships. This includes lack of skills in communication, which may be compounded by poor self-esteem. Lack of skills in assertion may lead to difficulties in establishing their rights, and can result in angry or violent outbursts.

Group therapy is ideal for training offenders in social skills and anger-management. Skills in both areas can be practised with role-play, and developed through feedback from others. Group members can role-play typical situations such as getting to know someone, or asserting their rights in an unfair situation, and can learn new skills from the modelling provided by others. Detailed 'packages' for running such groups are provided in relevant texts (e.g. Crawford & Allen 1979, Whitman & Quinsey 1981).

Offenders who are unable to assert their needs appropriately may resort to violence. Some may use threats, while others damage property or physically harm other people. Such behaviour is a major concern for those who experience it. Effective treatment for such clients includes education about anger, recognition of 'warning signs', and the development of self-control strategies. Learning to express anger appropriately is important, and group members need to be affirmed when they successfully demonstrate achievements in this area.

Learning relaxation and stress-management skills also is often an integral part of anger management, as is learning to control drug and alcohol intake.

Many useful books have been written about anger management. One which we have found particularly valuable is *The Hitting Habit* by Jeanne Deschner (1986).

Reintegration

When both abuser and victim come from the same family, reintegration of the offender back into the family can be a very difficult part of therapy. Several issues need particular attention. Foremost is the safety of the survivor and of other family members. They must feel safe as well as be safe; they must feel confident in their ability to assert themselves and to say 'No' to any unwanted attention; and they must feel confident of the support and protection provided by others. Clear rules and boundaries must be agreed on by all concerned, such as rules relating to touching, being alone with a child, access to bedrooms and bathroom, and access to pornography. Limits also might be placed on subjects which can be discussed, to avoid embarrassing or intimidating the child who was abused.

The offender should be making significant progress in a treatment programme, however, before their return to the family is considered. They should have fully disclosed the details of their offending, have taken total responsibility for the abuse, and have developed strategies to keep themselves safe from reoffending. Full consideration of these factors, combined with an appropriate period of separation, can help to avert the potential distress of the whole family.

Regardless of how much care is taken, however, reintegration is likely to be difficult. It may be helpful to consider the return of the offender to the family home as an experiment, the success of which is to be reviewed after a specific period of time. It is also important for the family to know that they can have the offender officially obliged to leave the home, at least temporarily, should any difficulties arise.

Relapse prevention

Usually formal treatment for offenders is necessary over a period of one to two years. It is necessary, however, for the abuser to monitor his own behaviour for the rest of his life. Techniques for use by therapists and offenders to prevent relapse are described by Pithers (1990) and Salter (1988).

By the end of therapy the offender should have developed strategies for relapse prevention. These enable him to recognize at an early stage any situation where he is at risk. He also should have plans for appropriate action when this occurs, for example, avoiding situations where he is left alone with children.

CONCLUSION

Many factors contribute to sexually abusive behaviour, and assessment procedures must identify the specific factors operating for each individual offender. To be effective, treatment must be comprehensive and involves a combination of methods that address beliefs, emotions, behaviours, and lifestyle difficulties.

Treatment of offenders differs from other forms of therapy because the therapist takes a non-negotiable stand against the client's abusive behaviour. It involves a delicate balance between forming a therapeutic relationship and confronting denial. Supervision with other therapists who have specialized in offender therapy is necessary to adequately meet the needs of these clients.

If the offender does not receive treatment the pattern of offending is likely to continue. Over a period of time one abuser can commit hundreds of offences (Abel *et al.* 1985; Krauth & Smith 1988). Re-abuse rates are high because of the gratification inherent in the act. The treatment of offenders is of major importance in preventing sexual abuse.

PART 7

GENERAL ISSUES FOR COUNSELLORS AND COUNSELLING

13

ISSUES FOR
THERAPISTS

In our work with sexual abuse many issues impact on the therapist's ability to provide a quality service. In this chapter we consider the most important of these issues:

- Survival as a Therapist
- Working as a Team
- Agency Issues.

SURVIVAL AS A THERAPIST

Sexual-abuse counselling has many rewards for the therapist, but at times it can be distressing, demanding, and emotionally painful. It can also be extremely discouraging as we hear a seemingly never-ending number of horror stories and witness time and again the consequences of abuse. In order to take care of our clients and to provide them with the quality service they need, we first need to take care of ourselves. We can do this in a number of ways and we describe here the most useful of these.

Maintain a balance in our lives

With the demands of the work and the constant pressure of more people seeking assistance, we can find sexual-abuse counselling taking over more and more of our lives. How many therapists have not at some time fitted in an extra appointment, gone without a lunch break, or given up time set aside for something else in order to see a client in crisis? While this is not a problem when it happens occasionally, when it happens regularly it is a recipe for 'burn-out'. Therapists who continually set aside their own needs eventually exhaust their energy supplies and seek alternative employment. They may, in fact, provide assistance for fewer people than those who restrict their workload and consequently continue their work with survivors over a longer period. It is important therefore to monitor the number of clients we see, and to maintain some balance in our caseload.

One way to maintain balance is to avoid wherever possible devoting a full working week to sexual-abuse therapy. Part-time work or a varied caseload which includes counselling for other problems can be helpful in limiting the stress associated with sexual-abuse therapy.

Another way to maintain a balance is to ensure that we have other interests and activities. Exercise is important to maintain physical and mental health, while relaxation is also essential to sustain our mental resources. Some therapists find structured relaxation exercises helpful, while others practise meditation regularly. Adequate sleep is important, as is a balanced diet. For some, spirituality provides further strength and balance to work in this area.

Having our own lives in order

The therapist working with clients who have been sexually abused should not have major issues of their own to deal with at the same time. This is important both for our own survival and for the quality of service we provide for our clients. A therapist with major stresses in their own life would be wise to take a break from sexual-abuse counselling until they were under less pressure themselves.

We all need a haven in our lives from the stresses of abuse counselling, and it is unlikely that we can continue successfully counselling abuse survivors if we do not have relatively stress-free times built into our regular routines. The type of refuge we provide for ourselves varies, depending on our individual needs, preferences, and options.

Acknowledge the pain and obtain support

Just as we continually encourage our clients to express their feelings, we too need a safe place where we can acknowledge the distress or anger we feel about the abuse of others. While at times it might be appropriate for our clients to see that we are touched by their stories, it is important that we do not add to their burden with our own pain. We need colleagues and/or friends with whom we can share our feelings and find support. It is important, therefore, that we do not work in isolation, and that we build some form of support group around us when this does not occur naturally.

Supervision

Another way of obtaining support is through supervision. Effective supervision is essential for therapists in this work, both in providing a check on ideas and methods, and in helping to create new solutions. It is potentially dangerous for any therapist, however experienced, to be working with abuse survivors without having in place some system for checking their work.

Supervision should be provided by a more experienced therapist, and both professionals should be of the same gender and culture to ensure that the needs of the therapist are met as fully as possible. It is also helpful for peers to meet together for consultation, and for sharing ideas and experience.

Wherever possible it is useful to have more than one supervisor in order to build on different skills. One supervisor may specialize in working with adults, for example, and another with children. One may have expertise in action-methods, while another may work predominantly with drawing or writing exercises. Provided that the contract with each supervisor is clear, and their philosophy and methods are consistent, it is possible to consult different people for help with different skills.

When a supervisor does not have the necessary skills, when the therapist outgrows the skills of the supervisor, or when supervisor and therapist are philosophically or theoretically incompatible, it is important that the contract is renegotiated. It might be changed to peer consultation, for example, or alternative arrangements might be made with another supervisor.

Clinical supervision should be regular, and should be with someone who is able to be honest, objective, respectful, and trustworthy. It should be separate from any personal counselling the therapist may choose to have. When personal issues overlap with clinical problems this needs to be made explicit. Therapist and supervisor can then discuss ways of dealing with the situation, and should seriously consider the possibility of referral elsewhere for personal therapy.

The use of a one-way screen is invaluable for supervision. It provides an immediacy and richness of information not possible with subjective reports of sessions from the therapist. Where use of a screen is not practical, audio or video recordings of interviews can be useful.

The client's permission for use of the screen or recording equipment is essential, so before requesting their permission we need to explain the reasons for using this equipment, and ensure that they feel able to refuse. This is a particularly sensitive issue for abused clients who may not find it easy to assert their rights.

There will be times, however, when we choose not to record a particular interview, because it would be inappropriate or because it could make the session too difficult for the client.

Feeling positive about our work

Supervision and training help us to provide a quality service for our clients which we can feel good about. When we are increasing our skills in any way we are stimulated and replenished. It is important therefore that we give priority to reading, discussion, and ongoing training. This is necessary not just for our clients, but for our own sense of well-being and pride in our work.

We also feel positive about our work when we know that it is effective. Frequently we witness dramatic changes made by survivors and their families. Sometimes this happens in an amazingly short period of time. Sometimes it requires courage and perseverance over an extended period. Either way it is encouraging and rewarding for the therapist who knows that they have helped to facilitate the changes that people make in their lives.

Respecting boundaries

We assist both our clients and ourselves when we respect the boundaries between us. It is part of responsible practice that we do not try to force the pace or agenda of therapy. It is not part of our job to impose decisions on our clients about how they should live their lives.

When we respect the rights of our clients, we appreciate the limits of our responsibility to them. This allows us to practise in an ethical and empowering way, while providing boundaries which protect both client and therapist.

Humour

While it may seem incongruous in relation to sexual abuse, humour can also play a useful role in therapist survival. Its use does not imply in any way that we are disrespectful of our clients or that we fail to appreciate the seriousness of the issues relating to abuse.

Humour provides a release from tension and a different perspective. It helps us to resist the pressures to be discouraged or defeated by sexual abuse. In order to avoid causing offence or being misinterpreted, however, we need to exercise some control over how and where humour is expressed. A joke which might be quite appropriate to share with a colleague, for example, might be totally inappropriate at a funding meeting or in therapy with a client.

Responsibility for change

Finally, for our survival as therapists we must acknowledge our own limitations. We are only a small part of our clients' lives, and we cannot force them to make changes. We do not know everything and sometimes we make mistakes. For a variety of reasons we do not always attain our goals in therapy. Sometimes we learn from these occasions and sometimes we need to seek further assistance, either for ourselves or for our clients. We hope that we can always do what we tell our clients to do — give ourselves credit for doing the best we could in the circumstances.

We need to acknowledge that we cannot solve every problem. Otherwise we set ourselves impossible goals and doom ourselves to constant failure and self-criticism. This in turn can impact on our work with clients.

WORKING AS A TEAM

There are a number of reasons why working as a member of a team is helpful for sexual-abuse therapy. These include support and peer consultation for the therapist, the input of different skills and perspectives from each team member, and the flexibility for team members to play different roles in working with the same family.

Support

An effective team provides a safe work environment for its members, a situation in which we can acknowledge the distress, the anger, the worries, and the self-doubts which most of us experience at times when working with abuse survivors. The team can validate and normalize these feelings, and provide reassurance and practical suggestions. It provides support, understanding, and appreciation from people who are familiar with the issues involved.

Supervision

Members of a team have ongoing access to supervision. When there are more experienced therapists on the team this may involve formal supervision and/or the opportunity for the less experienced to observe their work. When experience levels are more equal, peer consultation can provide a different perspective, a chance to check ideas, and input from different areas of specialist knowledge.

A team provides an excellent opportunity for training new therapists. It allows them to take as little or as much responsibility as they are capable of, while other team members ensure that the client gets all the assistance they need. In such cases use of the one-way screen is invaluable. For example, the less experienced therapist can observe how a team member conducts an interview, while carrying out useful tasks such as taking notes, operating video equipment, or monitoring specific behaviours. Alternatively, the less experienced therapist may be in the interview room with the client, while an experienced team member is available to prompt or intervene as necessary from behind the screen.

Providing different perspectives

With or without a one-way screen, the team provides a diversity of experience that inevitably leads to different perspectives on problems and different ideas about solutions. While the screen is not essential for this process, it does provide team members working outside the room with a little more distance from the therapy. This enables them to observe different reactions from the client or family, to think about questions not being asked or needs not being addressed, and to begin to think of solutions rather than having to focus on questions that need to be asked.

When the group dynamic works well the diversity of perspectives and experience in a team enhance creativity and provides a forum for checking ideas. There is consequently less chance of missing anything important or of making mistakes.

Flexibility of roles for team members

When we work from a family-systems perspective we often arrange separate sessions for the abuse survivor, for their family, and for individual family members. A team approach allows us to provide a different therapist to meet fully and more satisfactorily the different needs of each sub-system within the family without any possible conflict of roles for the therapist. The survivor's therapist, for example, might want to be there just for the child, with a focus on helping them to feel empowered to deal with the trauma of abuse. At the same time the parents' therapist may be working on helping the parents to feel empowered to deal with behaviour problems which have occurred as a result of abuse.

In such cases, the same appointment time is provided whenever possible for both child and parent to be seen by their respective therapists. This allows for the possibility of spending part of the session together to discuss mutual concerns and to exchange information. It also provides the family with the convenience of a single appointment for two separate sessions.

Similarly, in the case of an adult client, sometimes it is easier for one therapist to do the individual work with the survivor, while another does any couple counselling or individual therapy with other family members. In this way individual needs are met when each person concerned has their own therapist. Once again possible conflict of roles is avoided. Role conflict may occur, for example, if a client needs to be challenged within couple or family counselling but affirmed and supported in their individual sexual abuse therapy.

Avoiding difficulties in teamwork

When a team is not working well, there is a danger that team members seeing different family members become aligned in family conflicts and consequently take opposing positions in team discussions. This is less likely to occur when all team members are operating from a systems perspective, and are maintaining regular contact and open communication with one another.

It is helpful if team meetings are held before and after each interview to exchange information, plan the session, and review progress. With family interviews, in particular, it can be helpful to schedule a team meeting during the session in order to pool ideas and to formulate therapeutic plans. The family may be offered refreshments, a chance to tend to small children, or simply an opportunity to take a break from the intensity of the interview situation while the team is meeting.

Regular team meetings which are separate from family interviews are also important, because they help to make the work more manageable. It is at these meetings that issues concerning team members can be raised. Meetings are a chance to sort out differences, to share information, to consult about clinical or philosophical problems, to provide training and/or supervision, and to plan for the future. Planning covers a wide variety of issues, such as arranging appointments for the team to see a family, suggesting interventions, and discussing future directions of the agency. Without a specific regular time to address these issues, stress levels rise and decision-making is likely to be rushed and made in a way that excludes some of those most concerned. Team meetings strengthen the team by making it more united and effective.

Power issues in teamwork

Difficulties can arise in teamwork when power or status between team members is distributed unfairly. Sometimes counsellors are trained in different disciplines (e.g. psychiatry, social work) which provide them with unequal status on the team, but which do not necessarily provide an accurate reflection of levels of competence for sexual-abuse therapy. Sometimes power is distributed unequally according to gender or culture, rather than to skill base.

When power or status on a team is distributed unequally, it is helpful to make this explicit through team discussion, and to be clear about the reasons behind it. Reasons based on different levels of skills, experience, or responsibility may be accepted by team members, but when the reasons for unequal distribution of status are not accepted by any team member, this should be questioned, and discussed by all. Some renegotiation of job description, power, and responsibility may be required.

It is essential that we do not replicate in our teams the abuse of power which is inherent in the abuse that we work with. All team members must feel valued and empowered to develop competence and confidence within the team.

Composition of an effective team

It is possible, and perhaps even desirable, for team members to have different strengths and to play different roles within the team. For example, some people are better at working with offenders, some are better at working with survivors, and some may specialize in work with families. It is essential, however, that all team members share the same philosophical and political beliefs about sexual abuse. It is not possible for a team to function effectively while harbouring incompatible basic beliefs about responsibility for abuse, for example, or about the processes of therapy and healing.

Individual team members may prefer to use different models or tools for therapy. This adds richness and flexibility to the team, provided that they respect one another's work and are willing to discuss their differences openly. Respect, trust, and consideration are basic components of a good team, and need to be nurtured continually.

When there is no team

While many therapists are working in agencies where they have colleagues who can form a team, others are working in relative isolation. It is possible, of course, to do effective therapy without a team, but it may not be quite so easy.

Many people have found creative ways of forming some sort of team to provide them with support, supervision, and shared resources. Like-minded therapists working alone or in separate agencies can arrange to meet regularly. They may arrange to work together at specified times, either on a paid or an exchange basis, meet for peer consultation, or go together to see the same supervisor. In more remote areas contacts can often be made through relevant journals or newsletters.

When it is not possible to form a team, time out from counselling to attend conferences, update on recent literature, get additional training, or visit other agencies should be a priority. In this way the therapist makes useful contacts and enjoys the benefits of intellectual stimulation and the input of practical ideas. If we are to continue working effectively in this challenging field it is important that we find ways to stimulate our interest, and maintain the development of our skills.

AGENCY ISSUES

There are a number of important policy issues for any agency that provides counselling for sexual abuse. In effect this applies to just about every coun-selling service, because a history of sexual abuse can be part of almost every type of problem for which counselling is sought. Most counselling services need to be prepared to deal with disclosures of sexual abuse from their clients.

When we refer to agencies in this context, we are talking about services of all sizes, social services with hundreds of employees as well as therapists working alone in private practice.

Philosophical/political attitudes to sexual abuse

It is important for the training of staff and the effective provision of service to clients that therapy is based on an unambiguous agency philosophy about sexual abuse. Sexual abuse is not an area where it is possible to be value-free or politically neutral. Consensus amongst staff about our beliefs and values is important, and we need to make these explicit, and be pre-pared to defend them where necessary.

For example, the agency as a whole needs to have a policy about the safety of children, the rights of clients, and about where responsibility for abuse lies. The particular philosophical base which we advocate includes the following general statements:

- The responsibility for abuse lies totally with the abuser.
- The safety of the survivor is the first consideration.
- Sexual abuse is a serious problem in our society, both in its extent and its potential effects.
- People who have been sexually abused are entitled to quality coun-selling that is both culturally and gender appropriate.

- Therapy should respect the rights of clients and should not compound abuse in any way.

Ethical basis for counselling

Agency policy should make explicit the ethical obligations of staff. As with the philosophical and political statements, these could be made available in written form for staff and clients. They might include policies about confidentiality, violence, sexual abuse of clients, and about procedures for dealing with complaints.

When a therapist is working outside an agency that has clear procedures and guidelines, it is important that they join a professional society (e.g. an association of counsellors, psychologists, social workers, etc.) which has its own ethical requirements. This provides some protection for both members and their clients.

Confidentiality

Agency policy on confidentiality needs to describe both the extent and the limits of confidentiality. As previously mentioned, clients need to know that confidentiality will be broken if we consider that someone is at risk. We do not feel bound by confidentiality, for example, if we believe that there is a risk that the offender may abuse again, if we were concerned that anyone may attempt suicide, or if there is a risk to others from the sexually inappropriate behaviour of a client.

Protocol for dealing with disclosures

Those working with sexual abuse survivors need to have a clear policy for dealing with disclosures. Legal requirements vary from country to country, and sometimes within countries from state to state. A requirement for mandatory reporting, for example, leaves the agency with few options. With mandatory reporting the choices to consider focus on how the client and/or family can be best supported through this process. We may choose to accompany them to the police station, for example, or to put them in touch with a statutory social worker whom we know to be sensitive and competent. We may make the initial report ourselves, to pave the way for a client who is anxious about dealing with statutory agencies. In any case we need to be well informed about the legal obligations on both client and therapist, and about the procedures which will be set in motion once a report is made.

When reporting is not mandatory, often it is still advisable. Without some form of statutory intervention it is unlikely that an offender will accept responsibility for abuse or willingly seek treatment. They may then present a continuing risk to our client or others. Legal intervention can also be a way of validating our client's experience. It can provide formal acknowledgment that they have been wronged and that the abuser is responsible for what happened.

On the other hand, an agency policy of mandatory reporting may deter some people who have been abused from seeking help. For many reasons they may be unwilling to put themselves or others through the experience of coping with the justice system. They may feel unable to talk about the abuse to officials such as police or statutory social workers; they may be unwilling to give evidence in court; or they may be very fearful of repercussions on themselves or others — ambivalence towards the offender or loyalty to the family, for example, may restrain them from forcing the offender to face the legal consequences of his actions. With mandatory reporting the only choice for some survivors is to remain silent, or to unwillingly take a step which could compound their experience of abuse.

In order to assist those who otherwise would not seek help, an agency may prefer a policy which leaves them with some flexibility about reporting abuse. In some cases it may be preferable to work overtime providing support and assistance until the client feels ready and willing to report.

Networking

Contact with other services involved in sexual-abuse counselling is important for all agencies, regardless of size.

Whether we work as therapists in isolation or within an agency which employs many counsellors, we need up-to-date information. This includes information about other resources, shifts in government policy, procedures involved in reporting to statutory agencies, the latest research, and ideas for improving our work. By networking with other agencies we can share our information and benefit from the discoveries of others.

Networking might involve circulating newsletters, attending conferences, meeting regularly with other agencies, or less formal contacts by telephone and personal communication. It also occurs through supervision and peer consultation.

Networking can be time-consuming, and therefore needs to be recognized as a legitimate and valuable activity within an agency. Priorities may need to be established about the most productive forms of networking. These may depend on the needs of the agency and/or the interests of the individual therapist.

In larger agencies various staff members may adopt different roles, pooling their information at regular meetings. For example, one person may take responsibility for keeping current information about other services, one may maintain up-to-date information on financial aspects such as funding or fees, one may gather information from journals, and another may attend regular meetings with other agencies. In such situations not only the therapists but also administrative and managerial staff may be involved in networking.

Networking is also useful politically, because it enables agencies to take a united stand on issues of common concern. When changes to legislation are being considered, for example, we are more effective if we co-ordinate any action to be taken amongst those agencies affected.

Surviving the 'backlash'

Another benefit of networking is that it can support both individuals and agencies in facing the 'backlash' which occurs regularly in society against sexual-abuse survivors and counsellors. Publicity about 'false allegations' and 'false memories' can raise doubts in the community about all disclosures. Therapists, for example, have been portrayed as persuading clients that they were abused, and as eliciting highly suspect disclosures.

We do not wish to minimize the effects of a false allegation on all concerned, and we do not condone any practice which may persuade clients to mistakenly believe that they were abused. Our concern is that such incidents are relatively few compared with the number of genuine allegations.

Reports of false allegations tend to make it even more difficult for those people who have been abused to be believed, and tend to discredit the many counsellors who work ethically and competently. The major issues that we face are not the false allegations, but the enormous difficulties for survivors in speaking out, being believed, and getting the assistance they need.

Publicity about false allegations contributes to the social marginalization of sexual abuse issues, and thereby to lack of funding and general lack of support for counsellors. Agencies must become involved in providing information for the community, through the media or through provision of training. They must also be ready to respond to attacks which are based on sensationalism, self-interest, or lack of understanding. Decisions must be made about which attacks are best ignored, and which require an immediate response.

We also need to consider how we can support other counsellors or agencies when they are being subjected to unfair criticism and blame.

Evaluation

All therapists can benefit from an effective form of evaluation of their work. Feedback from clients is useful for our own development, and as a measure of client satisfaction. Feedback from clients provides a valuable addition to feedback from supervisors and peers. It contributes to our ability to provide a quality service for our clients by identifying areas of success and areas which need improvement.

Depending on the nature of the questions asked, evaluation can also provide information for research projects. It can help to identify the elements of effective therapy and develop our knowledge about sexual abuse and the healing process.

Obtaining useful and valid information requires a professionally designed evaluation questionnaire. Co-operation between the therapist and the questionnaire designer is necessary to ensure that the information is relevant and obtained in a sensitive manner. Consultation with survivors is also important when designing an evaluation questionnaire.

Such a questionnaire can be sent to clients as a follow-up after therapy. Generally, more reliable information is obtained when the client is not approached directly by the therapist, as feelings about the therapist may influence the client's ability to be objective. Some form of confidentiality must be guaranteed regarding the identity of the client and the information they have supplied.

14

EPILOGUE:
The Future of
Sexual-abuse Counselling

While different communities have different needs and priorities, few have totally satisfactory services for those who have been sexually abused. Issues which we believe most commonly require attention are discussed in this final chapter.

EMPHASIS ON WORK WITH THE FAMILY

Most therapists today acknowledge the importance of the family's response to childhood sexual abuse. With both adult and child clients we recognize the power of the family to help or hinder the healing process. We also see the many ways that family members can be affected by a disclosure about abuse of a child. Family members may need information or counselling in order to help the survivor more effectively. They also provide information which helps the therapist to be more effective.

Unfortunately, however, awareness of these issues has not always influenced the practice of therapy. Therapists continue to see children either individually or in groups, without providing any integrated service for their families. Others work with adult survivors, without taking the family system fully into account, and without offering any form of couple or family counselling.

As therapy for sexual abuse develops into the future, there is a need for greater emphasis on family work. It is essential that we develop a more integrated approach to therapy which acknowledges the interconnectedness of family members, addresses the needs of all those affected by abuse, and recognizes the crucial role they can play in the healing process.

MALE THERAPISTS

Developing awareness of the prevalence of sexual abuse of boys has not been followed by an adequate increase in services for gender-appropriate counselling of males. There is a need for more men to become involved in sexual-abuse counselling, and for agencies to give more priority to training male therapists.

CULTURALLY APPROPRIATE SERVICES

There is an increased recognition of the importance of culturally appropriate counselling services. This requires the availability of therapists from the same cultural background as their clients, working in ways that acknowledge and respect their own specific beliefs and values.

An experience of each client's particular culture is necessary for making effective connections with them. Without it, there cannot be full understanding and respect between therapist and client. It is also important for understanding the issues involved, for negotiating therapeutic goals, and for determining the style of therapy which is likely to be most appropriate and helpful.

A more diverse range of services therefore needs to be developed to meet the needs of the various cultural groups within our communities. This is important in work with both sexual-abuse survivors and offenders.

CRISIS SERVICES

When abuse is first disclosed immediate help is often required for both the person who was abused and their family. They all may be in a state of crisis and need information about what needs to be done, what resources are available, how to respond to a child, and how to ensure the safety of all concerned. Time and again we see the benefits of crisis services in alleviating the distress of both survivor and family at the point of disclosure. Ensuring that they receive appropriate help at this stage is a major step towards making therapy as brief and as effective as possible, and helps to avoid unnecessary suffering.

Sadly, our awareness of these facts has not always made crisis services available for all those who need them. In many places they are under-funded and unable to meet the needs of their community. Consequently, significant 'burn-out' amongst crisis workers is also a common problem, and delays can occur for clients who need immediate assistance.

If our politicians are serious about dealing with violence and abuse, they need to acknowledge the value of crisis services at a government level. Crisis services must be provided with the security of adequate and ongoing funding if, in the long term, we are to avoid far greater emotional, social, and financial costs.

EDUCATION

The seeds of sexual abuse lie in societal attitudes. Abuse is more likely to occur in any society which does not accord equal power to women, which does not recognize the rights of children, and which ascribes to men roles which emphasize dominance and self-gratification.

As with other forms of abuse, sexual abuse is inevitable in a society where power is distributed unfairly according to such criteria as gender, age, or culture. The rights of women and children to say 'No' to abuse need to be valued by all members of society. In addition, we need to foster attitudes that encourage men and boys to learn ways of relating to others which are based on equality, respect, sensitivity, and co-operation.

From an early age children need to be taught attitudes which do not support sexual abuse. This involves more than safety education or such simple prescriptions as 'sexual abuse is wrong'. It involves a critical analysis of power and oppression, of gender roles, human rights, violence, and social justice.

TEACHING CHILDREN TO KEEP SAFE

There is also a need for government-funded agencies to provide more education specifically aimed at keeping children safe from sexual harassment and abuse. This requires the production of pamphlets, books, and videos, and the distribution of such material to parents, schools, kindergartens, day-care centres, and medical professionals. It involves increasing awareness within the community generally about sexual abuse, and training educators in how to most effectively teach children the skills required.

Safety education not only helps to prevent sexual abuse, but also facilitates disclosures, thereby enabling more children to receive the help they need.

TREATMENT FOR OFFENDERS

Offenders are likely to abuse many people if they do not receive appropriate counselling. Recidivism rates for untreated sex offenders have been estimated to be as high as 60 per cent within the first three years of release from prison (Krauth & Smith 1988).

To be most effective, treatment of offenders should begin as soon as a problem is identified, and should involve a comprehensive treatment programme of individual, group, and family work. Adolescent offenders need to be directed to a treatment programme before they develop a lifetime pattern of abusive behaviour. Programmes for adults need to be provided both within the community and within the prison setting. It is not sufficient to punish an offender for sexual abuse. They must be directed to join a treatment programme if further offences are to be prevented.

Attention also needs to be paid to children who are behaving in sexually inappropriate ways. Teaching them to control their behaviour must be a priority if we are to avoid the risk of them developing into the abusers of the future.

While all this may seem self-evident, the availability of suitable programmes remains totally inadequate in many places. Severe funding restraints limit both the development of programmes and the training of sufficient numbers of counsellors.

Until we provide programmes for offenders which are comprehensive, accessible, and effective, we are contributing as a society to the perpetuation of sexual abuse.

RESEARCH

Perusing the literature on most aspects of sexual abuse we continually find the phrase 'there is a need for more research'. Controversy continues over such basic issues as prevalence rates, reliability of disclosures, and the benefits of various forms of therapy. Little has been done in terms of cross-cultural studies or comparisons of rates of abuse within various communities and socio-economic groups.

Research helps us to define priorities and to improve our knowledge base. It is essential for the ongoing development of therapeutic and prevention programmes.

The role of government

Development within any of the areas referred to in this chapter is dependent on acknowledgement of the problems relating to sexual abuse, and commitment of funding to provide adequate services to deal with it.

Therapists worldwide often are dependent on governments and the funding agencies they establish to provide the means to help those who have been abused, their families, and the offenders. As therapists we can heighten awareness of abuse within the community, we can make submissions, and lobby those responsible for making policy. Ultimately, however, it is the responsibility of governments to ensure that services are in place.

Conclusion

While it is impossible to obtain reliable statistics, many people believe that the rate of sexual abuse is increasing, and not just being reported more frequently. This would not be surprising given the increased availability of pornography that objectifies women and feeds sexual fantasies about women and children. In order to deal with sexual abuse in our society, major changes in social attitudes are required, along with a commitment of funds for education, research, prevention, treatment of offenders, and therapy for those who have been abused.

While much remains to be done, it is encouraging to note the achievements of the last two decades. Sexual abuse has been widely acknowledged as a serious problem, and the voices of those who have been abused have finally been heard. Information about sexual abuse is now readily accessible, and services have multiplied in a way that previously we would not have considered possible. There is a growing number of skilled therapists, and a growing number of options for those seeking help.

Therapists can work to help maintain this momentum, and to address the issues discussed above. However, major change only will occur when the wider society takes responsibility for dealing with sexual abuse, and with the attitudes that allow it to continue.

REFERENCES

Abel, G. C., Mittelman, M. S., & Becker, J. V. (1985). 'Sexual offenders: results of assessment and recommendations for treatment'. In M. H. Ben-Aron, S. J. Huckle, & C. D. Webster (eds.). *Clinical Criminology: The Assessment & Treatment of Criminal Behaviour* (191–205). M & M Graphic, Toronto.

Anderson, J. A., Martin, J., Mullen, P., Romans, S., & Herbison, G. P. (1993). 'Prevalence of childhood sexual abuse experiences in a community sample of women'. *Journal of American Academy of Child Adolescent Psychiatry*, 32(5), 911–919.

Annon, J. S. (1974). *The Behavioural Treatment of Sexual Problems* (vol.1 Brief Therapy). Enabling Systems, Honolulu.

Araji, S. & Finkelhor, D. (1986). 'Abusers: a review of the research'. In D. Finkelhor and Associates (eds.). *A Sourcebook on Child Sexual Abuse*. Sage, California.

Atkinson, J. & Raeburn, J. (1987). *Superhealth Self-relaxation Programme*. Mental Health Foundation of New Zealand, Auckland.

Badgley, R. (1984). *Sexual Offences against Children: Report of the Committee on Sexual Offences against Children and Youths*. Government of Canada, Ottawa.

Baker, A. W. & Duncan, S. P. (1985). 'Child sexual abuse: a study of prevalence in Great Britain'. *Child Abuse and Neglect*, 9, 457–467.

Bandler, R. & Grinder, J. (1979). *Frogs into Princes*. Real People Press, Moab, Utah.

Barbaree, H. E., Marshall, W. L., & Hudson, S. M. (eds.) (1993). *The Juvenile Sex Offender*. Guildford Press, London.

Bass, E. & Davis, L. (1988). *The Courage to Heal: A Guide for Women Survivors of Child Sexual Abuse*. Harper & Rowe, New York.

Bateson, G. (1972). *Steps to an Ecology of Mind*. Ballantine Books, New York.

Bateson, G. (1979). *Mind and Nature: A Necessary Unity.* Bantam Books, New York.

Becker, J. V. (1988). 'The effects of child sexual abuse on adolescent sexual offenders'. In G. E. Wyatt, & E. J. Powell (eds.). *Lasting Effects of Sexual Abuse.* Sage, California.

Beitchman, J. H., Zucker, K. J., Hood, J. E., da Costa, G. A., Akman, D., & Cassavia, E. (1992). 'A review of the long-term effects of child sexual abuse'. *Child Abuse and Neglect,* 16, 101–118. USA.

Benson, H. (1975). *The Relaxation Response.* Morrow, New York.

Bernstein, D. A. & Borkovec, T. D. (1973). *Progressive Relaxation Training: A Manual for the Helping Professions.* Research Press, Champaign.

Blume, E. S. (1990). *Secret Survivors: Uncovering Incest and its After Effects in Women.* Wiley, New York.

Bourne, E. J. (1990). *The Anxiety and Phobia Workbook.* New Harbinger Publications Inc., California.

Browne, A. & Finkelhor, D. (1986). 'The impact of child sexual abuse: a review of the research'. *Psychological Bulletin,* 99, 66–77.

Clayton, G. M. (1993). *Living Pictures of the Self: Applications of Role Theory in Professional Practice and Daily Life.* I.C.A. Press, Melbourne.

Coale, H. W. (1992). 'The constructivist emphasis on language: a critical conversation'. *Journal of Strategic & Systemic Therapies,* 2, 12–26.

Coleman, E. (1988). *Integrated Identity for Gay Men and Lesbians: Psychotherapeutic Approaches for Emotional Well-being.* Harrington Park Press, New York.

Corsini, R. J. (1984). *Current Psychotherapies.* Peacock Inc., Illinois.

Crawford, D. A. and Allen J. V. (1979). 'A social skills training programme with sex offenders'. In M. Cook & G. Wilson (eds.). *Love and Attraction* (527–536). Pergamon Press, New York.

Crowe, M. (1982). 'The treatment of marital and sexual problems: a behavioural approach'. In A. Bentovim, G. Barnes, & A. Cooklin, A. (eds.). *Complementary Frameworks of Theory and Practice* (vol. 1). Academic Press, London.

Davis, L. (1990). *The Courage to Heal Workbook: For Women and Men Survivors of Child Sexual Abuse.* Harper & Rowe, New York.

Davis, L. (1991). *Allies in Healing.* Harper Collins, New York.

Davis, M., Eshelman, E. R., & McKay, M. (1982). *The Relaxation and Stress Reduction Workbook.* New Harbinger Publications, California.

Deisher, R. W., Wenet, G. A., Paperny, D. M., Clark, T. F., & Fehrenbach, P. A. (1982). 'Adolescent sexual offence behaviour: the role of the physician'. *Journal of Health Care,* 2, 279–286.

Deschner, J. P., (1986). *The Hitting Habit: Anger Control for Battering Couples.* Free Press, New York.

de Shazer, S. (1985). *Keys to Solution in Brief Therapy.* W. W. Norton & Co., New York.

de Shazer, S. (1988). *Clues: Investigating Solutions in Brief Therapy.* W. W. Norton & Co., New York.

Durrant, M. & White, C. (eds.) (1990). *Ideas for Therapy with Sexual Abuse.* Dulwich Centre Publications, Adelaide.

Elliott, M. (1985). *Preventing Child Sexual Assault: A Practical Guide to Talking with Children.* Bedford Square Press, London.

Erickson, M. H. & Rossi, E. L. (1979). *Hypnotherapy: An Explanatory Casebook.* Irvington, New York.

Faller, K. C. (1987). 'Women who sexually abuse children'. *Violence and Victims,* 2(4), 263–276.

Farrelly, B. & Sebastian, A. (1984). *Child Sexual Abuse.* Adelaide Rape Crisis Centre, Adelaide.

Finkelhor, D. (1984). *Child Sexual Abuse: New Theory and Research.* Free Press, New York.

Finkelhor, D. (1986). 'Abusers: special topics'. In Finkelhor, D. & Associates. *A Sourcebook on Child Sexual Abuse.* Sage, California.

Finkelhor, D. (1990). 'Early and long term effects of child sexual abuse: an update'. *Professional Psychology: Research and Practice,* 21(5), 325–330.

Finkelhor, D. & Browne, A. (1985). 'The traumatic impact of child sexual abuse: a conceptualisation'. *American Journal of Orthopsychiatry,* 55, 530–541.

Finkelhor, D., Hotaling, G., Lewis, I. A., & Smith, C. (1990). 'Sexual abuse in a national survey of adult men and women: prevalence, characteristics and risk factors'. *Child Abuse and Neglect,* 14, 19–28.

Friedrich, W. N. (1990). *Psychotherapy of Sexually Abused Children and Their Families.* W. W. Norton & Co., New York.

Friedrich, W. N., Beilke, R. L., & Urquiza, A. J. (1988). 'Behaviour problems in young sexually abused boys'. *Journal of Interpersonal Violence,* 3, 21–28.

Furman, B. & Ahola, T. (1992). *Solution Talk: Hosting Therapeutic Conversations.* W. W. Norton & Co., New York.

Gale, J., Thompson, R. J., Moran, T., & Sack, W. H. (1988). 'Sexual abuse in young children: its clinical presentation & characteristic patterns'. *Child Abuse and Neglect,* 12, 163–170.

Garland, R. J. & Dougher, M. J. (1990). 'The abused/abuser hypothesis of child sexual abuse: a critical review of theory and research'. In J. R. Feierman (ed.). *Pedophilia: Biosocial Dimensions,* (488–509). Springer-Verlag, New York.

Gavey, N.(1991)'Sexual victimization prevalence among New Zealand university students'. *Journal of Consulting and Clinical Psychology*, 59(3), 464–466.

Giaretto, H. (1982). *Integrated Treatment of Child Sexual Abuse: A Treatment and Training Manual*. Science and Behaviour Books, California.

Gil, E. & Johnson, T. L. (1993). *Sexualized Children: Assessment and Treatment of Sexualized Children and Children Who Molest*. Launch Press, Rockville, USA.

Gilligan, C. (1982). *In a Different Voice*. Harvard University Press, Cambridge, Mass.

Gilligan, S. (1987). *Therapeutic Trances: The Co-operation Principles in Ericksonian Hypnotherapy*. Brunner/Mazel, New York.

Goldner, V. (1992). 'Making room for both/and'. *The Family Therapy Networker*, 16(3), 35–61.

Gonsiorek, J. C. (1985). *A Guide to Psychotherapy with Gay and Lesbian Clients*. Harrington Park Press, New York.

Gordon, D. (1978). *Therapeutic Metaphors*. Meta Publications, California.

Grinder, J. & Bandler, R. (1981). *Trance-formations: Neurolinguistic Programming and the Structure of Hypnosis*. Real People Press, Utah.

Groth, A. (1979). *Men Who Rape: The Psychology of the Offender*. Plenum Press, New York.

Grubman-Black, S. D. (1990). *Broken Boys/Mending Men: Recovery from Childhood Sexual Abuse*. TAB Books, Florida.

Haley, J. (1973). *Uncommon Therapy*. W. W. Norton & Co., New York.

Hatcher, C. & Himelstein, P. (eds.) (1976). *The Handbook of Gestalt Therapy*. Jason Aronson, New York.

Heiman, J. R., LoPiccolo, L., & LoPiccolo, J. (1984). *Becoming Orgasmic: A Sexual Growth Programme for Women*. Prentice Hall, Sydney.

Jacobson, E. (1938). *Progressive Relaxation*. University of Chicago Press, Chicago.

Johnson, T. C. (1989). 'Female child perpetrators: children who molest other children'. *Child Abuse and Neglect*, 13(4), 571–585.

Johnson, T. C. (1991). *Understanding the Sexual Behaviours of Young Children*. (SIECUS Report), August/September.

Johnson, T. C. & Berry, C. (1989). 'Children who molest: a treatment programme'. *Journal of Interpersonal Violence*, 1(2), 185–203.

Kilman, P. R. & Mills, K. H. (1983). *All about Sex Therapy*. Plenum Press, New York.

Knopp, F. H. (1984). *Retraining Adult Sex Offenders: Methods and Models*. Safer Society Press, New York.

Krauth, B. & Smith, R. (1988). *Questions and Answers on Issues Related to the Incarcerated Male Sex Offender: An Administrator's Overview*. US Department of Justice, Washington, DC.

Lambie, I. D., Simmonds, L., Houlahan, C. K., & Robson, M. (in press). 'A comprehensive treatment programme for adolescent sex offenders: outdoor wilderness group therapy, on-going group therapy, family therapy and individual therapy'. *Child Abuse and Neglect*.

Lankton, S. (1980). *Practical Magic*. Meta Publications, California.

Leupnitz, D. A. (1988). *The Family Interpreted: Feminist Theory in Clinical Practice*. Basic Books Inc., New York.

Lew, M. (1988). *Victims No Longer: Men Recovering from Incest and Other Sexual Child Abuse*. Harper Collins, New York.

Long, S. (1986). 'Guidelines for treating young children'. In K. MacFarlane & J. Waterman *et al*. (eds.). *Sexual Abuse of Young Children*. Guildford Press, New York.

Loulan, J. A. (1984). *Lesbian Sex*. Spinsters/aunt lute, San Francisco.

Luthe, W. (ed.) (1969). *Autogenic Therapy*, (six vol.). Grune & Stratton, New York.

McCarty, L. M. (1986). 'Mother–child incest: characteristics of the offender'. *Child Welfare*, 65(5), 447–458.

Maltz, W. (1991). *The Sexual Healing Journey: A Guide for Survivors of Sexual Abuse*. Harper Collins, New York.

Marshall, W. L., Laws, D. R., & Barbaree, H. E. (eds.) (1990). *Handbook of Sexual Assault: Issues, Theories, and Treatment of the Offender*. Plenum Press, New York.

Masters, W. H. & Johnson, V. E. (1970). *Human Sexual Inadequacy*. Little, Brown, Boston.

Minuchin, S. (1974). *Families and Family Therapy*. Harvard University Press, Cambridge, Mass.

Minuchin, S. (1991). 'The seductions of constructivism'. *The Family Therapy Networker*, 15(5), 47–50.

Moreno, J. L. (1975). *Psychodrama* Volume One: Foundations of Psychotherapy. Beacon House Inc., New York.

Morgan, L. (1986). *Katie's Yukky Problem*. Papers Inc., Auckland.

Morgan, L. (1987). *Megan's Secret*. Papers Inc., Auckland.

Parks, P. (1990). *Rescuing the Inner Child: Therapy for Adults Sexually Abused as Children*. Souvenir Press, London.

Pithers, W. D. (1990). 'Relapse prevention with sexual aggressors: a method for maintaining therapeutic gain and enhancing external supervision'. In W. Marshall, D. R. Laws, & H. E. Barbaree (eds.). *Handbook of Sexual*

Assault: Issues, Theories and Treatment of the Offender, (343–361). Plenum Press, New York.

Resick, P. A. & Schnicke, M. K. (1990). 'Treating symptoms in adult victims of sexual assault'. *Journal of Interpersonal Violence*, 5(4), 488–506.

Rosen, S. (ed.) (1982). *My Voice Will Go With You: The Teaching Tales of Milton H. Erickson, M.D.* W. W. Norton & Co., New York.

Roughan, P. & Jenkins, A. (1990). 'A systems developmental approach to counselling couples with sexual problems'. *The Australian & New Zealand Journal of Family Therapy*, 2(3), 193–201.

Russell, D. E. H. (1983). 'The incidence and prevalence of interfamilial and extrafamilial sexual abuse of female children'. *Child Abuse and Neglect*, 7, 133–146.

Salter, A. C. (1988). *Treating Child Sex Offenders and Victims: A Practical Guide.* Sage, California.

Saphira, M. (1985). *The Sexual Abuse of Children* (2nd edn). Papers Inc., Auckland.

Saphira, M. (1987). *For Your Child's Sake: Understanding Sexual Abuse.* Reed Methuen, Auckland.

Search, G. (1988). *The Last Taboo: Sexual Abuse of Children.* Penguin, London.

Seghorn, T. K., Prentky, R. A., & Boucher, R. J. (1987). 'Childhood sexual abuse in the lives of sexually aggressive offenders'. *Journal of the American Academy of Child and Adolescent Psychiatry*, 26, 262–267.

Seymour, F. (1987). *Good Behaviour: A Guide for Parents of Young Children.* G.P. Books, Wellington.

Simmonds, L. & Houlahan, K. (1991). *An Integrated Programme for Adolescent Sexual Offenders.* Leslie Centre, Auckland.

Summit, R. C. (1983). 'The child sexual abuse accommodation syndrome'. *Child Abuse and Neglect*, 7, 177–193.

Tharinger, D. (1990). 'Impact of sexual abuse on developing sexuality'. *Professional Psychology: Research and Practice*, 21(5), 331–337.

Watkins, W. & Bentovim, A. (1992). 'The sexual abuse of male children and adolescents: a review of current research'. *Journal of Child Psychology and Psychiatry*, 33(1), 197–248.

Watzlawick, P., Weakland, J., & Fisch, R. (1974). *Change: Principles of Problem Formation and Problem Resolution.* W. W. Norton & Co., New York.

White, M. (1986). 'Negative explanation, restraint and double description: a template for family therapy'. *Family Process*, 25(2), 169–184.

White, M. (1988). 'The process of questioning: a therapy of literary merit?'. *Dulwich Centre Newsletter*, (Winter 1988). Dulwich Centre Publications, Adelaide.

White, M. (1989). 'The externalizing of the problem and the re-authoring of lives and relationships'. *Dulwich Centre Newsletter*, (Summer 1988-89). Dulwich Centre Publications, Adelaide.

White, M. & Epston, D. (1989). *Literate Means to Therapeutic Ends*. Dulwich Centre Publications, Adelaide.

Whitman, W. P. & Quinsey, V. L. (1981). 'Heterosexual skill training for institutionalized rapists and child molesters'. *Canadian Journal of Behavioural Science*, 13, 105–114.

Williams, A. (1991). *Forbidden Agendas: Strategic Action in Groups*. Routledge, London.

Zeig, J. (ed.) (1980). *A Teaching Seminar with Milton H. Erickson, M.D.* Brunner/Mazel, New York.

INDEX

abusers *see* offenders
acknowledging that abuse
   occurred
   as a part of healing 31–3
   by families 74, 83
   difficulties in 32
action methods in therapy 52,
   116–21, 208–10, 215
   see also rescue scene
addictions *see* alcohol and drug
   abuse
adolescents
   effects of abuse 185–91
   issues for parents of 182–3
   issues for therapists working
     with 191–9
   specific issues relating to
     abuse 184–99
affirmation
   acknowledging the
     client's/family's strengths
     and resources 35, 48, 61,
     76–7, 90, 98, 140, 144,
     154, 162, 210, 213

progress in therapy 133, 140
agency issues 290–4
aggressive behaviour
   as a response to abuse 47,
     171, 173, 182, 90
   distinguishing between anger
     and 40–1, 105,167
   setting limits on 174–5
Ahola, Tapani 217–20, 222
alcohol and drug abuse, as a
   response to sexual abuse
   47, 171, 182, 188–9
ambivalence towards the
   offender 37, 41, 110, 158,
   192, 198
anchoring a resource 240–2
anger
   as a response to abuse 188,
     189
   expressing in therapy 40–1,
     43, 56, 128, 131, 174–5
   towards a non-abusive parent
     41, 173–4, 190–1
   see also catharsis